# ANZAC
## THE UNAUTHORISED
## BIOGRAPHY

CAROLYN HOLBROOK is a research fellow in the School of Social Sciences at Monash University. She completed a PhD in history at the University of Melbourne in 2012, for which she was awarded the Dennis Wettenhall Prize for the best thesis in Australian history and the Australian Historical Association's Serle Award in 2014. She has previously worked as a food and wine journalist and a policy adviser in the Department of the Prime Minister and Cabinet.

# Praise for *Anzac, the Unauthorised Biography*

For the centenary of Anzac, Carolyn Holbrook has written
an adventurous and judicious study of how for good and ill a
war on the other side of the world has entered into Australian
consciousness. She ranges widely and digs deep to track what
scholars, creative writers, politicians, filmmakers and families
have made of the phenomenon. With great skill she charts
the ebb and flow of remembrance public and private, and
ends with an eloquent plea for the separation of myth from
history. The book deserves a place on the shelf alongside the
writings of Charles Bean and Bill Gammage.
— *Ken Inglis*

A fine and robust attack on the birth-of-the nation view of
Australia, Gallipoli and the Great War. We are in Holbrook's
debt for helping us see how important it still is to honour
those who died in that catastrophic war without honouring
war itself.
— *Jay Winter*

You must be clever to write a book like this. You must know
the history and the evidence it depends on, then go behind
it to explore the historians who wrote it, then go beyond
them to the times, places and circumstances which led them
to write as they did. Carolyn Holbrook does this brilliantly,
illuminating the vast difference between the past and history.
'What use is history?', people ask. They ask it because history encloses them tightly, like breathing, but in this splendid
book Carolyn shows how artfully history is made, and how
much it makes us who we are.
— *Bill Gammage*

Memories of the Great War are all about us – powerful, insistent and all too often unreflective. Carolyn Holbrook looks back over its commemoration over the past hundred years in histories and memoirs, novels and films, ceremonies and monuments, orations and arguments to show a richer and more complex legacy. There have been many accounts of the Anzac legend: now we have its history.
— *Stuart Macintyre*

At last – a biography of the bastard son of war and nationalism. Now we understand what a life he's led, and what a dance he's led us …
— *Peter Stanley*

*Anzac, the Unauthorised Biography* is the first comprehensive study of how the history of the Great War has been written during the twentieth century. It makes a significant contribution to the study of the war in Australia as it charts the shifting understandings and responses to the war over time. Eloquently written, this compelling and important book provides an insightful and perceptive reflection on how each generation has interpreted the meaning of the war and how it has shaped understandings of Australian history over several decades.
— *Joy Damousi*

# ANZAC

## THE UNAUTHORISED BIOGRAPHY

### CAROLYN HOLBROOK

NEWSOUTH

A NewSouth book

*Published by*
NewSouth Publishing
University of New South Wales Press Ltd
University of New South Wales
Sydney NSW 2052
AUSTRALIA
newsouthpublishing.com

National Library of Australia
Cataloguing-in-Publication entry
  Author: Holbrook, Carolyn, author.
  Title: Anzac, the unauthorised biography / Carolyn Holbrook.
  ISBN: 9781742234076 (paperback)
        9781742247007 (ePDF)
        9781742241814 (ePub/Kindle)
  Notes: Includes bibliographical references and index.
  Subjects: World War, 1914–1918 – Historiography.
    World War, 1914–1918 – Australia – Historiography.
    World War, 1914–1918 – Participation, Australian.
    Nationalism and collective memory – Australia.
    Australia – Historiography.
  Dewey Number: 940.394

*Design* Josephine Pajor-Markus
*Cover design* Xou Creative
*Printer* Griffin Press

Extract from Vance Palmer's poem 'The Farmer Remembers the Somme' (1920) on page 86 is used with permission of the Estate of Vance Palmer.

This book is printed on paper using fibre supplied from plantation or sustainably managed forests.

# CONTENTS

# FOREWORD

## The Hon. Kim Beazley, AC

World War I, the Great War, changed everything. It was in essence European but it manifested in the Middle East, Africa and Asia though with less salience than its global successor, and in many ways outcome, World War II. It cut loose empire, destroying nationalisms in Europe, and sowed their seed in the increasingly challenged remnant European empires. It spawned massive challenges to democracy from left and right in communism and fascism. It opened the door to global superpower status to the United States, giving political pre-eminence – adding to what was, for a long time, economic pre-eminence – to that nation.

With so many massive changes wrought globally it is only to be expected that a small though heavily engaged participant like Australia would see its society and its thinking deeply influenced. This has been the case and the key symbol of that influence is Anzac Day. Carolyn Holbrook treads old ground anew in her 'unauthorised biography'. Each generation of Australian social, political and military historians walks to this altar and lays at its feet their accusations, their frustrations, their satire, their fury and their homage. Its mythical strength is our Hotel California. You can check out but you can never leave. In a lengthy political and now short diplomatic life I have witnessed a multiplicity of national days and veterans' days. None has so powerfully, movingly, reverentially gripped a national mind as Anzac Day, despite the fact that Australians are the most laidback and irreverent of folk. Americans are identified by Australians as harbingers of triumphant nationalism and idealisers of the serving men and women. They are. Compare, however, their commemoration of Memorial Day and the 4th of July with Anzac Day and they don't begin to climb the hill we sit atop. They do around Thanksgiving but that has a totally different mood and purpose.

Particularly at our foundation we could regard ourselves as among the world's great social experiments. We had become so famous for social advance after our first decade that Lenin felt he had to write a cautionary pamphlet about us lest our siren song seduce the European socialist movement. Though our devotion to the mother country was great and reinforced an intensely racialist, survivalist outlook, we struggled to break away from her military institutions with our own. We established early a fundamentally different view from Britain of the grand strategy of Asia–Pacific security. Our much greater concerns about Japan wove through that relationship up to 1951. Though in the solemn umbra of the consequences for our society of the Great War, we remained an innovative and creative nation with a pragmatic temper. So powerfully, however, has Anzac gripped our imagination, in a hundred years no commemoration of any achievement has been able to supplant it. Perhaps if Federation day was not the 1st of January, there might have been a chance there. Certainly our celebration of Federation's centenary was impressive. However for most Australians that celebration was a learning experience. For Anzac, we know. There are down periods, as Carolyn Holbrook reveals, but the magnetic power remains. Revival is easy.

I think there are two reasons for this, though this timely study has many more. The first is the Anzac commemoration was a 'bottom-up' not 'top-down' manifestation. The drive came from returning servicemen taking up the cause from the Gallipoli men redeployed to Egypt. In recent times it has been embellished by a variety of war commemorative dates, an active Department of

Veterans Affairs and the outreach of a brilliant war memorial. In recent years it has been folded into a more clear-cut sense of Australian nationalism. Politicians have ridden the Anzac legend but its engine is of a populist combustion. Veterans remain in control. I spent my childhood attending the main Anzac ceremonies with my father, then every year as a member of parliament. Until I travelled to Gallipoli with Bob Hawke I had never seen a politician speak at one. Though I have spoken at numerous gunfire breakfasts and a few little local ceremonies in my electorate – though I was defence minister for five years and opposition leader for six – I have never been a speaker at a main event until my time as ambassador in Washington. Anzac Day belongs to the Australian people through the veterans, and they hold their charge with reverence and determination. As the previous American ambassador to Australia said with some surprise, he found it a 'sombre day'.

The second reason goes beyond the day, though is based on it. That goes to the capacity of the legend to develop a broad tent. The sentiment around it has been capable of an attack from a gender and racial perspective, and from the left on social and pacifist grounds, where refreshment is sought from commemorations of ground-breaking Australian achievements in democratic rights and social programs. Brilliant attention has been given to these efforts. The wash of some of them is to be found in the following pages.

They have not succeeded because the Anzac legend has been spread to a multiplicity of events in subsequent Australian engagement in wars and foreign deployments. Each generation of veterans picks up where the last left off, reinforcing the commitment. Massively important was World War II, its veterans now almost gone. Australia believed itself fighting for its survival in a way not obvious in World War I, though we were rightly then concerned with the success of British arms. World War II was in gender and racial terms heavily inclusive. Women were engaged more broadly in the armed services and massively in production. Our production was critical for the functioning of MacArthur's South West Pacific Area command and crucial for the feeding of Britain. The Aboriginal population entered our armed services in numbers and were vital for labour and surveillance in our threatened north. Ours was a mobilised population in a national effort. Most Indigenous Australians are more comfortable with Anzac Day than they are with Australia Day. Women are deeply integrated into our current armed forces. Their massive contribution to the sharp end of the World War II home front in war production and logistics, let alone the services, removes the edge of masculinity from key features of the legend. Australians like history including their own. Whether or not they agree with Carolyn Holbrook's conclusions, they will enjoy the read.

# ACKNOWLEDGMENTS

During the preparation of this book I have had the privilege of working closely with three eminent Australian historians: Joy Damousi, Stuart Macintyre and Kate Darian-Smith. Joy provided the intellectual ballast for my interest in the Great War and its psychological traces, and has helped me navigate the vast literature. The modesty with which Stuart bears his encyclopaedic knowledge of history is matched by his willingness to share that knowledge with others. The book has benefited from the guidance that Kate has provided in its transition from doctoral work.

Historians, former politicians, colleagues and descendants of men who fought in the Great War have shown enthusiasm for this project and I am extremely grateful for their interest and expertise. I thank Professor Bain Attwood, the Hon. Kim Beazley, Professor Geoffrey Blainey, Ms Julie Cattlin, the Rt Hon. Malcolm Fraser, Professor Bill Gammage, the Hon. Bob Hawke, Ms Jo Hawkins, the Hon. John Howard, Professor Ken Inglis, the Hon. Paul Keating, Ms Winsome McDowell Paul, Dr Michael McKernan, Dr David Noonan, Professor Sharon Pickering, Professor Peter Stanley, Professor James Walter and Dr Bart Ziino. I thank Monash University for its financial support for the publication of this book.

I have been very fortunate to work with the staff at NewSouth Publishing. Phillipa McGuinness has been an enthusiastic and inspiring advocate of my research, while Emma Driver has ably guided the manuscript through production. My copy editor Jean Kingett brought to the project not only her expertise in grammar and expression, but the great benefits of her experience and counsel. Designer Josephine Pajor-Markus deserves recognition for the clarity of her design, while Xou Creative have produced a striking cover. I also thank Jo Hawkins for suggesting the title.

Thank you to Annabelle and John Holbrook, John R Holbrook, Jennifer Holbrook, Sally Holbrook Marko, Susan and Craig Readhead, Tony Barker, Robbie Campo, Sarah Q Murray, Sharyn Rowlands, Amanda Hopps, Maria-Luisa Coulson and Angela Franich for your interest and encouragement during the writing of this book. The Great War probably doesn't seem so great any more to Catherine and Sarah Forsyth: I am grateful for your forbearance. To Anthony Forsyth, whose support has made this project so enjoyable, I thank you especially.

# THE ANZAC ASCENDANCY

In the weeks preceding Anzac Day 2013, the former Chief of the Australian Defence Force and current Governor-General, Peter Cosgrove, appeared in a television advertisement called 'Excuses'. Images of Australian soldiers, past and present, were juxtaposed with the voices of contemporary Australians explaining why they were not going to the Anzac Day dawn service: 'I'd go if it wasn't so early'; 'I just wouldn't know where to park'; 'Look, it's all just a bit too hard to be honest'. Cue Peter Cosgrove: 'This Anzac Day, there is no excuse. Along with raising a glass, we are asking you to attend your local dawn service'.[1] I was stunned. Here was a retired general, speaking in an advertisement funded by a brewery, attempting to shame Australians into attending a military ceremony. Not only that; in a nation where drinking is a serious social problem he was making a connection between the Anzac legend and alcohol.

The advertisement is a striking example of a phenomenon that has been well documented by historians: the extraordinary currency of the Anzac legend in contemporary Australian society. In this instance, a brewery was prepared to donate $1 million dollars a year to the RSL (Returned and Services League) and Legacy in order to associate its product with Australia's most powerful brand: Anzac. There are many other examples of the Anzac ascendancy: the enthusiasm with which politicians attach themselves to the tradition; the popularity of books with war themes; the hundreds of thousands of people who do not need to be exhorted to attend dawn services.

Sport seems to have a particular affiliation with the Anzac

tradition. In 2001 the national cricket team travelled to Gallipoli, where players re-enacted a match played by the diggers on Shell Green and learned about the place 'where the spirit of Australia really came from'. The hugely popular 'Anzac Day clash' between the Collingwood and Essendon AFL football clubs, devised in 1995, honours the soldiers with a minute's silence and a rendition of the Last Post. The Anzac Medal is awarded to the player who 'best embodies the Anzac spirit'. The then Collingwood coach, Mick Malthouse, famously criticised his team for letting 'down the Anzacs' when they lost the match in 2009.[2]

The potency of the Anzac story is apparent also in the popularity of the Gallipoli 'pilgrimage'. Thousands of Australians, many of them in their early twenties, attend the Anzac Day dawn service at Gallipoli each year. So great is the demand expected to be for the centenary dawn service in 2015 that the government has introduced a ballot system to restrict numbers to 10 000. It is not uncommon at the televised dawn service to see Gallipoli 'pilgrims', wrapped in the national flag, moved to tears by the ceremony. When I see these pictures, I wonder what emotional buttons are being pushed to induce such strong feelings about men who died so long ago. Patriotism? Jingoism? Perhaps the suffering of the soldiers provides a vicarious outlet for personal distress.

The catalyst for this book was a question: why are Australians of the twenty-first century so emotionally attached to a military event that took place nearly one hundred years ago? The question does not imply disdain, rather fascination and intrigue. It is a question that suggests a host of others: Has the Anzac legend always enjoyed such prominence and prestige? What would the diggers whose remains lie at Gallipoli make of the flag-draped mourners of 2014? Would Charles Bean, who produced the twelve-volume *Official History* of the war between 1921 and 1942, be pleased that his revered Anzacs are so well remembered a century later? Or would he cringe at the cynical commercialism of Carlton & United Breweries and the crassness of comparing football with battle?

*Anzac, the Unauthorised Biography* is my attempt to answer these questions by tracing the history of the way that Australians have thought about the Great War. Historians have written previously about how *aspects* of the Great War, such as the raising of war monuments and the patterns of commemoration and grieving, are remembered. This book offers a new perspective, both in the range of its timescale and the scope of the evidence it considers. It attempts to beat all that has been previously 'imagined' about the Great War into a meaningful shape.

Some might wonder 'Why dedicate a book to examining something as esoteric as the history of an idea'? Over the past few decades, scholars around the world have turned increasingly to the study of memory. Borrowing the methods of psychoanalysis, historians recognise that the study of what people *believe* happened – their *memory* of an event – can be as instructive as the study of 'what actually happened'. Thus, the meanings that Australians have ascribed to the Great War over the course of a century are a valuable record of the history of Australian identity, nationalism, politics and culture during that time.

The Great War (1914–18) was a monumental event in the history of Australia. When the war began in 1914, the Australian nation was just thirteen years old, with a population of less than five million people. Of this small, overwhelmingly British-derived population, 330 000 men served overseas in the Australian Imperial Force (AIF). Sixty thousand men were killed in the war and 167 000 were recorded as wounded. In addition to the physical harm, contemporary understanding of war trauma suggests that most of the returned men would have been suffering psychological distress and a good proportion would have acquired the symptoms that we now classify as post-traumatic stress disorder.

The legacy of the war extended far beyond the damage wrought on the battlefield. At home, the struggle over the introduction of conscription cut deep divisions into Australian society, between middle class and working class, between Protestant and Catholic, between English and Irish, between soldier and 'shirker'. The Labor Party was all but destroyed by the conscription issue. Following the departure of the pro-conscriptionists in 1916, it governed federally for just two of the next twenty-five years.

An immense amount has been produced about the Great War over the past ninety years, in forms ranging from monuments and museum exhibitions to histories, novels and films. I have necessarily been selective for the purposes of this study, choosing evidence that best illuminates several major themes. I have examined academic histories, newspaper reportage, soldier memoirs and fiction, film, family history, and political commemoration. At various points I have used oral testimony gathered from academic historians, family historians and former politicians to enhance the written record. I have not considered aspects of war memory that have received substantial attention elsewhere, such as monuments to the Great War, its display in museums, the changing observances of Anzac Day or the role played by returned servicemen's organisations.[3]

The book proceeds chronologically, with the opening chapter setting the context for Australian responses to the Great War. It looks at the various forms of Australian nationalism that existed around the turn of the twentieth century, and how Australians of both radical and British loyalist affiliations craved the test of battle that would ratify psychologically Australia's claim to nationhood. The issues of nationalism and war are considered through an examination of Australian attitudes to the Boer War and its commemoration.

If the Boer War proved a disappointment for Australians craving a martial baptism, the Great War was more than adequate to the task. The historiographical interregnum that existed immediately following the war was ended by two histories: one written by an ardent imperialist, Professor Ernest Scott, and the other by an Australian nationalist, the official historian Charles Bean. How did these differing loyalties affect the history these men wrote?

By the 1930s, as the great boom in books written by Europeans about the war was waning, Australian soldiers began to record their experience in memoir and fiction. I ask whether the Australian appetite for modernist European books, such as *All Quiet on the Western Front*, was replicated in a desire to read about the Australian experience in the new-fangled realist style.

Next came the collision between socialism and memory of the Great War in Australia, which I present through the work of three radical nationalist historians: Russel Ward, Ian Turner and Geoffrey Serle. These men were caught between conflicting loyalties to class and nation. They were drawn to the distinctive Australian qualities displayed by the diggers – disregard for authority, larrikinism, egalitarianism and mateship, yet they rejected the British connection that drew Australia into the Great War, and were disillusioned by the conservative nature of the Anzac legend. How did these radical nationalists resolve these contradictions when they wrote the history of the Great War?

During the 1960s and 1970s, commemoration of the Great War declined, to be followed in the 1980s by an unpredicted revival. Why did Anzac fall so dramatically from popular favour and how did it begin the spectacular rise to the status it enjoys today? In seeking to explain the re-emergence of the Great War, I look particularly at the influence of Bill Gammage's book, *The Broken Years*, and Peter Weir's film, *Gallipoli*.

Gammage's pioneering emphasis on the personal stories of the soldiers was given momentum by the boom in family history in the 1980s. There was a sudden surge in the publication of the letters and diaries of soldier-fathers, uncles and grandfathers.

How can we explain the increased popularity of these family histories? To what extent are family historians motivated by the belief that their stories have national historical significance, and to what extent are they influenced by international trends in memory studies and trauma psychology?

Political commemoration plays an increasingly significant role in shaping our opinions of the Great War. Before Prime Minister Bob Hawke's trip to Gallipoli with a group of elderly veterans in 1990, politicians were participants in war commemoration, but they were not instigators of it. That role was filled by the returned men themselves. This chapter investigates the reasons for the massive increase in political involvement in war commemoration, and the ways in which various prime ministers have sought to tailor our military history to their ideological ends. There is evidence gathered from interviews with the former prime ministers Malcolm Fraser, Bob Hawke, Paul Keating and John Howard, and the former defence minister and leader of the Labor Opposition, Kim Beazley.

Two principal themes recur throughout this book. The first is the historical contingency of war memory. In other words, far from being anchored to the events of 1914–18, memory of the Great War has drifted on the currents of Australian history. Thus, the nation-making war fought by bushman-soldiers for the maintenance of the British Empire became, in the eyes of the Vietnam generation, a tragic debacle that was glorified each Anzac Day by a group of racist, chauvinist old boozers. Fast forward to 2014 and the nation-making war has been revived, only now, the imperial and militarist elements have been muted and the stories of mateship, courage and trauma are greatly amplified. The history of the Great War in the Australian imagination demonstrates that we should remain vigilant against the selectivity of our memories and constantly seek to measure the distance between memory and 'what actually happened'.

The second principal theme, closely related to the first, is the way that various ideologies and beliefs have washed through Australian history and tinted our war memory. Pseudo-scientific beliefs about race sustained the original Anzac legend; our British race patriotism was built upon a belief in the superiority of the 'British race'. The Marxist claim that the war was a product of the corrupt capitalist system and a disaster for Australian progressivism ultimately sank beneath the weight of nationalist pride. The Holocaust simultaneously buried racial 'science' and uncovered new ways of remembering the Great War, which placed value on personal testimony and emphasis on the traumatic effects of the war. Contemporary Australian war memory is an unlikely amalgam of nationalist sentiment and trauma psychology.

The series of Great War centenaries to be held from 2014 to 2018 provides the ideal setting in which to record the patterns its memory has whittled into the Australian psyche. This book encourages readers to put aside the commemorative frenzy in order to set, not merely the Great War, but our memory of it, into historical context. The war began just thirteen years after Federation and 126 years after Europeans arrived to settle Aboriginal lands. That European roots are tamped so lightly into Australian soil explains why we stare so intently into the past. For one hundred years, Australians have sought their reflection in the Great War. This book tells the story of what we have seen.

# 1

# BEFORE 1914:
# NATIONALISM AND WAR

WHY DO SO MANY AUSTRALIANS BELIEVE that their nation was born on a battlefield in Turkey on 25 April 1915, rather than in Melbourne on 1 January 1901 when six colonies became one Commonwealth? If the nation had to be born on a battlefield, why was it not born on the South African veldt during the Boer War, in a campaign that coincided exactly with Federation, rather than at Gallipoli fourteen years after Australia came into official existence? The attitudes that Australians have held towards the Great War of 1914–18 for a hundred years have been influenced in large part by how they understood war at the turn of the twentieth century. This chapter considers the crucial link between nationalism and war commemoration *before* 1914, through an examination of Australian involvement in the Boer War.

Anxious nationalism is the curse of settler societies such as Australia. These societies struggle to conform to the conventions of nationalism that developed in eighteenth- and nineteenth-century Western Europe. Those conventions place an emphasis on the historical past of the nation, something that settler societies conspicuously lack. The French-Canadian scholar Gérard

Bouchard has proposed that there are three ways in which set-tler nations have dealt with 'the problem of historical time': they have borrowed the history of their mother country, they have co-opted the history of the indigenous population, or they have rejected the need for history in the making of the nation. Aus-tralia is a clear example of the first solution; Mexico illustrates the second, and the United States the third. While riding on the coat-tails of the mother country lends instant 'strength and credibility' to a fledgling nation, the price to be paid, according to Bouchard, 'can be enormous: bound to imitation and depend-ency, the founding culture settles into an inferiority complex that stifles its creative potential'.[1]

Bouchard's analysis has the ring of truth, though it does not allow for the varying shades of Australian nationalism that exist-ed in the late nineteenth century, and the fact that an Ameri-can-style repudiation of the mother country was arguably pres-ent to some extent from the early years of settlement. While loyalist Australians clung to their British heritage and basked in the reflected glory of racial superiority, as evidenced by the 'largest and greatest' empire in the history of the world, there had developed by the 1880s and 1890s a vocal section of the population that denounced the British connection. It seemed to these people that Australians were a different type from Britons: tall, strong, athletic, loyal, practical, unaffected, informal and irreverent (the national type was assumed always to be male). The icon of this radical nationalist movement was the bushman and its hymns were the ballads, poems and songs that took the bush and the bushman as their subjects. By 1900 the *Bulletin* magazine was bringing the stories and poems of writers such as Joseph Furphy, Bernard O'Dowd, Henry Lawson and 'Banjo' Pat-erson to a circulation, in both rural and urban areas, of 80 000. It cultivated a mockingly anti-British sentiment and professed the view that Australia ought not to cling 'to the coat-tails of a respectable old body in the Northern Hemisphere', because it 'possesses in itself the materials for a great Republic'.[2] Despite the popularity of the 'bushman's bible', as it was known, in the years between 1890 and the Great War, the *Bulletin's* vocally expressed republican and anti-imperialist opinions remained minority views.

Whether they were imperial loyalists, radical nationalists or 'independent Australian Britons' (in the words of the parliamentarian Alfred Deakin), European Australians subscribed readily to the conventions of nationhood. During the middle of the nineteenth century, those British-derived conventions encompassed a benevolent liberalism and faith in international peace. However, by the last quarter of the nineteenth century the military threat posed by the unification and rise of Germany had led to a more aggressive form of British nationalism. In addition to the escalation of imperial rhetoric and monarchical pomp, British nationalism was infused with the ideas of social Darwinism, an ideology that applied the biological theories of natural selection and evolution to human societies. The concept of 'nation' became conflated with that of 'race', and a host of categories such as 'the British race' and the 'higher and lower races' appeared. The naturalist Charles Darwin had decreed that the fittest, by which he meant those animals best adapted to their local environment, survived in nature by a process of natural selection. When transferred to the human sphere, social Darwinism conceived the fittest humans as those who were physically strongest and morally the most courageous. If the measure of a nation's or a race's fitness for survival was its moral and physical strength, then the logical test was war. Blood must be spilled in the drawing of the physical and psychological boundaries of the nation; only then had it proved its fitness for survival in the great war of the races, according to the laws of science.

If war was the true test of nationhood, then Australia felt

keenly its deficit. The Australian colonies' martial dearth com-
pounded a sense of disquiet about their lack of history. Writing
in 1890, the respected Victorian educator and politician Charles
Pearson espoused a common view:

> There is very little that is romantic or picturesque in the
> early history of a penal settlement on a continent peopled
> by some of the lowest savages known ... We miss the grand
> procession of the ages; the conflicts of Church and State; the
> wars of rival nationalities; the relations of baron and knight
> and serf; all the colouring and light that we find in Chaucer,
> or Froissart or Shakespeare.[3]

School textbooks were frank about the lowly status of the colonies in the hierarchy of nationhood. The *Royal Readers* taught
children that 'Australia is essentially a new region, containing no
human beings but a few of the lowest race of mankind'. In the
century or so of British settlement in Australia, there had been no
heroic wars or bloody revolutions. It did not occur to European
Australians that their conflict with Indigenous peoples might be
understood as a form of warfare, let alone that the long inhabita-
tion of the continent by Aborigines might constitute 'history'. It
followed therefore that 'Australia has no history, but that of a few
squabbles with the Colonial Office'.[4]

Some, like the Federation poet George Essex Evans, tried to
muster pride in Australians' 'bloodless flag' and the fact that theirs
was 'Free-born of nations, / Virgin white, / Not won by blood nor
ringed with steel'.[5] But the sentiment of the journalist and author
AG Hales more accurately represented the view of the majority:
that nationhood was not achieved until 'mothers have sent their
firstborn / To look death on the field in the face ...' and there is 'a
soldier's grave for our dead'.[6] It was Henry Lawson, the short story
writer and balladist, who articulated most famously the baying

for baptismal bloodshed. *The Star of Australasia* eschewed conflict on the frontier and dismissed the achievement of peaceful federation, warning Australians to 'boast no more of our bloodless flag'. This sensitive man of radical political sympathy foresaw the glorious moment when 'The Star of the South shall rise – in the lurid clouds of war'.[7]

White Australians of the nineteenth and early twentieth centuries understood themselves to be participants in a scientific experiment that the world was watching with interest. A great race had been transported to a new environment, 'where snow was almost unknown, and where a hot summer sun baked and parched a thirsty soil'. The vexed social Darwinian question that lay at the core of Australians' unease about their nascent nationhood was how that 'mighty race' would fare 'beneath bright and unclouded skies'. Would it maintain 'the determination, self-reliance, energy, and enterprise … that had been the guarantee of England's greatness'? Or would the 'fatal influence of a warm but enervating climate' see the transplanted Britons 'degenerate into a weak, lazy, and inferior race of men, unfit to be classed amongst the world's great peoples?'[8] Only the test of war could answer that fraught question.

Australians would not have wished for war so fervently had their impression of battle borne close relation to reality. The end of the nineteenth century was a high watermark in the romanticisation of warfare. Young Australians, like Britons, were steeped in what the cultural historian Graham Dawson has called the 'pleasure culture' of war.[9] The values of physical strength and prowess, courage and loyalty, emotional stoicism and sacrifice for monarch and Empire were celebrated in everything from popular literature and school textbooks to sporting pursuits, schoolyard ceremonies and children's toys.

In Britain, the adventure story genre was particularly influential in breeding young men for battle. The weekly magazine, the *Boy's Own Paper*, for example, while not explicitly militaristic or jingoistic, promoted the values of patriotism, gentlemanliness and stoic masculinity to generations of young men in Britain and around the Empire. There were rollicking adventure stories, all with happy endings, and pages of practical information about morally sanctioned pursuits, such as stamp-collecting, photography, fishing, bee-keeping, taxidermy and aviary building. Should all these physical activities fail to distract boys from the temptation of 'secret vices', they were advised to take a cold bath.[10]

The many pages of the *Boy's Own Paper* devoted to games, particularly to rugby and cricket, did much to encourage fanciful notions of war. W Cecil Laming's popular poem, 'Play the Game', which compared the 'schoolboy pluck' of the rugby field to 'the British pluck' of the battlefield, appeared in the magazine.[11] To Laming and the impressionable young readers of the *Boy's Own Paper*, sport and war summoned the same qualities of physical and moral courage. Whether in the scrum or on the battlefield, the rallying cry was the same: 'Play up! Play up! And play the game!'

Young Australians were exposed to this idealisation of war, both through their consumption of British publications such as the *Boy's Own Paper* and through literature produced at home. For most Australian schoolchildren of the late nineteenth century, school textbooks were the principal source of reading material; for some, they were the only source. Nelson's *Royal Readers* had been amended to cater for antipodean tastes, but their content still betrayed their British origins. The sturdy blue books were infused with the optimism of the age and assumptions of British good sense, justice and superiority. Dispersed among the poems, songs and lessons on technology and natural science were passages about British military victories and patriotic heroes. The *Commonwealth School Paper* and the various state *School Papers* responded to growing calls for more local content and proved exceedingly popular. The early *School Papers* typically ploughed more benign ideological ground than the *Royal Readers*, though there were exceptions.

In 1901, the Victorian Education Department embarked upon a project designed to increase patriotic sentiment among school-children. It was felt that the introduction in schools of a weekly flag ceremony around the British Union Jack would encourage 'devotion to the Sovereign, love of country and respect for the laws'.[12] The Department issued detailed instructions for the ceremony, including a labelled diagram.

The Reverend William Henry Fitchett would no doubt have approved of the ceremony; the state was generally far too subtle in its execution of the imperial mission for the loyalist tastes of the preacher, journalist and principal of Melbourne's Methodist Ladies' College. In 1896 Fitchett was commissioned to compose a series of articles for Melbourne's *Argus* newspaper about significant battles in British history. The articles were received enthusiastically by readers and prompted calls for them to be compiled in pamphlet form, 'so admirably calculated' were they 'to nourish the noble sentiment of patriotism, which is such a powerful factor in binding together the component parts of our grand empire'.[13] Readers' wishes were fulfilled the following year when *Deeds that Won the Empire* appeared. Fitchett's preface articulated his concern that young Australians were insufficiently inculcated with the martial glories of the warrior race to which they belonged: 'There is a real danger that, for the average youth, the great names of British story may become meaningless sounds, that his imagination will take no colour from the rich and deep tints of history. And what a pallid, cold-blooded citizenship this must produce!'[14]

*Australians at the turn of the twentieth century were primed psychologically for war.*

If Fitchett's efforts to 'nourish patriotism' are measured in book sales, then he was stunningly successful. Australians of the late nineteenth and early twentieth centuries were far more likely to be immersed in William Fitchett's 'red-coat dreamings' than they were in the words of writers such as Henry Lawson, 'Banjo' Paterson or Steele Rudd.[15] And Fitchett's appeal did not end at Australian borders. *Deeds that Won the Empire* was embraced eagerly around the Empire, selling an extraordinary 100 000 copies in its sixpenny edition and running to seventeen impressions of its six-shilling edition by 1904. It became prescribed holiday reading at Harrow and Winchester and was placed in the libraries of all warships in the Royal Navy.[16]

Australians at the turn of the twentieth century were primed psychologically for war. This war would prove that they were not the degenerate spawn of convict stock, but a thriving offshoot of the mother race. The war of Australian imaginations would be fought in the style of the battles described in the *Boy's Own Paper* and *Deeds that Won the Empire*. When war between Britain and the Boers was declared in October 1899, Australians would be given the opportunity to measure the war of their imaginations against reality.

Tensions between the rebel South African states and Britain had been festering for a more than a decade before war broke out. When gold was discovered in the Transvaal in 1886 tens of thousands of *uitlanders*, a few hundred of them from Australia, but most from Britain, arrived to pan for their fortunes. The Boer government of the Transvaal refused to grant the franchise and other citizenship rights to these *uitlanders*, whose numbers greatly exceeded those of the Boer population by the late 1890s. The Boers feared, justifiably, that Britain would use the enfranchisement of *uitlanders* to wrest back political control of the resource-rich republic and the neighbouring Orange Free State.[17] It was Britain's professed outrage at the treatment of the *uitlanders* that led eventually to the outbreak of war.

Each of the six Australian colonies sent contingents to fight in the South African war. After Australia federated on 1 January 1901, its first national military force, the Australian Commonwealth Horse, was recruited and despatched. Half of this contingent arrived after a peace treaty was signed and the rest saw little action. The public response to the initial despatch of soldiers to South Africa was enthusiastic, often wildly so. More than 300 000 people lined the streets of Sydney to cheer the first New South Wales contingent as it marched to the docks, at least double the number that turned out a year later when the six colonies federated into a nation.[18]

Critics of the war were relatively few, but they were outspoken. Despite efforts by conservative newspapers, politicians and commentators such as Reverend Fitchett to portray all opponents of the war (or 'pro-Boers' as they were often called) as anti-British, this was far from the case. Arnold Wood, the professor of history at the University of Sydney, rejected Britain's aggressive foreign policy, though not the imperialist project itself. Wood had been raised as a Congregationalist in Manchester and was influenced by the Nonconformist liberalism of John Bright and Richard Cobden, which advocated an ethical foreign policy. He believed that international co-operation could ensure the triumph of peace over conflict. From the outset, he was suspicious of British motives in South Africa and expressed his opposition to the war in letters to the Sydney *Daily Telegraph*: the greatness of Britain's Empire should not be measured by 'the extent of the land it could devastate, and "annex", nor by the richness of the gold mines it could secure for its capitalists', but by 'the righteousness of its rule'.[19]

The radical Irish Protestant and member of the Victorian parliament, Henry Bournes Higgins, was another outspoken critic of British conduct. Though not the demonstrative imperialist that Arnold Wood was, Higgins bore Britain no grudge. While the

Victorian Premier George Turner advised his parliamentary colleagues not to 'inquire too closely into the justice of the quarrel'
with the Boers – Britain was, after all, 'the greatest, most mag-
nanimous, most Christian and civilized country in the world' –
Higgins wanted to know what precedent there existed 'in international law for one nation to compel another nation to take its
subjects and make them its own? What precedent there is for one
nation to compel another to naturalise its subjects?'[20] A parliamentary motion to send a contingent to South Africa was carried,
with Higgins and twelve other members dissenting.

Like everyone else, Higgins expected the war to be a quick
and brutal affair: 'There is an empire on the one side, which has
250 times at least the strength of the little Boer republic', he told
the Victorian parliament. However, the imperial forces soon discovered that their enemy was not the 'cowardly kind of veldt
pariah' and 'degenerate offshoot of a fine old parent stock' that
British propaganda had suggested. He might 'not wear a stand-
up collar, nor an eyeglass, nor spats to his *veldtschoon*', but the
Boer was proving himself to be a mighty foe.[21] Seizing the initiative, the Boer farmer-soldiers laid siege to the strategic towns of
Ladysmith, Kimberley and Mafeking in British-controlled South
Africa in the first weeks of the war. Within the space of five days
in December 1899, which came to be known as Black Week, the
British were beaten at the battles of Stormberg, Magersfontein
and Colenso. The mantle of invincibility that Britain had worn
since Waterloo had slipped.

People around the Empire were stunned by Britain's poor
showing and then stung into action. In Australia, jingoistic
patriotism took the place of gentle enthusiasm. Amid fear that
Germany, France or Russia might exploit Britain's vulnerability
and make a grab for its colonies, 26 000 Australian men joined
militia groups and rifle clubs to prepare for invasion.[22] Even the
*Bulletin* temporarily abandoned its position that the war was a

Jewish-inspired capitalist conspiracy against the working man and declared that this was now 'a genuine case of the "empire, right or wrong"'. HB Higgins was shouted down when he reiterated his anti-war stance at a campaign meeting in Geelong. Members of the audience waved Union Jack flags and jeered: 'You are a Boer!'[23] Higgins, who had the misfortune of seeking re-election when war fever was at its highest, lost his seat in parliament.

The British military responded to the defeats of Black Week with the deployment of unprecedented numbers of troops and a call for more contingents from the colonies. Men with bush and horse skills were requested specifically, as they would be better suited to the mobile, dispersed warfare of the South African plains than the mostly urban volunteers of the early contingents. Private benefactors and colonial governments sorted through the thousands of 'squatters, boundary-riders, shepherds, shearers, and prospectors' who offered themselves for service. These men became known as the Bushmen's Contingents and were felt to be 'truly representative and characteristic of the Colonies'.[24] The first of these 'Australians of the Bush', the New South Wales Imperial Bushmen, arrived in South Africa in May 1900, just as the town of Mafeking, which had been under siege by the Boers, was relieved.

The great news of Mafeking rang out around the Empire. An ebullient Reverend Fitchett burst into a classroom at Methodist Ladies' College to break the glorious news. The girls went 'mad with excitement ... marching around the garden, ringing every available bell in the College and using handkerchiefs as substitutes for flags'.[25] It seemed to most observers that the crisis was over, that victory was imminent and British pre-eminence had been rightfully restored. But Britain had underestimated its enemy once again. Anxious to avoid confrontation in battles they had little chance of winning, the outnumbered Boers instead concentrated their efforts on frustrating British lines of supply. Lord

Kitchener, who had replaced Lord Roberts in command of the British military effort, introduced his own unconventional methods to counter the Boers' guerilla warfare. Thus began the protracted, final phase of the war, during which imperial soldiers evicted Boers from their property, set fire to their buildings and belongings, and incarcerated Boer men, women and children in dire concentration camps.

When news of the burning of a Boer farm and the cruel treatment of its inhabitants reached Australia in late 1901, Arnold Wood felt compelled to enter the public debate once more, asking readers of Sydney's *Daily Telegraph*: 'Is there not in Sydney enough English patriotism to protest against a policy that is bringing everlasting infamy upon the English name?' With a group that included the New South Wales Labor rebels William Holman and Arthur Griffith, and the *Bulletin*'s editor James Edmonds and literary editor AG Stephens, Wood formed the Anti-War League with a view to influencing public opinion and ending the war. His alliance with avowed anti-imperialists such as Edmonds and Stephens caused him some consternation and likely made him an easier target for the conservative opponents who were circling. Wood looked in danger of losing his academic chair when the Senate of Sydney University censured him for espousing views that were 'unworthy of a professor of history, whose utterances ought to be marked by strict impartiality and freedom from passion'. Reverend Fitchett did not hide his contempt for Wood, observing that 'undergraduates are, in all lands, very inflammable material, and if many professors followed Professor Wood's example, the universities would break into patriotic flame from one end of Australia to the other'.[26]

However, Fitchett's assessment of public sentiment was more than a little optimistic. The tide of patriotism that had peaked after Black Week was fast receding. Arnold Wood hung onto his professorial position with some help from the Prime Minister,

Edmund Barton, who was a member of the university Senate and, although unsympathetic to Wood's view, felt strongly about his right to hold it. Criticism of the British war effort increased as the methods employed by Kitchener bore less and less resemblance to the image of war that Australians carried in their imaginations. Soldiers were supposed to die glorious deaths on the battlefield, not waste away deliriously 'before the sickle of that grim reaper – Enteric', wrote a disenchanted soldier.[27]

Soldiers returning from their South African tours gave first-hand accounts of life on the veldt. 'The practical experience is so very different to the theory which we have learned in our drill-books', observed Arthur Tremearne. 'Why did we ever come?' asked Corporal JHM Abbott:

> This isn't charging into battle. This isn't getting the Victoria Cross. Where is all the 'pomp and circumstance of war'? Where are the bands and martial music to play us into action? Where are the clouds of drifting smoke we've read about? Where's that 'thin red line,' and all those gorgeous uniforms that used to make war picturesque, and romantic and spectacular? Where's anything but dirt, and discomfort, and starvation, and nigger-driving? Who wants to participate in a shabby war like this?

Measured against 'Waterloo, Inkerman, Gettysburg, Gravelotte or Mukden', wrote Abbott, even the great march on Pretoria seemed like 'a larrikin heaving half a brick at a policeman'. The sardonic humour of a Tasmanian officer's observation that 'We cleared the country by burning all farm-houses; and the poultry fell to the victors', only emphasised the fact that Kitchener's methods were far less noble, gallant and glorious than Wellington's.[28]

William Fitchett had no moral qualms about Kitchener's methods. In fact, he told a Methodist conference that there had never been a war 'in which there was so earnest an attempt to carry it on with humanity and kindness to the enemy'. What exercised Fitchett's mind was the performance of the Australian soldiers: had they measured up to the standards of British military prowess that he had detailed in *Deeds that Won the Empire*? How did the colonials compare with the 'hardy and dashing men of the Imperial Light Horse or .... the sturdy riders of the Imperial Yeomanry?'[29]

Fitchett's desire to be told what gallant and noble soldiers his countrymen made was a sentiment common to many of his compatriots. The despatches of Lord Roberts and Lord Kitchener from South Africa made headlines in Australia whenever they included praise of the Australians, no matter how fleeting or incidental the references to their 'soldier-like manner' or 'soldierly qualities'.[30] The British command sensed the colonials' need for martial gratification and took trouble to oblige; the stroking of delicate colonial egos was a small price to pay for the 83 000 troops that South Africa, Australia, New Zealand and Canada contributed over the course of the war. But Australians never received the emphatic proof of military competence that they craved. Their performance in comparison with that of Britons and other colonials was made more difficult to gauge by the practice of merging colonial contingents into existing British regiments. And while the Western Australians and New South Welshmen earned accolades for their 'gallant deeds' at Diamond Hill, and the New South Wales Imperial Bushmen were heralded by Kitchener for their stoicism during the siege of Elands River Post, the performance of other Australian soldiers was less worthy of praise.

Major-General SB Beatson, who led the 5th Victorian Mounted Rifles, was one British commander who conspicuously failed to comply with the implicit code of buttering up the colonials. Eighteen members of the regiment were killed and at least forty wounded when the reposed Victorian troops were rushed by a small group of Boer commandoes at Wilmansrust farm on 12 June 1901. The rest of the men either surrendered or fled. When Beatson heard of the fiasco he called the Victorians a 'fat-arsed, pot-bellied, lazy lot of wasters' and 'white livered curs'. And as if accusations of military cowardice were not difficult enough to bear, three members of the regiment were found guilty of inciting to mutiny for encouraging their fellow soldiers to refuse to serve under Beatson. The men's death sentences were commuted to imprisonment by Kitchener and they were released after some 'nudging' from the Australian government. The fact of the court martial was unknown in Australia until its details appeared in the Melbourne *Age* at the end of September 1901. Amid the confused and shame-filled reports of Wilmansrust, there were murmurings of discontent about the way Beatson had behaved, and at the arrogance of Britain in failing to inform Australia officially about the courts martial before their details appeared in the press. These criticisms of British behaviour came from more than just predictably anti-imperial sources such as the *Bulletin*. Opposition to the war was strongest in the churches, Irish communities and labour organisations, though the historian Craig Wilcox judges that 'it never won more than a strong foothold in any of these spheres'.[31]

The release of the Wilmansrust three probably prevented the issue from becoming as notorious as the case of the Bushveldt Carbineers a year later. The news of the executions of Harry Morant and Peter Handcock for the murder of Boer prisoners reached Australia at the same time as news of their courts martial – four weeks after they were killed by a firing squad on 27 February 1902. When the Barton government asked Britain for more details of the affair, Kitchener responded with a desultory and disingenuous telegram. But if some Australians sensed that Britain had not acted fairly in the matter of the Bushveldt Carbineers, their voices were barely heard above the chorus that rushed to uphold Britain's conduct, disown the English-born Morant and point out that the men were serving, not under an Australian flag, but in an irregular regiment that had been raised in South Africa. Not surprisingly, Reverend Fitchett reported that the British response found 'stern and universal endorsement in Australia'. Less predictable was the *Westralian Worker*'s conclusion that Kitchener 'had no choice to but dispatch' those 'murderers and ruffians'. Almost alone among Australian voices, the *Bulletin* took up the cause of its former contributor, Harry Morant, predicting that he 'will certainly be an Australian bush hero of the future, his statue in the Valhalla where the venerated Ned Kelly and Starlight wear their haloes unabashed'.[32] If Australians had strained at the colonial bit in the 1880s and 1890s, their response to the Bushveldt Carbineers incident shows how confined that nationalist impulse was. It would take half a century for the murdering Harry Morant to be recast as 'Breaker Morant', martyred maverick, and make true the *Bulletin*'s prediction. But in 1902, Australians had no need for an anti-imperial hero. It was easier just to forget the whole shameful episode.

*After the initial wave of excitement and the jingoism of Mafeking, Australian enthusiasm for the war in South Africa had waned.*

On 31 May 1902, Britain and the rebel republics signed the Treaty of Vereeniging, bringing to an end nearly three years of fighting. The war that Alfred Deakin had hoped might become Australia's 'spiritual equivalent of the American War of Independence' had petered out to an inglorious spectacle of farm burning, civilian imprisonment and sporadic guerilla engagement.[33] After the initial wave of excitement and the jingoism of Mafeking, Australian enthusiasm for the war had waned. How would a war that had begun with such promise and ended with the scandal of the Bushveldt Carbineers be remembered?

As the Australian troops returned from the Cape to meagre crowds, a few brave souls were prepared to declare that the great question about Australian civilisation had been answered, that Australians had shown the world they 'were not degenerate sons of the gallant race from which they sprung', but 'worthy descendants of that noble stock'. Some even went further, claiming that the Australians had proved themselves superior to British stock: 'the renewed, reinvigorated reproduction of the old race'. The colonials, so this version went, were better horsemen than the famous British cavalry, and more able to adapt to the harsh conditions on the veldt than the 'unduly rigid' Tommies. According to Corporal Abbott, the Australians were teaching regiments that had seen Waterloo and Balaclava how to 'play this particular game as it should be played'.[34]

Australian minds were also turning to the role of the historian. Reverend Fitchett felt confident that 'Someone with an adequate historical imagination will, in due time, write the story of "What the Australians did in South Africa"'. The Reverend's failure to nominate himself for the task reflected disinterest rather than modesty. The new Commonwealth government fielded offers from several people eager to fill the role of official historian. The war had another year left to run when Melbourne journalist Frank Wilkinson wrote to the Minister for Defence and his department offering his services for the important task 'of converting into permanent, consecutive form the brilliant records of Australia's first campaign'. In Wilkinson's view, 'the Govt cannot afford ... to allow such an important phase in the history of Australia to pass into oblivion without a permanent record'. But the Barton government was less sure than Wilkinson. The British War Office was already in the process of collecting and collating records, both its own and those of the colonies, for an official history: 'This History will of course be the Official History of the War, and it is difficult to see what advantage would be gained by the Commonwealth Government having an historian of its own', advised the defence department. The prime minister concurred;

while having 'no doubt of Mr Wilkinson's ability to write a good history of the nature proposed by him, I do not feel at liberty to expend funds of the Commonwealth on the undertaking'.[35]

Wilkinson, however, was not prepared to let the matter rest, and sought out a powerful ally in Edward Hutton, the commander of the Australian army. Hutton advised the Department of Defence that a history would 'have a great effect in moulding National character' and went so far as to suggest to Prime Minister Deakin a structure and marketing plan for the publication, which could be distributed to 'Schools of Art, Mechanics Institutes, Public Libraries, Government Offices, State Schools, &c'. If the book were written by 'a well-known and competent literary authority – such for instance as Dr Fitchett', he anticipated it would 'command ready sale and be read with keen interest', not merely in Australia, but also in 'all the Libraries of the Mother Country as well as other portions of the Empire'.[36]

Sensing that he was fighting an uphill battle with the prime minister, General Hutton enlisted the Governor-General, Lord Tennyson, to his cause. Like Hutton, the Governor-General baited his hook with the patriotic potential of war commemoration, telling Prime Minister Deakin that a history of the South African campaign would 'largely contribute to harmonizing and consolidating the very strong feelings of patriotism and of self-sacrifice which form so important a force in the moulding of a young People'. Whether ingenuously or otherwise, Deakin responded positively to Tennyson's 'happy' and 'timely suggestion', then failed to act on it.[37] Deakin's successor as prime minister, George Reid, lent similarly glib support to the idea of an official history.

Why were Australian politicians so ambivalent about commemorating the Boer War? The infancy of the Commonwealth seemed to work against rather than towards the cause of national commemoration. During the early years of federation, Commonwealth governments were sensitive to claims of financial profligacy and aware of criticism directed at the 'incorrigible' British War Office for its official South African history: the *Age* wondered whether the 'purpose of so costly a record' might be 'to disguise the complexion of military incompetency'.[38] Hutton and Tennyson's advocacy of the history was set against a background of financial and political constraint: the Commonwealth was constitutionally required to remit 75 per cent of its revenue from customs and excise duties to the states until 1911. The Defence Minister John Forrest was battling to steer his second effort at a defence Act through parliament and governments were preoccupied with settling into place other cornerstones of the federation, such as social security and arbitration.

Yet parsimony only partly explains why the official history was not commissioned until the approach of the war's hundredth anniversary. In 1902, the nation-state had not yet assumed its role as commemorator-in-chief. Just as contingents for the Boer War were raised by an ill-defined combination of state and private initiatives, so there existed no clear demarcation between the state and private citizens in matters of commemoration. Writing about memorials in *Sacred Places*, the historian Ken Inglis observed that 'Nobody expected federal, state or municipal governments to pay ... The grieving and the celebration were understood to be a communal rather than official responsibility'. As the expectations and urgings of Frank Wilkinson, Lord Tennyson and Edward Hutton show, this conventional understanding of the state's (lack of a) role in commemoration was changing. The British had produced their first official history after the Crimean War, basing it upon the Prussian model, which used official histories as a means of improving military performance.[39] But the Boer War was not a sufficiently memorable war to prevent Hutton's proposal for a history falling through the cracks between private and public sponsorship.

The ambivalence and apathy of the new Commonwealth government were not shared by Tasmanians, who began building their 'National Memorial' when the war still had a year to run. The Tasmanian monument was completed in 1905, a year after South Australia's and three years after Western Australia's, making those three 'non-eastern' states the only ones to complete memorials before 1914. Pondering this pattern of commemoration, Ken Inglis wondered whether Perth, Adelaide and Hobart had more compact and unified elites, which could better galvanise political and financial support than the more pluralist cities of Sydney, Melbourne and Brisbane.[40] Certainly it seems that the eastern states, which hosted more deeply rooted nationalist sentiment and greater opposition to the South African campaign, were less interested in remembering a war that was waged for dubious British interests.

Queensland's memorial to the Boer War was finally unveiled in 1919, following a difficult fundraising process that had begun in 1901. After a ten-year hiatus, Victorian veterans began preparations for a monument. Their committee had no difficulty extracting a promise of money from the state government, but was then faced with the problem of an indifferent public, for whom the war was a fading memory.[41] Insufficient funds meant that the committee was forced to replace its plan for a grand hexagonal monument guarded by six bronze lions with a simple granite obelisk. The memorial was unveiled in 1924: 'In Memory of the Australians who fell in the South African War ... Fighting for the Unity of the Empire which is our Strength and Common Heritage'. Four crouching sandstone lions, representing the 'nobility and strength of the British Empire', were added in 1952 after more money was raised.

Victoria was not the last state to raise its Boer War monument. In 1940, under the headline 'Deferred Honour', the Melbourne *Argus* thought that it seemed 'very strange' that 'only now has

Sydney erected a memorial to the 6000-odd New South Wales men and women who assisted in shaping a new era in South Africa'. Money had been collected sporadically over a period of thirty years for the memorial, which was situated on Observatory Hill in The Rocks. As Australia braced itself for another world war, which would transform its relationship with Britain, this simple sandstone block monument was dedicated to those volunteers 'who responded to the Empire's call'. The crowd sang, without the irony suggested by the elapsed decades, Kipling's 'Recessional', with its admonition: 'Lest we forget – lest we forget!'[42]

Monuments of stone would prove a longer lasting tribute to the war than South Africa Day, which was inaugurated in 1902. The day did not commemorate a significant battle for Australian soldiers – for there was none – but rather the anniversary of the Canadian charge at Paardeburg in early 1900, which marked the first time colonial troops participated in an imperial war. Australian soldiers indicated their disinterest by staying home in large numbers and South Africa Day was forgotten thereafter.[43] Its failure was not an indication that Australian soldiers were uninterested in remembering the war. Rather, it was testament to the complexity of the imperial relationship. Most Australians revelled in their Britishness, but did not want their Australianness to be subsumed completely by their imperial identity.

*Most Australians revelled in their Britishness, but did not want their Australianness to be subsumed completely by their imperial identity.*

They did not share the imperial federationist aspirations of British statesmen such as Joseph Chamberlain, Cecil Rhodes and Alfred Milner and the federation movement's chief publicist, the author Rudyard Kipling. Australian soldiers wanted to remember a version of the war that was distinctly Australian (and flattering of Australian soldiering), albeit built upon the racial foundation stones of King and Empire.

The war that returned soldiers preferred to remember was recorded most accurately by Corporal JHM Abbott in his 1902 memoir, *Tommy Cornstalk*, a book imbued with the fashion for scientific categorisation of the late Victorian and Edwardian ages. For Abbott, the Boer War provided a unique opportunity to compare the 'human product' of the New World with that of the Old: an opportunity that would not present itself again until the 'Great War comes'. The product of the New World was 'Tommy Cornstalk', Abbott's prophetic fusion of the Australian bushman and the archetypal European soldier hero. Cornstalk was deep-chested, slimly built and long of limb. He thought more about sport and holidays than work and valued physical over intellectual pursuits: 'A man who cannot read is far less to be pitied than one who cannot ride'. Upon comparison with his British counterpart, Tommy Atkins, Abbott found Cornstalk to be a superior fighting specimen, though he was not without his faults, if disrespect for authority and a reluctance to bend to military discipline could be considered faults: 'It seems to him bitterly hard that he is required to salute a man whom he may not consider at all his better'. In fact, according to Abbott, Cornstalk 'considered himself to be rather a better man than most other men'.[44]

Uniquely among Australian memoirists of the Boer War, George Witton was willing to uncouple his remembrance entirely from the imperial wagon. The former Bushveldt Carbineer had escaped the death penalty given to Morant and Handcock in early 1902, but was sentenced instead to life imprisonment for his involvement in the murders of Boer prisoners. Though he was released from prison in 1904, Witton remained bitter for the rest of his life about his treatment by the British military. *Scapegoats of the Empire*, published in 1907, cast Lord Kitchener as an expedient villain with the blood of two innocent men on his hands, rather than in his usual role of soldier hero. Harry Morant and Peter Handcock played the martyred heroes who were killed to appease German outrage at the murder of a German missionary. The book ran to at least two editions and inspired a rumour, never proved, that the Australian government was buying copies in order to repress criticism of Kitchener and the British government.[45] George Witton's characterisation of himself as an innocent betrayed in *Scapegoats of the Empire* found some sympathy among the Australian public, though Australians were more likely to see his betrayers as Morant and Handcock than the British military. Witton died in 1942 and did not live to see his story capture the imagination of a public newly attuned to anti-British tales in the 1960s. His ashes are interred at Lutwyche Cemetery in Brisbane. The road that runs alongside the cemetery is called Kitchener Road.

⊹⊱⊰⊹

Five years after the end of the Boer War the British journalist Alfred Buchanan wrote in his essay on antipodean society, *The Real Australia*, that people ought to sympathise with the 'little Australian ... He has so few materials with which to build. He has no national flag, no history, no bead-roll of fame, no justification for enthusiasm of any kind'. But the most gaping deficit for the 'little Australian' looking to 'nourish the flame of patriotic sentiment' was that 'The altar has not been stained with crimson as every rallying centre of a nation should be'.[46] It was as if South Africa had never happened.

In 1899 the Boer War had been welcomed by the majority of Australians as their test of nationhood and racial worth: the soldiers' performance under fire would furnish proof of whether the British race was evolving or degenerating in its strange new setting. The test, Australians imagined, would be something like Waterloo: men would fire rifles at the enemy or rush towards them on horseback, testing their physical strength and courage in the calamity of battle. As steel pierced the chests of these brave men, they would feel an 'undercurrent of hot joy to know they fell as soldiers love to fall, face forward to the foe'.[47] But South Africa was very different from Waterloo, and Kitchener's victory was not swift, emphatic and gallant as Wellington's had been. Popular responses to the war were rooted more in anticipation of Australia's pending martial baptism, than in the cause for which the troops went to war. When the baptism proved to be something of a fiasco, the public simply lost interest. For the new Commonwealth government, preoccupied with setting up the young nation-state, the Boer War did not justify the expense and effort of commemoration. Yet the lessons of the veldt were learned. From 1911, boys and young men were drilled for military service, and the minds of future soldiers were filled, as never before, with the propaganda of Empire. However, Waterloo, not South Africa, was the allegorical centre around which the martial culture was instilled in the minds of the young.

If the Boer War had been a more personally devastating war for a greater proportion of Australians, then it would have been better remembered. But the hysteria of Black Week and the jubilation displayed at the relief of Mafeking were evidence of the existence of an equally powerful emotion, dormant by the end of the war, which influenced people's desire to remember or forget. Australians craved the test of war that would make legitimate their claims to nationhood. The nation-making war that finally came in 1914 embodied the contradiction that lay at the heart of Australian nationalism: the very nation that it sought to distinguish itself from was the nation whose approval it craved. When they came to write the story of the Great War, the first historians would deal with this paradox in profoundly different ways.

# 2

# 1916–1936:
# EARLY HISTORIES OF THE GREAT WAR

WHEN GREAT BRITAIN DECLARED WAR ON Germany on 4 August 1914, there was never any question that Australia would lend its support to the British war effort. Australian forces saw their first action the following month when they seized German New Guinea. During 1915 they fought unsuccessfully in Turkey in an Allied campaign to capture Constantinople, and subsequently in the Middle East and on the Western Front in France and Belgium. Of a national population of approximately five million in 1914, 330 000 people served overseas in the Australian Imperial Force (AIF). Sixty thousand soldiers died, two-thirds of them on the Western Front, and 167 000 were recorded officially as wounded. While Australians felt immense pride in the fighting capacity of their soldiers, industrial unrest and conflict over conscription caused a degree of division and hostility at home that had never before existed and has never been seen since.

Such was the scale and extent of destruction of the Great War that there was none of the apathy or contention that had characterised attempts to commemorate the South African campaign. Even so, during and immediately after the Great War, there existed an historiographical interregnum – a pause in the recording of the Australian story. How would this war be remembered? What place would it occupy in the history of the young Australian nation?

This chapter considers the earliest attempts to write the history of Australia in the Great War. The first historians, Ernest Scott and Charles Bean, brought to their tasks divergent views about Australian nationhood and drew very different conclusions about the place of the war in Australian history. The two men were obliged to confront their ideological differences when they collaborated on the domestic volume of the *Official History of Australia in the War of 1914–1918*, the eleventh of a twelve-volume series of which Bean was editor and principal author. Neither Scott's story of imperial resolve nor Bean's tale of national baptism proved particularly resilient in the face of Australia's conscription crisis. However, their efforts, both individual and combined, show how the war could be used in the service of two very different kinds of nationalism.

Ernest Scott was an unlikely professor of history. Born illegitimately in 1867, he was raised in the East Midlands of England by an old grandfather and a housekeeper. As a sensitive young man with a flair for words, Scott soon abandoned his religious faith, along with early plans to become a teacher. He found work as a radical journalist in London and married Mabel Besant, the daughter of the famous feminist, Fabian and sometime theosophist, Annie Besant. In 1892 the Besant-Scotts migrated to Melbourne, where Ernest edited the local theosophy journal and the couple became advocates for women's suffrage. Mabel told a town hall meeting in 1894 that 'a woman should not only be her husband's housekeeper, the nurse of his children and the darner of his stockings, but his helpmate and companion'.[1] Soon after Mabel expressed such progressive aspirations for marriage, the Besant-Scotts' relationship faltered when she converted to Catholicism. For more than a decade, Ernest and Mabel lived in miserable cohabitation, until Mabel returned to England in 1909 with their daughter.

This upheaval in Ernest Scott's personal life (the hyphenated name was soon discarded) coincided with an ideological transformation. He began to shed his radical skin, finding new friends among the progressively minded 'independent Australian Britons' who shone brightly in pre-Federation Melbourne, men such as Melbourne University law professor Harrison Moore, barrister Frederic Eggleston, businessman Herbert Brookes and barrister and politician, Alfred Deakin. Having renounced his mystic socialism, Scott found his moral bearings in the cause of British imperialism. This new faith stood for principles that guaranteed 'to mankind the largest measure of freedom, justice and righteousness'.[2]

Ernest Scott witnessed the creation of the Australian nation from his vantage point as a journalist and later as a Hansard reporter for the Victorian and federal parliaments. Federation and the process that preceded it only confirmed to him that the destiny of Australia lay in the perpetuation of its British heritage and values. Scott pursued this conviction through his membership of the Round Table, an organisation that existed to promote closer ties between Britain and the Commonwealth. In an article for the organisation's journal, he derided the notion that the dominions should endeavour to establish identities apart from Britain: 'How do you aspire to a distinctive national character? I have heard a certain type of young Australian talk like that, and it made me feel as if the Pilgrim Fathers had called a meeting on the Plymouth Rock and voted by a majority to speak through their noses'.[3]

Watching and describing British civilisation being sown into Australian soil by his friends and associates, Scott wondered at the dealings of fate. What good fortune had led the British, rather than the French or the Portuguese, the Dutch or the Spanish, to settle this land? Without religion to answer his existential musings, Scott turned to history. The publication of *Terre Napoléon* established him as a pioneer of rigorous archival history and of the study of the Australian past. After consulting previously ignored French records, he overturned decades of historiographical convention by proving that French maritime expeditions of the early nineteenth century served scientific rather than acquisitive purposes. Scott never again hit historiographical pay-dirt as emphatically as he did with *Terre Napoléon*, but the faith he had acquired in the scientific method and the acclaim he garnered sustained him through monographs on the French explorer *Lapérouse* and the English navigator Matthew Flinders.[4]

It was on the basis of these books and numerous scholarly articles that in 1913 the 45-year-old *Hansard* reporter was appointed to the chair of history at the University of Melbourne. One of the first matters the new professor attended to was the negotiation of a generous commission from Oxford University Press to produce a school textbook of Australian history. Such books had become essential accessories to the burgeoning system of state education, wherein history was the primary means of civic instruction.[5] Scott was the first academic historian to attempt a book of Australian history, which would challenge him to extend his expertise beyond the European exploratory period. For the purposes of this broad historical survey, intricate knowledge of archival material and historiographical gainsaying would not count for so much as the articulation of a cogent and concise argument about the course of Australian history. So what did this lapsed-radical British emigrant have to say about the history of Australia? And how would he work the dramatic events unfolding in the northern hemisphere into his national narrative?

In January 1915 Ernest Scott began drafting, chapter by

chronological chapter, his survey of Australian history. The country was newly at war. Australia's forces had seized German colonies in the Pacific, its navy had forced the German cruiser *Emden* to run aground on the Cocos Islands, and the first contingent of soldiers was training at Mena camp in Egypt with the Giza pyramids and sphinx as its backdrop. Scott's manuscript was probably somewhere in the middle of the nineteenth century, elucidating the reasons for the end of transportation or the dawn of colonial constitutional government, when press reports described Australian deeds at Gallipoli in breathless headlines. Scott's happy story of a nation and a race that had stumbled through dark beginnings towards an enlightened liberalism had been granted a perfect ending: from 'a blank space on the map' there was now 'the record of a new name ... that of Anzac', he wrote in the Preface to *A Short History of Australia* in July 1916.[6]

But despite Scott's decision to enclose the *Short History* between the bookends of European discovery and the 'Great European War', its thematic architecture was left intact and its content barely altered in light of unfolding events in Turkey and France. The half-page and two hundred words that Scott devoted to the war reported with unmistakable pride that 'Australia flew to arms on the instant', putting paid to German predictions that it would declare independence and become a republic: 'They might as truthfully have prophesied that Yorkshire would declare its independence, or that Manchester would become a republic'.[7]

The *Short History* described in some detail how Australia's first armed force of the Great War, the Australian Naval and Military Expeditionary Force (AN&MEF), combined with New Zealand forces to seize German territories in the Pacific in the first weeks of the war.[8] However, Scott attached less significance to events on the Dardanelles Peninsula in Turkey during 1915, which had reached their conclusion by the time he drafted his final chapter early the following year. He described Australian actions against the Turks in the Middle East and at Gallipoli in a single sentence:

> Australian troops fought in resisting the first Turko-Teutonic
> attack on Egypt, and took a leading part in the assaults on
> the Gallipoli Peninsula – where the coincidence that the
> initials of the Australian and New Zealand Army Corps spelt
> Anzac, gave rise to a name that added a new marking to the
> map and signified things which history will not allow to fade
> from memory.[9]

For Scott, the poorly conceived and executed British-led attack
on the Dardanelles was a minor aspect of the great battle against
Prussian militarism. His book was silent on the flurry of Australian nationalist pride that followed the events of 25 April 1915
and he certainly did not consider the 'assaults on the Gallipoli
Peninsula' to have induced the birth of the Australian nation.

Scouring the war experience for proof of imperial unity rather
than national distinction, Scott found it in the way that Australia rushed to the aid of Great Britain. This was not a new and
significant chapter in Australian history, but an incident within
the greater story of 'Imperial Relations'. The war was an affirma-
tion of ideals that had been settled at Waterloo. Great Britain
was Europe's pre-eminent colonial and naval power, and whatever significance this war had lay in ensuring that Britain and its
Empire crushed German pretensions to that status.

Scott's interpretation of Australia's role in the Great War was
entirely consistent with the principal theme of the *Short History*:
the triumphant tale of the perpetuation of the British race, after
an uncertain beginning, in a new environment. It did not matter
that Australians lacked a meaningful history of their own, for
'British history is their history, with its failings to be guarded
against and its glories to be emulated'. Australians had no cause
to distinguish themselves from Britons with contrivances such as

the martial baptism, for their nation and its (white) inhabitants were but 'a southern reflex of the type of civilization flourishing in the British Isles'.[10]

Sales of the *Short History* were excellent; it was destined to become the standard history textbook in Australian schools for the next three decades. Reviewers seemed obliged that a university professor had applied himself to the meagre subject of Australian history and praised the work, though some of the more conscientious noted errors of fact and regretted the fleeting attention paid to Australian literature.[11] The imperialist tone of the book and its scant coverage of the war were not remarked upon, even by the *Sydney Morning Herald's* reviewer, who noted in passing that Gallipoli was the occasion at which Australia 'attained its full stature of nationhood'.[12]

New editions of the *Short History* were published in 1918, 1919 and 1921. Despite the tumult of the debate over whether to introduce conscription in Australia, Scott made no amendment to the brief account of the war provided in 1916. It was not until 1927 that he revised his *Short History* to include a chapter on the Great War, by that time, nine years past. The new, penultimate chapter was slotted in between existing ones on 'The Commonwealth' and 'Imperial Relations'; thus the book still ended with its original treatise on British racial genius.[13] In the eleven years that had elapsed since Scott became the first historian in Australia to write about the war, other voices had been added to the record. While the book's bibliography reflected this growing literature, Scott's interpretation of the war was unswayed by the nationalist slant of much of it.[14]

Scott's expanded account of the Gallipoli landing in the 1927 edition of the *Short History* would surely have sustained the attention of the schoolchildren for whom it was primarily written:

The sun shone from a cloudless blue sky upon the sparkling
waters of the Aegean as the ships moved inshore. From the
land batteries a hail of bullets spattered the sea, and shells
from heavy howitzers screamed through the air, dealing out
death to many of the men in the boats which dashed through
the shallow waters from the transports to the shore.

The Boy's Own–style description of Australian soldiers 'Singing
and shouting' as they scaled the cliffs at Anzac Cove probably
owed something to John Masefield's account. The English poet
and writer had described the troops singing 'Australia will be
there' in his famous book Gallipoli, which Scott listed in his bibliography. Despite the failure of the Gallipoli campaign, Scott
concluded that the Australians performed 'a great feat of arms
not eclipsed for daring and endurance by any during the war'. He
allowed that the Australian soldiers displayed 'reckless courage',
'heroic fortitude' and 'stubborn valour', and were 'splendid men
in the pink of condition', though he stopped short of Masefield's
observation that they were unsurpassed 'for physical beauty and
nobility of bearing'.[15] This hymn of praise, sung as it was in the
romantic rhetoric of pre-1914 war literature, remained silent on
the matter of nation-making. Gallant soldiers the Anzacs made,
but to suggest that their deeds forged a nation would be akin to
calling a meeting of the Pilgrim Fathers on Plymouth Rock.

Scott made only cursory mention of Australian martial deeds
in France in the new chapter on the Great War. Sir John Monash,
who led the Australian Corps in 1918, would have been flattered
by Scott's lengthy and laudatory account of his intellect and abil-
ities as a commander. The professor was sure to list in his bibliography the work of his friend and occasional dinner guest at the
Scotts' Brighton home.[16] But despite Scott's flattering portrait of
Monash, the general's self-aggrandising version of history in The
Australian Victories in France in 1918 was quite different from Scott's.

Pre-empting much of what Bean would say in the *Official History*, Monash ventured that the military proficiency of the Australian soldier, of which he made a great deal, was fostered by the democratic institutions under which he was reared, an education system that taught him to think independently and practically, an instinct for sport and adventure, and the opportunity for 'creating a great national tradition'.[17] Scott was not interested in posing questions about the idiosyncrasies of the Australian soldier, let alone in answering them.

Scott had little choice but to deal in his new chapter about the war with conscription and its consequences. There was no doubt where the professor stood on the issue. He had signalled his support for the concept of compulsion as early as April 1915, a position entirely consistent with the fact that he aligned Australia's strategic interests exactly with those of Britain. Scott delivered a lecture to members of Melbourne University's Historical Society in September 1917, almost a year after the failure of the first conscription referendum and shortly before Prime Minister Hughes announced that a second vote would be held in December. Scott likened Australians' resistance to conscription to that of 'a small boy putting his finger to his nose in face of his mother, and being saucily proud of his impudence'. But there would come a time, he warned, when they 'must accept the responsibility which is the moral consequence of their nationality'.[18] For a fierce loyalist such as Scott, the failure of the second referendum, by a slightly greater margin than the first, could only be explained by the moral inadequacy of a large portion of the Australian public, many of whom were Catholic and working class. How could a democratic system of government function if the people to whom it was

*The* Short History's *grand theme of the triumphant unfurling of British civilisation in Australia was compromised by the failure of the two conscription referenda.*

magnanimously granted did not exercise their rights responsibly?

Scott's revision of the *Short History* in 1927 left untouched his original rhetoric about Australian race pride and the nation flying to arms 'on the instant' upon the outbreak of war. But the *Short History*'s grand theme of the triumphant unfurling of British civilisation in Australia was compromised by the failure of the two conscription referenda. The professor was fierce in his defence of Prime Minister Hughes, whose determination to introduce conscription was due to the fact that he recognised the Great War's 'fateful significance for Australia ... only a churlish and rancid opponent would deny that his fervent Celtic temperament was deeply stirred by the war'. It would have been churlish of the gentlemanly Scott to register what he believed to be the true reason for Australians' failure to implement compulsion: the impudence and irresponsibility of a good part of its population. He recorded the results of the conscription votes without embellishment or explanation, noting that the issue had caused 'an intensity of bitterness exceeding anything known in Australian politics hitherto', but made no mention of the reasoning of those opposed to it. Nor did he mention the name of the anti-conscriptionists' most prominent and controversial spokesperson, the Catholic Archbishop of Melbourne, Daniel Mannix.[19] Lacking grist for his loyalist mill, Scott sought solace in select and unadorned facts, a technique he would revisit in his collaboration with the official historian, Charles Bean.

While Ernest Scott was expounding to his students on the moral necessity of conscription in the Australian spring of 1917, Charles Bean, in his dual roles as official correspondent and official historian-to-be, watched the 4th and 5th Divisions advance under a creeping barrage upon Polygon Wood near the Belgian town of Ypres. Almost six thousand Australians were killed and wounded in the successful attack of 26 September 1917. Among the dead were two of Bean's dear friends from childhood. The strain of the war was taking its toll on his nerves, but Bean pressed on, fortified against complete collapse by his determination to bear witness to the deeds of the Australian soldiers.[20] His mission to celebrate Australian distinctiveness was at least a match for Scott's evangelistic imperialism.

Charles Edwin Woodrow Bean was born into a respectable British–Australian family in Bathurst in 1879. His early education was at the faux-British All Saints College in Bathurst, which was run by his headmaster-father. By the time the family returned to Britain in 1889, the eldest son Charles was already 'a boy in love with England and Empire'. He was an eager student of tales of British military glory with, according to his brother, a 'great power of imagination ... he could draw out of his head, from early boyhood, and so often as not it was battle scenes he drew'. During winters spent in Brussels, Edwin Bean would take his sons to fossick around the battlefield of Waterloo, where they collected imagined relics – 'probably bits of farm harness', Bean reflected decades later.[21] Charles completed his schooling at Clifton College in Bristol, alma mater of the British generals Douglas Haig and William Birdwood, the imperialist poet Henry Newbolt and Bean's father Edwin. After graduating with second-class honours in classics and a law degree from Oxford, Bean failed (like his father before him) to gain admission to the Indian Civil Service. Denied the Oxford First he must have coveted and rebuffed by Britain's bureaucratic elite, Charles Bean decided (again, like his father) to chance his luck in Australia.

Landing back in Australia in 1904 after a fifteen-year absence, Bean worked, among other things, as an assistant to various circuit judges with whom he travelled around rural New South Wales. His observations as a 'new chum' about the recently federated nation were published in the *Sydney Morning Herald* as a series of articles under the heading 'Australia'. In contrast to Ernest Scott's observation made a decade later that 'There are differences [between Britain and Australia], but they do not at present go deep', Bean declared in 1907 that the Australian was emphatically 'not an Englishman'. Physically, he (it was always a male) was different from the Briton: 'a tall, spare man, clean and wiry ... with a certain refined ascetic strength'. His character was 'the simplest imaginable. The key to it is just this – that he takes everything on its merits, and nothing on authority'. This 'Briton reborn', the author implied, was at least equal, if not superior, to that from which he had sprung.[22]

Bean's creative and curious mind was better suited to journalism than law, a fact he acknowledged when he became a junior staff reporter at the *Sydney Morning Herald* in 1908. His skill for observation and unusual ability as a writer were rewarded by his editor TW Heney, who despatched him to the New South Wales countryside to write about the Australian wool industry. Dismayed at first by the dreary-sounding assignment, Bean quickly realised that 'the most important product of the wool industry was men; it was responsible for creating some of the outstanding national types'. The assignment yielded two books – *On the Wool Track* (1910) and *The Dreadnought of the Darling* (1911) – both of which were powered by Bean's fascination with the Australian male. Englishmen had long ago 'thought out and settled' their national ideal – 'the gentleman'. In the man of the interior, Australians had found an archetype upon which their nation could be built. They were consciously forming their ideals from those standards of 'pluck, hardiness, unaffectedness, loyalty, truthfulness [and] hospitality' set by the men 'in the pastoral industry and at the diggings'.[23]

If Bean used Britain as a point of comparison with the emerging Australian nation, he was never critical of the mother country. Unlike the radical voices of writers for the *Bulletin* such as Henry Lawson and Joseph Furphy and the *Bulletin* editor JF Archibald, Charles Bean's affection for Australia was not felt at the expense of Great Britain (though later that would change). Bean sounded as earnest as Professor Scott when he explained in 1913 what the Union Jack represented:

> [It stood] For generosity in sport and out if it; for a pure regard for women, a chivalrous marriage tie, a fair trial, a free speech, liberty of the subject and equality before the law; for every British principle of cleanliness in body and mind, in trade or politics, of kindness to animals, of fun and fairplay ...[24]

The difference between Charles Bean and Ernest Scott's views about Australia's British heritage was one of emphasis rather than substance. While Scott placed this heritage at the centre of the Australian story and sought to diminish differences between the centre and the periphery, Bean's mission was to document the differences between the two.

Charles Bean's thesis about the emergence of an 'Australian Ideal' drew from the ideologies of nationalism and racial hierarchy, which had been made more brutal by the rivalry between European empires for colonies, markets and arms. Bean had pitted his 'Australian Ideal' against the vicissitudes of fire and flood and drought, and he had emerged triumphant. But what this nascent version of manhood needed, according to the widely held conviction of the age, was to prove his mettle in the fires of battle. The opportunity came in 1914 and, when Bean was elected as the official correspondent for the AIF by his peers in the Australian Journalists' Association, the Australian male had gained his greatest advocate.

At the request of the Minister for Defence, George Pearce, Bean agreed to write the history of the AIF in addition to his journalistic duties. In December 1918 Charles Bean estimated to his parents that the history would 'certainly take 5 years (or 4 anyway) to write'; it ended up taking twenty-four years. The first volume of the *Official History* was published in 1921 and the last in 1942. Bean himself wrote six of the volumes, about Gallipoli, France and Flanders. He edited others on the navy, the flying corps, Rabaul, Sinai and Palestine and domestic affairs. With Henry Gullett, he annotated a volume of photographs.[25]

Emboldened by the success of his prewar publications, Bean was adamant from the outset that his official history would be different from conventional military histories. He was not interested in the machinations of generals and politicians, but 'in what actually happened at the cutting edge of the military machine' where soldier was pitted against soldier, character against character, National Ideal against National Ideal. The history would not be a military history, but a national history, 'read by my nation as long as it exists'. Bean's decision to pay unprecedented attention to front-line soldiering earned him a reputation as an unusually democratic war historian, but his motivation was nationalist rather than democratic sentiment:

> as war – even more than other disasters – still affords a
> plain trial of national character, it was necessary to show
> how the Australian citizen reacted to it. This could be done
> only by recording not merely the decisions of generals and
> governments, but also the manner in which those decisions
> worked out through the ultimate machinery of men's nerves
> and muscles at the fighting edge, where nation grated against
> nation.[26]

In telling the story of great incidents such as 'the Landing, Lone Pine, the Evacuation and so on', Bean felt that his words were simultaneously constructing the Australian nation upon a featureless landscape: 'The foundations must be deep and solid, the structure firmly morticed, and it is with a feeling of intense relief that one puts the last stone on each established monument'. In the final paragraphs of the *Official History*, published in the middle of another world war, Bean did not resile from the theme that he had first articulated more than two decades earlier. After passing the great test of war:

> Australians watched the name of their country rise high in the esteem of the world's oldest and greatest nations. Every Australian bears that name proudly abroad today; and by the daily doings, great and small, which these pages have narrated, the Australian nation came to know itself.[27]

Australian historians have recorded the sins, mostly of emphasis and omission, which Charles Bean committed in *The Anzac Book* and the *Official History* in order that his 'Australian Ideal' could be shown to have passed emphatically the greatest 'trial of national character'. Lloyd Robson, for example, undermined Bean's contention that Australian soldiers' prowess derived from their rural backgrounds when he demonstrated that only a small proportion cited occupations in primary industry on their enlistment papers. As the Anzac legend began its resurgence during the 1980s, historians of the baby boomer generation who had been radicalised by the Vietnam War challenged what they perceived as the militarism and political conservatism of the Anzac legend. David Kent argued that Charles Bean was a highly selective editor of *The Anzac Book* and consciously crafted an image of the Australian soldier as tough, loyal, ill-disciplined and sardonic. Alistair Thomson has documented the controversy that arose when Bean deemed that a draft of the official British history of Gallipoli placed too much weight on the Australian shirkers who gathered on the beach on the day of the landing. After details were leaked to an hysterical press, the British official historian James Edmonds was quick to place diplomatic serenity before historical accuracy and toned down the criticism, to the point where even Bean thought it had gone too far.[28]

As Thomson has shown, Bean often complained during the war that British military leaders underplayed Australian military successes.[29] This resentment was part of a broader antipathy that he was developing towards aspects of British society. In the privacy of his diary, Bean wished for a cleaning-out of the British class system and the abolition of the monarchy, 'because it perpetuates the snobbery which paralyses England'.[30] Despite his eligibility, he refused to wear an officer's Sam Browne belt with his captain's uniform because it represented to him 'all that is worst in the snobbishness of the British army'. Nor was Bean an immediate convert to the cause of conscription, despite the explicit wishes of the British political and military leadership. Indeed, he seems only to have decided in favour of compulsion once he learned that his hero, the chief staff officer in the AIF, General Brudenell White, was a conscriptionist. Bean shared with John Masefield, the English author whose *Gallipoli* propaganda piece had thrilled the Australian public when it described the Anzacs as men who 'walked and looked like the kings in old poems', a growing distaste for the inequities of British society. When the two spent a weekend together in London in mid-1917, Bean discovered that they shared the view that 'the best thing the world can get out of the war – especially Britain – is a revolution'. Masefield had a fascination with Australians that matched Bean's and thought that rather than letting the young race perish in the war, these fine specimens should be sent back home and leave 'the old race [to] die'.[31] It is unlikely that Bean would have subscribed to such a drastic sentiment, but his conversations with Masefield illustrate the extent to which he had prised himself loose from the British embrace. When Charles Bean came to collaborate with Ernest Scott on the domestic volume of the *Official History*, the editor would have to confront not only Scott's loyalist sympathies, but the discrepancies between his own thesis of Australia's martial baptism and the disturbing domestic events of 1916 and 1917.

In one of the more fanciful passages in *The Story of Anzac*, Charles Bean wrote of the war that 'so completely did it absorb the people's energies, so completely concentrate and unify their effort, that it is possible for those who lived among the events to say that in those days Australia became fully conscious of itself as a nation'.[32] In moments of greater frankness, Bean was capable of admitting that Australians were, in fact, far from united by their war effort, that there was a great divide between those who served and the 'shirkers' who stayed at home, that industrial unrest and class antagonism were significant problems, and that the issue of conscription divided the country almost down the middle. Bean had applied his great thesis about the evolution of a race of 'new Britons' to the men of the AIF, but he could not arrange the facts of conscription to fit his theme. It was not just the shame of the failed conscription referenda that perturbed Bean but the aspersion that the rejection of conscription cast upon his own volumes and, by extension, the men of the 1st AIF. His story of a nation of natural warriors was not well served by that nation's inability to produce volunteers sufficient to supply the frontline and its failure to coerce them by means of conscription. In the clamour of Anzac idolatry it could easily be forgotten that six out of every ten eligible Australian men between the ages of eighteen and forty-four *did not* enlist for war.[33]

Though Bean's original plan for the *Official History* did not include a volume about internal Australian affairs, the official historian acceded without fuss to the wishes of his political masters on the matter. The Nationalist government led by WM Hughes was eager to ensure that its effort during the war, particularly its position on conscription, was a matter of public record; if someone were to be blamed for the fiasco it would not be them. The concept of a dedicated volume about home affairs (written by someone else) pleased Bean as it 'left me free to discard nearly all political questions and devote myself to the AIF in the field', which was where his interest lay. Bean accepted the suggestion that his former editor at the *Sydney Morning Herald*, TW Heney, should write the domestic volume. Heney's editorials in the *Herald* during the war confirmed that he was 'sound' on the conscription issue, a fact that no doubt influenced his choice by the government. Bean counselled Heney about his particular responsibility as gatekeeper of the conscription issue: 'it is the effort in Australia rather than the effort abroad which is subjected to criticism by the outside world, and which requires an especial degree of understanding'.[34]

When Bean briefed Heney for the role, the official historian had not yet realised the magnitude of the task. Gradually he came to comprehend the range of sources that would need to be examined in order to present a record of domestic affairs sufficiently complex and sophisticated to stand alongside the operational volumes. Unlike Bean, however, Heney failed to make the intellectual transition from journalist to historian. His manuscript relied too heavily on newspaper reports and presented only the perspective of New South Wales. Heney failed to consult Commonwealth records adequately or to speak to people involved in key events. After reading a draft, General White wrote to Bean: 'The work is neither record nor history. It is merely a newspaper article – and not much better informed than the average newspaper product!' When Bean abandoned his decade-long effort to coax a decent book from Heney in 1928, he was determined to enlist someone possessed of academic rigour who could lift the journalist's superficial account 'onto a higher plane as a literary and historical work'. He was also keen to recruit 'someone other than a

*The issue of conscription divided the country almost down the middle.*

"Cornstalk" [New South Welshman]' in order to counter Heney's Sydney bias. When the poet and professor of English Archibald Strong declared himself unavailable to take on the work, at Strong's suggestion Bean turned to the eminent historian Ernest Scott.[35] Bean and Scott had articulated distinctly different versions of the war. What would be the outcome of collaboration between an academic whose inclinations were uncompromisingly imperial and an official war historian who was moving in the opposite direction?

Charles Bean again misjudged the scale of the task when he estimated to Ernest Scott that the manuscript of 240 000 words should take approximately one year to complete. Scott thought that he might require a bit of extra time: 'One ought not to feel that one could not spare time to follow up a trail. But subject to that consideration, I should think that a year would be nearly sufficient'. In addition to Heney's manuscript, which Scott was free to use as he saw fit, he would consult parliamentary debates and papers, newspapers, defence records, personal collections such as that of former prime minister WM Hughes and official government papers in Canberra. Bean must have felt relief that at last he was dealing with a real historian when Scott flagged his intention to talk to politicians such as Hughes, George Pearce and Joseph Cook in order to canvass a wide range of opinion about the matter that stood at the heart of the enterprise: conscription. Scott 'would even venture to approach [Catholic Archbishop of Melbourne, Daniel] Mannix, and show him the pages in which he was referred to, if he would consent to look at them'.[36]

After reading a draft of the first chapter late in 1928, Bean took the opportunity to spell out Scott's responsibility as author of the domestic volume: 'the reader should, by the time he has finished the book, understand the Australian attitude and outlook – our independence and habit of thinking for ourselves'.[37] He believed that Scott might cite this Australian independence of mind – a characteristic Bean had been claiming and documenting since the early 1900s – to explain the nation's failure to adopt conscription. But Scott was not open to special nationalist pleadings on the matter of conscription, because he countenanced no significant delineation of strategic interest or character between Australians and Britons. When he finally came to deal with conscription, his earlier undertakings to deal with the issue 'patiently and fully' had been forgotten.

Upon reviewing Scott's work, Bean became concerned at its overwhelming bias. He spent the early part of 1934 inserting more balance into Scott's draft and confided to Robert Garran, long-time secretary of the Commonwealth Attorney-General's Department, the onerous nature of the task: 'As I was not in Australia during the war, it has been a pretty big job – indeed, I have done little else since Christmas'. He was dismayed at the absence of an account of the principles of the anti-conscriptionist case and cautioned Scott that any justifiable charge of bias 'would wreck the history'. He found a statement of the former Labor prime minister Andrew Fisher's views and secured advice from Henry Boote of *The Australian Worker* and the Presbyterian minister AJ Prowse, 'both of whom are solid men'. Scott acquiesced to his editor's insertions – he was hardly in a position to protest – but drew the line at including a photograph of Archbishop Mannix in the book.[38]

The writing of *Australia During the War* proved to be a far more convoluted process than either man had anticipated. Bean was surprised and dismayed to discover how many factual errors the esteemed professor's manuscript contained: 'numerous minor inaccuracies – as to dates, figures, personal details, etc … as well as a certain number of more important ones', he told Scott. He worried that Scott would think him 'over-fussy', but his fastidious nature would not allow him to leave any stone unturned. Although Scott was weary of the task and preparing for a grand tour to the United

States and Europe with his wife Emily, Bean was relentless. He thought the book dealt inadequately with such matters as taxation, outbreaks of disorder in the camps, the funding of an Australian arsenal, munitions workers, comfort funds other than the Red Cross and repatriation, and requested more information.[39] In his turn, Scott worried that the book was becoming dull beneath its burden of facts, but still he cheerfully indulged Bean's obsessive drive for detail and precision.

In the second half of 1933, leaving Bean and his staff to labour over his still-incomplete manuscript, Ernest Scott set out on his tour of the United States and Europe. The itinerary included a visit to Sir Ronald Munro-Ferguson, who had been Governor-General in Australia and a friend of Scott's during the war. Munro-Ferguson died while Scott was crossing the Atlantic, but his widow allowed the charmed professor to peruse her husband's archive at will. If Scott's enthusiasm for the official history had been waning, this unexpected trove of documentation seemed to revive it. Scott dashed off a letter to Bean. There was proof that the Governor-General made up his mind 'independently of ministerial advice' to grant Prime Minister Joseph Cook a double dissolution in June 1914. Here was the chance to prove the author Berriedale Keith wrong on the 'DD question'; this new material was so 'interesting'

*If Charles Bean wrote the* Official History *from the trenches of Gallipoli and the Western Front, Ernest Scott's* Short History of Australia *was written from Waterloo's Butte du Lion.*

and 'important' that it warranted a new chapter in the already bloated manuscript, to be titled 'The Governor General'. Best of all, there was a letter from the papal delegate to the Governor-General that criticised Archbishop Mannix's utterances about the conscription issue. Scott told his editor that the new material would 'brighten up a book which has to deal with

such subjects as wool, wheat and metals, which are not material for lively reading'. He also wrote to Major Treloar at the
War Museum: did he want one of Munro-Ferguson's uniforms
for display – the khaki or the full dress general's uniform? Perhaps he should ask for both: 'they will be objects of interest in
your Museum – especially if you could get good wax figures of
[Munro-Ferguson] made to wear them'.[40]

There was no doubt that Munro-Ferguson was a significant
figure in the domestic story of the war. In addition to his crucial
role in matters of security, all communication between the British
government and the Prime Minister of Australia passed through
the office of the Governor-General until late in the war. Munro-
Ferguson's meticulously maintained records allowed Scott unusual insight into the processes of government decision-making,
but his decision to compress this archive into a new chapter
was surely made because he could not face the painstaking task
of integrating pertinent material within the existing manuscript.
The separate biographical chapter sat awkwardly within a book
that was organised around themes and issues, and proved as
obsequious as Scott's communications to Bean suggested it would
be. Scott's description of the Governor-General's personality –
'Humourous [sic], fond of conversation … he could cap any tale
with a better one, and talk flowed freely in his presence' – was
clearly derived from fond personal reminiscence. He thought
that Munro-Ferguson's 'splendid presence' (indeed, his resemblance to portraits of Sir Walter Raleigh) could be explained by
'race, training and a certain distinction of mind'.[41] The historian's
capacity to judge what was relevant to his project and what was
of personal interest had abandoned him. And while Professor
Scott fawned, his editor drowned his anxieties about the quality
of the book in a sea of facts. Bean acceded to the new chapter
despite his concern that he would not be able to check Scott's
work for errors, given that the archive on which it was based

was in Scotland. Such errors, he told Scott, would discredit the history as a whole.[42]

Ernest Scott's conclusion to Volume XI of the *Official History* put the conscription matter to one side when it claimed that 'The patriotism evoked by the war was singularly bright and pure'. For the final paragraph of the now-voluminous book, the professor chose a moving metaphor about the legacy of the war on Australian society: 'It was affirmed by dependable witnesses within the last thirty years that the marks of the waggon-wheels of Major Mitchell's expedition when he made his famous journey in 1836 to "Australia Felix" were still visible in parts of the Wimmera Plains. Probably the marks of the war-chariots will still be visible in political and social life for a longer span of years'.[43] Those marks were discernible in politics, particularly on the Labor side, in the comradeship of the returned soldiers, and in the widespread aversion to rearmament. Though Scott did not mention it, the war chariots had left deep furrows also in the thesis of British race patriotism that informed his entire intellectual endeavour.

Scott's fear that his book had become dull beneath the weight of Bean's unrelenting pursuit of detail was confirmed upon its publication. The *Argus* was diplomatic in its description of an 'unvarnished tale' without 'illuminating passages', but *The Times Literary Supplement* was less restrained. It felt the book lacked 'narrative power' and that much of it was 'valuable chiefly for purposes of reference rather than for any historical judgement which it is designed to pass'.[44]

That Ernest Scott and Charles Bean failed to contrive a successful book about Australian domestic affairs during the Great War was not, fundamentally, a result of their ideological differences, but of their shared ideological assumptions. Scott's inclination was to throw impartiality to the wind and present an account that justified the actions of the pro-conscriptionists and lambasted those who were opposed. This version could offer no explanation for the failure of the conscription referenda other than that Australians had proved incapable of exercising their democratic rights responsibly. Bean drew the book back from this blatantly biased approach, but presented no explanation for the rejection of conscription. His suggestion to Scott in 1928 that the failed referenda might be explained by Australians' 'independence and habit of thinking for ourselves' was discounted by an author whose intellectual settings allowed him to see only interdependence and common kinship – British nationalism was 'an extension and completion of Australian nationality'.[45] The story of Australia during the war could perhaps have succeeded as a piece of narrative history if it had been told from a radically nationalist, anti-British perspective. Charles Bean flirted with such an approach, but baulked at endorsing the rejection of conscription.

⋄⊷⊚⊷⋄

In early 1919, before Charles Bean headed homewards to begin writing the *Official History*, he had indulged in a quick side trip to Belgium. After wandering around the battlefield of Waterloo that had so excited his imagination as a boy, Bean wrote to his parents: 'I went to the top of the mound and in Father's best style lectured to three Australian railway operating company men and an American officer whom I found there'. But after four and a half years of following Australian soldiers to the battlefields of Gallipoli, France and Flanders, Charles Bean's imaginative world was no longer anchored by the events of 18 June 1815. Waterloo would 'always be a very great battle in one's imagination because of the issues which were decided there', but one could not 'help but note that it seems a little battlefield after our huge ones'.[46]

If Charles Bean wrote the *Official History* from the trenches of Gallipoli and the Western Front, Ernest Scott's *Short History of Australia* was written from Waterloo's *Butte du Lion*. For him, the Anzacs' brave endeavour at Gallipoli on 25 April 1915 did not give Australians their martial baptism, but rather it sought to defend against Prussian militarism the British supremacy that had been won at Waterloo one hundred years earlier. The man of humble origin who had sampled Fabian socialism and theosophy before succeeding spectacularly under the auspices of British liberalism could not contemplate Australians charting a course away from 'the most majestic nationalism which has been attainable in all human history'.[47]

Ernest Scott did not get long to enjoy the 'days of delight' that he had so keenly anticipated when he retired from the University of Melbourne in 1936.[48] He received his knighthood in June 1939 and was dead six months later after a short illness. Charles Bean lived a long life, dying in his ninetieth year. On more than one occasion he was offered a knighthood, but declined to endorse a system that 'encourages false values among our people'.[49] Longevity gave him the privilege of testing his beliefs against history. By the time of the Second World War he had dismissed as 'old world ignorance' the claims of racial superiority upon which he had developed his thesis of the 'Australian Ideal'.[50] When he died in 1968, Charles Bean's history of the Great War seemed militaristic and anachronistic to a great many Australians but, unlike the imperial version of Australians in the Great War told by Ernest Scott in his *Short History*, it was not entirely lost to time.

# 3

# 1920s–1930s: THE GREAT WAR IN AUSTRALIAN LITERATURE

Australians lived with the legacy of the Great War in various ways during the 1920s and 1930s. Some people sought solace in the fine fighting reputation of the 1st Australian Imperial Force (AIF); that the war had shown Australians to be 'worthy of the breed' mitigated, to some extent, the scale of the calamity. Others coped by clinging tightly to the conviction that the Great War would never be repeated; that it had been 'the war to end wars'. In August 1937 the widow of a Great War officer wrote a letter to the *Sydney Morning Herald* denouncing a recently released book about the war called *A Brass Hat in No Man's Land*. Mrs Jean Robinson Guy wanted to see 'all such books of the horrors of the war, which robbed us all of our youth, homes, happiness, etc. banned … No one wants any such reminder of the Great War. What most of us crave is a little peace, and some reverence, to soothe an all too vivid memory. Such books can do no possible good'. Her plea to be allowed respite from her grief in forgetting provoked condemnation from another correspondent. AE Searle believed that 'books that expose the horrors of the war' were 'perhaps the best weapons possible in the hands of today's growing bands of world-peace advocates'. These peace activists 'aim, not at the soothing of our all too vivid memories: rather do we aim at probing our memories in order to be the better able to pass on our experiences to the wives and mothers of today's potential war victims'.[1]

As the correspondence between Mrs Guy and AE Searle suggests, books about the Great War were the subject of considerable controversy during the inter-war years. This chapter looks at the Australian response to the sudden rush of books from Europe about the war that began in the late 1920s, as well as the novels and memoirs that Australian veterans wrote. What kind of war did Australian soldiers write about? And why did they produce no equivalent of European modernist classics such as *All Quiet on the Western Front?*

Thursday 25 April 1929 passed quietly in the picturesque town of Ross in the Tasmanian Midlands. Locals gathered for the annual Anzac Day service around a granite pillar, upon which was mounted the figure of a digger carved from Carrara marble. The service began with a subdued rendition of 'God Save the King' – attendance was down from previous years due to bad weather. After special prayers for the King and Empire, sermons were delivered on the themes of 'Self-Sacrifice' and 'Courage'. The service closed with the singing of the poet Rudyard Kipling's 'Recessional', with its stern warning, 'Lest we forget – lest we forget!'.[2]

By the 1920s, Australian commemoration of the Great War evinced several distinctive characteristics. Remembrance had coalesced decisively around the anniversary of Australian troops' experience of battle in the Dardanelles on 25 April 1915. By 1927, the date had been gazetted as a public holiday in all Australian states, and the word 'Anzac' had been protected against

arbitrary commercial use as early as 1921.[3] Australians' preference for 25 April was in contrast to that of countries such
as Britain, France, the United States and Canada, whose commemorative rituals revolved around the anniversary of the end
of the war each November. Australian war commemoration still
drew on the rhetoric of Empire, though imperial affection was
more qualified than it had been in the initial years of the war.
The 'heads' who ran the war were often remembered as fools,
and the British soldiers as scrawny physical specimens, lacking
in dare and initiative. But a distinction was made between the
British army and its cause. Sixty thousand Australian dead had
been 'sacrificed' for something most people thought meaningful: the maintenance of the values of the British Empire. These
worthiest of causes – 'King and Empire' – were carved into the
stone of hundreds of memorials being raised in cities, towns and
tiny hamlets around Australia, with money gathered mostly by
public subscription. In its ritualised simplicity, a commemorative
structure built upon the foundations of Anzac Day, Empire and
monuments of stone served people's need to grieve in the immediate aftermath of the war.

During the war, especially in its early stages, there had been
a flood of imperialist, patriotic and anti-German writing in Australia, most of it of poor quality. Works like JD Burns' poem, 'For
England!' (1915), and Arthur Wright's novel, *The Breed Holds Good*
(1918), perpetuated the 'high diction' and imperialist rhetoric of
nineteenth-century war remembrance, but they were becoming
increasingly rare. A distinctly Australian voice was emerging,
which paid more heed to national than imperial motives. When
one character in Harley Matthews' short story 'The Dinkum Australian' says to another: 'You came to do your duty by the moth-
erland and for the great Empire and to uphold the honour of
the glorious old flag', the reply is indignant. 'Rot', cries Private
Frederick Pearson: 'We came for a fight, and for Australia'. Hugh

Knyvett's memoir 'Over There' with the Australians showed a similar shift from imperial to national identification, though the underlying assumption of British racial superiority remained unchanged. The immediate aftermath of the war saw a deluge of unit records, accounts of operations, and reminiscences, the best known of which was John Monash's The Australian Victories in France in 1918, but there were very few representations of the war in memoir and fiction.[4]

Existing alongside rituals of mourning was a visceral and often-expressed desire to forget about the war and get on with daily life. In a speech to a group of Sydney veterans in February 1931, Charles Bean acknowledged the widespread desire 'to obliterate all memory of the Great War, cut it out of our consciousness if that were possible'. Fred Farrall, one of the working-class Melbourne veterans interviewed by the historian Alistair Thomson for his book Anzac Memories, recalled in the 1980s that the war had 'slipped into the background' during the twenties and thirties. Farrall's recollection seems vindicated by the scant coverage allocated to the war in the most significant and celebrated work of Australian history published in the inter-war years – the eminent historian Keith Hancock's Australia. While praising the book's eloquent style and brilliant analysis of Australian society upon its release in 1930, reviewers thought more attention might have been given to matters such as education and the press. No-one remarked upon the fact that this 'striking picture of Australian aspirations, foibles and accomplishments' barely mentioned the Great War. Nor did they note that its formulation of national identity under the banner of 'Independent Australian Britons' paid no heed to Charles Bean's thesis of national baptism under fire.[5]

General distaste for 'the late unmentionable war' and a common mood for living in the moment were mirrored in the policies of successive federal governments, which accurately anticipated there were few votes in defence issues.[6] Conservative administrations under Stanley Bruce and Joseph Lyons sought refuge from the perceived Japanese threat in the imperial relationship. Construction of a naval base at Singapore began in 1923, but progressed in fits and starts during a period of economic frugality, wherein nations professed faith in the effectiveness of international co-operation and arms limitation. Labor returned to power briefly in 1929 after thirteen years in opposition, still bearing the legacy of the anti-conscription and anti-war fervour that followed the split between pro- and anti-conscriptionists in 1916. The Labor Prime Minister James Scullin suspended compulsory military training in favour of a voluntary part-time militia, and the strength of the army fell from 48 000 to 27 000 in one year. After peaking during and in the years immediately following the war, defence expenditure sat at around £6.43 million in 1925–26; by 1930–31 it had fallen to £3.86 million.[7] Labor pegged its security policy to a strong League of Nations but failed to bolster its rhetoric with financial and political support for the struggling institution.

The common desire among Australians 'to forget about the war and all that it means' was in close accord with sentiment in Britain and on the Continent.[8] But as the tenth anniversary of the Armistice passed, there came a sudden new willingness to remember. On 9 December 1928, a play called *Journey's End* began a two-night run at the Apollo Theatre in London. Set in a British dugout before the battle of Mont St Quentin in northern France, the play told the story of a group of officers struggling to live up to the ideals of public school gentility under the strain of trench warfare. It was written by RC Sherriff, a diffident and solitary insurance adjustor who had emerged from the trenches with his nerves barely intact. Sherriff's manuscript initially met with the usual indifference accorded to plays about the war. After several knock-backs, it eventually found favour with a small company that was dedicated to producing works of merit, regardless of their commercial potential.[9] Common wisdom about war plays was confounded when the opening night performance, starring an unknown young actor called Laurence Olivier, was rapturously received by reviewers and audience alike. On the strength of its critical notices, the production moved to the Savoy Theatre, where it settled in for a record-breaking 593 consecutive performances.

On the same day that *Journey's End* made its debut at the Apollo Theatre, the final instalment of a serialised novel about the war was published in *Vossische Zeitung*, a liberal daily newspaper in Berlin. The novel's author was a young German veteran of the Great War called Erich Maria Remarque. Remarque had dashed off the manuscript over five weeks during the autumn of 1927, in order, as he later explained, to restore his 'peace of mind'. *All Quiet on the Western Front* appeared in book form in Germany in January 1929, where it immediately became a phenomenal bestseller. It was published in Britain in March with a translation by a former Australian army officer, Arthur Wheen, and declared by the *Manchester Guardian* to be 'the greatest war book ever'. By September 1929 it had been translated into eighteen languages, including Russian, Polish, Finnish, Hebrew and Yiddish, and had sold more than 1.5 million copies.[10]

*All Quiet on the Western Front* was a much more confrontational work of art than *Journey's End*. Sherriff's play was critical of high command and frank about the terror men felt in the trenches and the fact that they sometimes used alcohol to cope, but at its heart lay a story about the tragedy of the war, rather than the futility of it. Remarque, on the other hand, did not spare his readers graphic detail, nor shirk from his message of despair and hopelessness. Despite these differences, Sherriff and Remarque both represented war in a radical new light that rendered pre-1914 notions of martial glory not only redundant but absurd. The poet Leon Gellert, who had been a soldier in the Great War and was now the literary critic for the *Sydney Morning Herald*, observed that 'the pendulum has swung from the heroic style to its opposite'.[11]

By early 1930 the boom in books from Europe about the war was in full swing. British publishing houses dominated the Australian publishing industry so that books published in Europe took only a short time to find their way to Australia: 'It is impossible to visit one's book club without finding additions to the list of war books [by] clever young men determined to outdo Remarque', wrote a Sydney journalist. The pages of the monthly journal *All About Books* were filled with reviews of soldier literature and publishers' advertisements spruiking 'the English *All Quiet on the Western Front*' and 'the greatest war book ever'. 'War books still!' wrote a reviewer in February 1930, when the rush was still months from exhaustion.[12]

*Never before had men been so open about war and its physical and psychological effects.*

There were certainly some writers and publishers who sought to jump on the Remarque bandwagon. The Australian-born writer Frederic Manning, who had served with the British infantry during the war, was pestered by his publisher to write about his experience, and eventually obliged with the critically fêted novel *The Middle Parts of Fortune*, later published in expurgated form as *Her Privates We*. But the publishing phenomenon was not driven purely by commercial motives. The passing of a decade since the Armistice had afforded many veterans the psychological perspective with which to describe their experiences in literary form. The American novelist Ernest Hemingway's *A Farewell to Arms* and the British poet and writer Richard Aldington's *Death of a Hero* both appeared in 1929, as did Robert Graves' *Goodbye to All That*. The self-serving frankness of Graves' autobiographical book put paid to his faltering friendship with the poet Siegfried Sassoon, whose lightly fictionalised *Memoirs of an Infantry Officer* were published to critical and popular acclaim in 1930.

Even more remarkable than the suddenness and intensity of this rush of war literature was the nature of some of the books that it produced, books 'largely based on actual trench experiences, seasoned with intimate psychological details showing the private soldier very much *au naturel'*, summarised a reviewer in *All About Books*.[13] Never before had the voices of the private soldier and junior officer been heard so resoundingly. And never before had men been so open about war and its physical and psychological effects.

The ruckus that the appearance of these frank and intimate war books caused in Britain and Germany was reported in Australian newspapers. In October 1929 the *Queenslander* noted that Erich Maria Remarque was 'the most discussed man of the day. Debates are held for and against him. He is worshipped and detested, exalted and decried'. As the first copies of *All Quiet* began to arrive from Britain in the latter half of 1929, Australians now had the opportunity to respond personally to this confronting new genre of 'realistic fiction'.[14]

On 15 January 1930, thousands of passers-by gathered in the centre of Sydney to watch the commotion as a detachment of police officers loaded stacks of books and photographs from a shop in Martin Place onto their patrol wagon. The following day, newspapers reported that the police raid had yielded approximately £1000 worth of obscene material. Among the stacks of books and photographs removed from the premises were Boccaccio's *Decameron*, Shakespeare's *Venus and Adonis*, a volume on birth control by Marie Stopes and several copies of a sensational new book about the Great War called All Quiet on the Western Front.[15]

The Martin Place police raid was ordered by the Nationalist state government, despite the fact that the Commonwealth Customs Department had examined All Quiet on the Western Front in mid-1929 and decided that it did not breach obscenity laws.[16] The New South Wales government's lone attempt at censorship stood no chance of halting the Remarque juggernaut.

An anti-censorship columnist in the *Sydney Morning Herald* noted the absurdity of the prohibition, given that the book was freely available in other states and had enjoyed 'a phenomenal sale' in New South Wales before its ban. Indeed, *All About Books* reported in September 1929 that *All Quiet* was finding as many buyers in Australia and New Zealand per capita as it had in Germany; total sales in the two countries within the first six months of its release were reported to be an extraordinary 50 000 copies.[17] The New South Wales ban was never enforced after the Martin Place raid and the policy was abandoned when Labor returned to office in November 1930.

So if thousands of Australians were reading *All Quiet on the Western Front*, what did they make of a book in which soldiers swore, drank, traded bread for sex and were killed in arbitrary and gruesome fashion? Outrage and affront were the emotions that tended to provoke readers to write to newspaper editors. But the fact that the historical record is mostly silent about the response of ordinary readers, despite the book being so widely read, suggests that its message fell on sympathetic ears. That judgment seems vindicated by the success of the Hollywood film of *All Quiet on the Western Front*, which was released in Australia in July 1930. Although the tone of the film was gentler than that of the book, it remained faithful to Remarque's story-line and featured realistic scenes of battle. Anticipating strong demand, His Majesty's Theatre in Brisbane scheduled three viewings a day, and was forced to extend its season indefinitely 'owing to the continued demand of the public'. Many patrons, it seems, were seeing the film three and four times over.[18]

Perhaps the enthusiasm with which the public responded to *All Quiet on the Western Front* accounted in part for the virulence of the conservative attack upon it. For a nation with 60 000 dead, memory of the war was called into service as an emotional salve to be applied in whatever form gave most comfort. People of

conservative outlook tended to find emotional solace in traditional moral values and codes of behaviour. Thus, the men who died at
war were remembered as uniformly brave and morally irreproach-
able warriors whose lives were given in meaningful sacrifice for
nation and Empire. The cursing, hedonistic and desperate crea-
tures of *All Quiet on the Western Front* could find no place within this
exclusive commemorative structure.

Antipathy towards Remarque was particularly strong among
those with military backgrounds. WD Joynt, a recipient of the
Victoria Cross, put forward a motion at a Legacy Club luncheon
arguing for the banning of war books that sought to commercial-
ise 'the horrible and the dreadful'. Joynt objected particularly to
Remarque's book: 'Not only was it loathsome and filthy, it was also
counterfeit, because it did not give a true picture of the behaviour
of a soldier in any army'. The Germans were gallant fighters, he
told his audience; if their army had been 'as Remarque depicted it
the war would have ended in six months'. William Joynt's motion
to outlaw Remarque's book and others like it was defeated, but
his grievance was echoed in other military fora. In March 1930
the Federal Executive of the Returned Sailors' and Soldiers' Imperial League of Australia (RSSILA) passed a resolution that the
Minister for Customs should 'prohibit war books which defamed
soldiers of the Empire'. The best means of appraising which
books were defamatory was to submit all war books to the official
historian, Mr Bean, for adjudication. Prime Minister Scullin was
unswayed by these calls for censorship. He had read Remarque's
book and 'believed that every word in it was true'. The filthiness
of its language was 'outweighed by the lesson it taught'.[19]

Concern was frequently expressed about the effect of these
loathsome war books on the emerging generation, which relied
on second-hand accounts for its impression of the event. William Joynt and others knew – very definitely – that *All Quiet on
the Western Front* was 'being read avidly by young people of both

sexes'. What would happen if a national emergency arose and the youth of Australia, filled with the pernicious ideas of Remarque and his imitators, were called to arms? As one commentator saw it: 'A diet composed solely of the brutal war books of recent years could have no other effect on the reader but complete revulsion against war. That incidentally is the intention of some of the post-war authors – to make war impossible by turning the young citizen against it'.[20]

In their desire to expunge these radical new modes of expression, critics turned to traditional literary forms. The *Boy's Own Paper* representation of war, which had peaked in the decades leading up to 1914, had been bled of credibility after the Somme and Passchendaele, but had not disappeared entirely from public rhetoric. The British statesman LS Amery, a former Secretary of State for the Dominions, was confident that this current fashion for 'stench warfare' writing would soon pass, 'and that the war would take its place as a marvellous effort and an amazing romance in which no part was more amazing than that played by the Australians'. This Fitchett-like conceptualisation of the war was tethered to Empire-building and its vindicatory ideologies of martial nationalism and racial superiority. Wherever the rhetoric of glorious warfare appeared, so too did declarations of British racial genius. A columnist in the *Canberra Times* berated the 'glass half empty' bias of the war books. Everyone knew that war was horrible, but 'out of its horrors came some of the most heroic deeds and self-sacrifice that the world has ever known … The flood of new war books casts serious blots on the name of the bravest soldiers'.[21]

In fact, it was the very lack of these traditional categories of remembrance – race, empire and nation – in books like *All Quiet* that so unsettled conservatives. For those who thought to look beyond the swearing and drinking, there was a profound, if naive, subversiveness in *All Quiet on the Western Front*. The frightened and miserable Germans of the novel did not square with wartime propaganda about the monstrous baby-bayoneting Huns. *All Quiet* 'gave us our first intimation that the German soldier had any feelings at all', wrote a journalist in the *Sydney Morning Herald*.[22] The enemy, Remarque's book implied, was not the group of soldiers huddled in the mud across no-man's-land, but a political system that had led men of all nations to awful, meaningless deaths. Conservatives around the world despaired as millions of readers cupped their ears to *All Quiet's* socialist undertone, just as the international financial system was failing.

The atmosphere of crisis and disillusionment generated by the Depression gave impetus to the radical message of the war books. A correspondent to the *Sydney Morning Herald* represented a common view: 'The truth is that the present crop of war books is not in any way an attempt to condemn the soldier … but to condemn war itself, and to show it up as well as we know how, in all its naked horror and stupidity, so that if possible our children may benefit by the lessons we have so terribly learned'.[23] Nora Cooper went on to note that 'most of these published protests against war books come from military men'. While the physical courage of these men could not be questioned, there was one thing they were unwilling to face, 'and that is the prospect of a world without any armies at all'. Cooper did not identify herself as a grieving mother or widow, though the tone of her letter suggests she was. Unlike the military men she criticised, her distress did not manifest itself in idealisation of fighting men and romanticisation of battle, but in the need to remember the Great War as full of 'naked horror and stupidity' and thus make its repetition less likely. Her letter drew a sharp response from a correspondent whose emotions were differently calibrated. 'A woman descendant of soldiers' took umbrage at Cooper's slight against military men. These 'men would gladly see a world of peace', she wrote, 'but dare not lay down the sword. Their spirits must still flame white hot in sacrifice – such dreadful sacrifice'.[24]

Australia's official historian, Charles Bean, stood to one side as the controversy raged, until a contribution to the debate by the British writer Major John Hay Beith unsettled his usual equanimity. Beith had decried writers such as RC Sherriff who depicted men as 'brutes and beasts, living like pigs and dying like dogs'. Such a bleak perspective, Beith said, belittled the men and overlooked their many virtues: 'The most admirable thing about the British soldier was his unconquerable cheerfulness and sense of humour in the utmost squalor, even in the face of death itself'. Bean begged to differ. His response showed how emphatically he had discarded the ideal of war he had formed during his childhood excursions to Waterloo: 'Where is the "cheerfulness", where is the "sense of humour" that touches the millions who have suffered, and reminds us of other millions who can suffer no more?' he asked. Bean was a man of stringent morals with a tendency towards idealisation of the Australian soldier. Yet he had personally witnessed the suffering of front-line soldiers and felt obligated to defend the authenticity of the war books. By describing accurately the experience of war, these books might sponsor peace: 'However grim the realities of war may be, let the world become enlightened by "these war books", rather than by war's humour and cheerfulness, so that the rising generations of man may know the truth, and strive for world peace with the determined resolve, "Never again!"'.[25]

By the end of 1930, the torrent of European war books had slowed to a trickle and Australian reading tastes returned to more prosaic fare. *All About Books'* list of recommended reading for January 1931 included *Don Bradman's Book of Cricket*, as well as works by well-known authors such as Henry Handel Richardson, John Galsworthy, Somerset Maugham and Arnold Bennett. Just as the local appetite for sensational war books seemed to be sated, Australian veterans were digesting the international literary genre and beginning to put their own memories to paper. Though Australians had demonstrated interest in the modernist literature coming out of Britain and Germany, it did not follow automatically that they would be keen to read Australian war books that struck the same tone of desperation and hopelessness.

The returned soldiers who wrote about the Great War in the 1930s were entering, mostly unwittingly, into an Australian literary culture poised awkwardly between its nationalist aspirations and its colonial legacy. Australian readers were far more likely to be reading romance and thriller novels imported from Britain and the United States than novels written, typeset and published locally; by the end of the Second World War only 15 per cent of books sold in Australia were of local origin. Australia was a vital market commercially for British publishers and during the interwar years imports from Britain grew to 'diluvian proportions'. Angus & Robertson became the main publisher of Australian fiction in 1930, but local authors were still much more commonly published in Britain than at home.[26]

The dominant British and American presence in literary production and consumption had the advantage of exposing Australian readers to the latest books from overseas. A 'middlebrow literary culture' of magazines, reviews, bestseller lists, prizes and book clubs developed to make sense of

*As home-grown war books began to appear in the 1930s, the gatekeepers of an emerging Australian intellectual tradition stood ready to appraise their literary merit.*

the mass of imported publications and steer readers towards the 'best new books'. Yet, cultural nationalists, such as the literary critic and writer Nettie Palmer, and her writer-husband Vance, resented the domination of imported books. Australians might have had access to the latest modernist literature from Europe and America, but the Palmers believed they ought to be reading about their own environment and encouraging the establishment of a literature that was, as the Australian writer Miles Franklin put it, 'of the soil as Russians are to their soil'.[27]

The Palmers were prominent among a small but vocal group of intellectuals, mostly of the left but occasionally of the right as well, that championed the cultivation of a distinctively Australian literature. They encouraged local writers as much through their ability to foster a sense of purpose and collegiality, as through their own criticism and creative writing. The Palmers lamented the decline of the nationalist impulse, expressed in ballads, poems, short stories and novels about the men who lived in the interior before the Great War. Since the departure of its literary editor, AG Stephens, from the *Bulletin* in 1906, that journal had ceased to be the staging post for Australian fiction. Haltingly, the towns, cities and suburbs were edging their way into Australian literary consciousness, but the Palmers still despaired at the public's taste for novels that contained 'obvious drama and ultimate sunshine', in the style of Steele Rudd's *On Our Selection* and Thomas Alexander Brown's *Robbery Under Arms*. The Australian reader, according to Nettie Palmer, wanted the novelist to be 'essentially an entertainer ... It does not ask him to be penetrating, or to trouble his head about style, or to have a view of life'. Nettie Palmer hailed the fact, in 1935, that local authors such as Henry Handel Richardson and Katharine Susannah Prichard were at last beginning to write about 'complex adventures of the spirit', rather than confining themselves to 'out-west' adventure-style novels that lacked psychological complexity and sophistication.[28]

Though the Palmers and other advocates of an Australian literary canon specified no subject matter for nationalist writers, one topic did present itself clearly. The Great War was now more than a decade past; the extremity of the experience would surely have been seared into the minds of those sensitive Australians whose job it was to forge a national literary tradition. As home-grown war books began to appear in the early 1930s, the gatekeepers of an emerging Australian intellectual tradition stood ready to appraise their literary merit. The distance between the nationalism of the battlefield and the nationalism of the salon was soon apparent.

Nettie Palmer unashamedly judged Australian books about the war against the best that had been produced in Britain and Germany – books like *Her Privates We*, *All Quiet on the Western Front* and *Goodbye to All That*. Among this company she found the 'first Australian reminiscent war book, apart from official histories and records like Sir John Monash's *The Australian Victories in France*' thoroughly inadequate. Palmer thought the characterisation in Donald Black's *Red Dust*, which was set in Palestine, especially poor. To her chagrin, the author's horse was 'a more important character' than his fellow soldiers, and the most poignant moment in the book came when Black was compelled to shoot Blackboy because the horses that the men had brought with them from Australia could not be transported home.[29]

Of greater literary merit was *The Desert Column* by Ion Idriess, a writer who had already established his reputation with popular Central Australian adventure stories, such as *Lasseter's Last Ride* and *Flynn of the Inland*. *The Desert Column* opened on the Dardanelles Peninsula but was set mostly in Palestine, where the author had served in the Australian Light Horse. While Idriess did not shy away from depicting gruesome aspects of warfare, his characters were inoculated against moral and psychological disintegration by their good-humoured comradeship. *The Desert Column* was greeted with gratitude and relief by Australian reviewers – gratitude that Idriess had produced an Australian war memoir of respectable quality and relief that he had not written a local version of *All Quiet*. The German novel was an unacknowledged presence whenever war books were discussed. Mr Idriess 'does not gloss over the worst experiences', wrote a reviewer in the *Queenslander*, but he did not feel the need, like 'so many writers, particularly from the ranks … to magnify what may be termed the "filth" of war while minimising the brighter aspects of it'. Another reviewer praised the 'marvellous spirit of comradeship, heroism and sportsman-ship' of the Australian soldiers in *The Desert Column*: Idriess' book was quite unlike other war books, which wallowed in 'a mixture of mud, oaths, explosions, blasphemy, drink, sex, and introspec-tion'. *Reveille*, the journal of the New South Wales RSSILA, noted that *The Desert Column* was as different in spirit from *All Quiet on the Western Front* as the men who wrote them: 'The suffering and horror of war, are, of course, in both, but Idriess has not dwelt on them. He never lost his optimism, nor his sense of humour, nor his interest in little things'. Nettie Palmer declared *The Desert Column* 'one of the Australian war books for which we have been waiting' and cited the strong endorsements of Charles Bean, the journalist and historian FM Cutlack, and the leader of the famous cavalry charge on Beersheba, General Harry Chauvel.[30] But her praise was forced. Palmer did not share the satisfaction of some of her main-stream colleagues that Ion Idriess was no Erich Maria Remarque or Robert Graves. Perhaps the 'sensitively written', nation-making war book after which she hankered would need to come out of the mud of France rather than the sand of Palestine.

By the mid-1930s Australia's principal publishing house, Angus & Robertson, had a catalogue of Australian war books to stand alongside its crowning achievement, Charles Bean's *Official History*. In 1936 the firm bundled together twelve of its war books – 'Epic Stories that Touch the Heartstrings!'; 'Deeds That will Echo Down the Centuries'; 'Volumes that can be handed down to your children's children!' – and marketed them as 'The Gallant Legion'. 'Send for them now and so salute the modern Odys-seus', shouted the advertisement. One in the series was Joseph Maxwell's *Hell's Bells and Mademoiselles*. *Reveille* had previewed the Victoria Cross winner's forthcoming book with enthusiasm the previous year: 'Joe is spending his winter nights writing a book that embodies not only his own amazing war experiences, but a vivid picture of the tragic and the lighter side of the great world drama of 1914–18'. Maxwell, the most highly decorated Australian soldier of the war after the renowned Harry Murray, was 'not following in the steps of other writers on the war. He is not seeking to cram a bewildering mass of horror into his pages. His war book promises to be something different. There are little fleeting glimpses of life out of the line'. The memoir received mostly glowing notices in the press and in military publications when it appeared in August 1932. Some reviewers were displeased with the author's frankness about prostitution and alcohol consumption, but thanks were given that *Hell's Bells* was 'not one of those unsavoury war books that emphasised only the ugly aspects of the war and left out everything about the noble qualities of loyalty to mates and devotion to duty'.[31]

There was no concept in *Hell's Bells and Mademoiselles* of Charles Bean's national initiation at Gallipoli, let alone of Ernest Scott or WH Fitchett's devotion to Empire – only the initiation of naive young men into the true nature of warfare – 'So here, in this dismal forbidding gully brushed by Death, lay glory! It was not the heroic, theatrical war of the history books'. Maxwell admitted frequently to 'being scared stiff', and also to the imperative to disguise that fear from one's comrades. He confessed to feelings of depression and desperation, but also described hedonistic moments when pleasures such as 'talcum powder in clouds, carmine lips, roguish smiles, and white-and-pink softness' took on an exaggerated meaning after a stint in the trenches.[32] Maxwell was exceedingly modest about his considerable martial achievements, but did embellish his larrikin credentials. For instance, he placed himself at the notorious 'battle of the Wazir' in Cairo, though he did not leave Australia until after the riot of early April 1915 had taken place.

From the vantage point of 1932, Joseph Maxwell recognised

'the futility of 1914–18; the insane folly that cost millions of lives and disorganized the whole world'. But for all its horror, the war was not without its virtues; it still exercised a 'peculiar fascination', a 'glamour' that the 'humdrum of civilian existence' lacked.

> Back through the years of disillusion flashes to the mind
> some cameo of heroism, some epic of self-sacrifice ...
> When Digger meets Digger the memory goes jogging back
> to the Peninsula or to the mud and blood and mad ruin of
> northern France. We talk war, we live war once again. Time
> has mellowed sorrows and dimmed the horror ... Out of the
> wreckage emerges nothing finer than the memory of that
> splendid comradeship of the troops.

Maxwell invited his readers, many of them former soldiers, to be complicit in his decision to 'remember with advantages' his experience of war. He asked them to join with him in illuminating the friendship and humour, the pursuit of mademoiselles and the pranks against the 'brass hats'; and to leave the awful memories in the shadows. Readers accepted Maxwell's invitation with enthusiasm; the first 10 000 copies of *Hell's Bells* sold out in three months and Angus & Robertson went on to reprint the book in 1932, 1933, 1936 and 1939.[33]

Nettie Palmer dismissed *Hell's Bells and Mademoiselles* as having 'one foot in fact and one in romance'. But such a reading ignored the gruelling descriptions of battle and stints in the trenches, and the emotional frankness that Maxwell served up in between acts of insubordination and propositions to young French women in *estaminets*. *Hell's Bells* was no *All Quiet on the Western Front*, but nor was it written in the *Boy's Own* style upon which the 1914 generation had been raised, in which battle was compared with cricket and rugby, and war was willed for the test of moral and physical courage it would provide. *Hell's Bells* would have displeased

WH Fitchett as much as it disappointed Nettie Palmer. John Monash informed Fitchett after the war that he had used the descriptions of famous British battles in *Deeds that Won the Empire* to 'considerable advantage on several occasions in stimulating the interests of the men in our military traditions at Gallipoli', Messines and Passchendaele, and 'during the victorious advance in 1918'.[34] Fitchett's prose could apparently still propel men into battle, but it could no longer be taken as a truthful representation of warfare.

Flushed with the success of *Hell's Bells and Mademoiselles*, Angus & Robertson published two volumes of war memoirs by soft-goods agent and former digger HR Williams. The titles of the memoirs – *The Gallant Company* and *Comrades of the Great Adventure* – suggested WH Fitchett and the *Boy's Own Paper*, but the narratives struck the same balance between realism and manful stoicism that characterised Maxwell's book, though they lacked the streak of larrikin humour that enlivened *Hell's Bells*. Like Joseph Maxwell, Harold Williams did not spare the reader from explicit information about his experience. The mud of the Somme 'drowned men's spirits with horror' and left the author 'windy' and close to breaking point on several occasions. Those who did succumb to shell shock were not judged as cowards, but as sensitive men unable to cope with the strain of war. While misery and hardship were recorded by Williams in the cause of authenticity, they did not lie at the heart of his message. The moral force of Williams' books lay in his love for his fellow soldiers. Salvation was not to be found in thoughts of Empire, or even of Australia, but in the 'companionship of men with hearts of gold, learning to live only for the hour, which enabled us to conquer the utter misery of our surroundings'.[35]

For Williams and Maxwell, remembrance was an act of will, a conscious decision to emphasise friendship over horror. In an era before the notions of trauma and catharsis were popularised, men were expected to suppress difficult emotions. There was no shame or subterfuge about the fact that returned soldiers might edit their memories in order to produce a war that they could live with:

> in looking back to those days, hardships, dangers and
> awfulness have become obscured by pleasanter memories.
> One has only to listen to a group of ex-servicemen
> conversing to realize how completely the rough jest, the
> hearty laugh or whimsical doings of former comrades remain
> vividly in their minds, while the horrors, peculiar to the front
> line, are never discussed.[36]

Williams' books were praised by mainstream Australian critics and popularly embraced; his first book was reprinted just two months after its release. The author also found favour in Britain: Eton had a copy of *The Gallant Company* specially bound in Moroccan leather for the college library and *The Times Literary Supplement* declared it 'one of the best half-dozen soldier's stories of the War to be found in any country'.[37] Books such as *Hell's Bells*, *The Gallant Company* and *Comrades of the Great Adventure* were prominent examples of a new kind of war writing that sat somewhere between modernism and what had gone before. These books were not overtly nationalistic; they did not boast outwardly about the martial feats of heroic Australian soldiers, but rather exuded a quiet pride in their achievements. Crucially, popular Australian war books portrayed men who had been sorely tested by war, but not defeated by it. The diggers were not all-conquering Odyssean heroes, but ordinary men with heroic powers of endurance.

The high-minded champions of an independent Australian literary culture were unimpressed by these mainstream, commercially successful publications. For Nettie Palmer, such books were not the profound works of literature upon which an Australian sensibility could be built. Perhaps the emotional complexity that nationalist intellectuals craved would only be achieved by the representation of an unrelentingly awful war. But could the author of a book proclaiming disenchantment with the event that gave birth to the nation, according to popular sentiment, also be a nationalist?

In the late 1920s, Leonard Mann, a former soldier of the AIF's 39th Battalion, was approached to write a history of his unit. Mann decided instead that he would write a novel about the Great War. The Melbourne barrister finished *Flesh in Armour* in 1931 but could find no-one to publish it, either in Australia or in Britain. Angus & Robertson declined the book on the basis that it could not be put 'into everyone's hands'.[38] Mann eventually resolved to finance the publishing of one thousand copies of the novel himself under the Melbourne-based Phaedrus imprint. The austere dustjacket of the original edition of *Flesh in Armour* posed a rhetorical question: 'WHY has the novel of the Australian Infantry not been written?'

> At last it is here; revealing much, valorous, pathetic and
> passionate. Frank Jeffreys went into action sustained by
> his love of Mary Hatton but his image of her was defiled.
> Though it is he who is the principal character, in truth the
> Platoon is the hero and its adventures the story.[39]

Frank Jeffreys was indeed the principal character of *Flesh in Armour*, but he was no conventional protagonist. Wracked by nerves and perennially close to collapsing under the strain of trench warfare, Jeffreys was a decent but solitary man, unable by temperament to form the bonds of camaraderie that nourished and sustained other members of his platoon. When Jeffreys discovered that his fiancée had had a sexual liaison with a fellow platoon member, his one source of comfort evaporated. After failing to support the brave and affable Jim Blount in a spontaneous attack on a rogue group of Germans, in which Jim was killed, Jeffreys moved to a quiet section of trench, held a grenade to his heart and pulled the pin.

Nettie Palmer was 'astonished' upon reading *Flesh in Armour*. Here was the Australian war book for which she had been waiting. Leonard Mann's command of the novel form and his 'fearless adherence to invigorating fact and his few passages of lyrical ecstasy' justified a surmise that Australians were 'now adult', she enthused in the *Argus*. The superior quality of Mann's book was recognised by other literary intellectuals, such as the *Bulletin*'s John Dalley, who declared *Flesh in Armour* to be 'one of the best war novels ever written'. The Australian Literature Society, whose aim was to 'seek out and crown meritorious work that might otherwise be overlooked', awarded Mann its gold medal for the best Australian novel of 1932.[40]

Spurred by Nettie Palmer's rapturous endorsement of the novel in *All About Books*, a reader rushed to procure 'a copy for weekend reading'. The reader's high expectations were dashed, however, when she came upon the incident, early in the book, in which Frank Jeffreys' fiancée, Mary Hatton, had sex with Charl Bentley in her parents' dining room. 'This tragedy, portrayed in lurid detail' besmirched 'the atmosphere of the whole book', the reader wrote in a stern letter to *All About Books*. Mr Mann would have better conveyed the spirit of the Australian infantry 'by giving us a picture of the wonderful comradeship which, in so many cases, remains unbroken to this day. He could have told of the hardships, the privations, the unendurable nerve-strain, and perhaps the soldiers would then have gathered their womenfolk about this book to hear "just this bit, and that bit", as we were gathered many times around Sherriff's *Journey's End*'.[41]

The editor of *All About Books* resolved to seek 'independent' arbitration about the value of *Flesh in Armour*. He asked a soldier 'who had been through it all' what he thought of Mann's book.

The soldier conferred with fellow veterans and all agreed that the book was 'a fair and accurate portrayal ... [W]e were not an army of Sir Galahads ... [and] it is just this recounting of only the glorious and heroic in war to the exclusion of all else that keeps alive the war spirit from generation to generation'. The opinion of 'Furnley Maurice' – the pen-name of the left-wing, anti-war poet, bookseller and publisher, Frank Wilmot – was also sought. Maurice obliged with a resounding endorsement of *Flesh in Armour*. He proclaimed the book a substantial piece of literature of the kind that Australia desperately needed: 'There is a realisation of the character that will some day make Australia a nation; and behind that realisation lies the suggestion that some day Australia will have a literature. The book has found a spirit'.[42] If the quest for this nation-making 'spirit' required the author to besmirch Australians' martial reputation, then so be it.

The correspondent who took exception to the tone of *Flesh in Armour* was not alone. The award of the Literature Society's gold medal to the book had inspired another Australian author, Frank Dalby Davison, to lobby Angus & Robertson to reconsider *Flesh in Armour*. Davison was furious to discover that the company still refused to publish the book, 'some wowser of a reader having advised against it'. In fact, the reviewer was scathing of the book that had so impressed Nettie Palmer and John Dalley: 'Of the War, the author tells us nothing we do not know. In fact it is rather tiring to read of it all again and in such detail. For the rest, the book had better never been written. Mann presents a picture of Aussies that will make decent Australians blush'. A reviewer in Hobart's *Mercury* had also detected the stench of *All Quiet on the Western Front* in Mann's novel. The author had fallen victim to the belief that 'it is necessary to portray accurately the days of war by including the vulgarity of speech that war begets, and the general laxity of thought engendered by those to whom killing becomes a daily habit and normal business'.[43]

The controversy over *Flesh in Armour*, such as it was, resembled that which had dogged *All Quiet on the Western Front* two years earlier. Nationalist intellectuals, concerned to develop a canon of Australian literature, admired the psychological sophistication of Mann's novel. Pacifists lauded its anti-war message. Moral conservatives and many of those with military affiliations preferred to remember the Australians as an army of Sir Galahads and found the book offensive. Meanwhile, the majority of the Australian public indicated a more tacit type of disapproval by ignoring the book altogether. Whereas Remarque's book had sold tens of thousands of copies, sales of *Flesh in Armour* totalled just 860 by 1937.[44] Despite its critical success, the novel languished, dropping out of print and out of mind throughout the 1930s.

Angus & Robertson had baulked at *Flesh in Armour* but did not shy away entirely from books in which the 'horrors' were not anaesthetised with strong doses of mateship and humour. They picked up Jack McKinney's novel *Crucible* when it won the Victorian Returned and Services League (RSL) Centenary Prize for the best novel about the war. *Flesh in Armour* had been widely expected to take the award, but the judges – who included the newspaper proprietor Keith Murdoch and General Harry Chauvel – preferred McKinney's interesting but less accomplished tale. The novel's principal character, John Fairbairn, did not enjoy the bonds of friendship that sustained Joseph Maxwell and HR Williams; he felt no pangs when he left his battalion for a cushy job away from the frontline. Fairbairn was a thoughtful, fearful and cynical man for whom the war was 'damned, colossal lunacy'. His last-minute realisation that the war had in fact made him 'a better and bigger man ... more of a man than he would ever have been in peace days' might have pleased the judges of the RSL prize, but seemed out of step with the mood of the rest of the novel. Like most of the men who chose to remember the war in fiction rather than memoir, McKinney was disturbed by his experience for many years afterwards – he 'was a man of many parts until the war took a lot of the kick out of him', noted *Reveille*.[45] McKinney became a peace activist, philosopher and, eventually, the husband of the poet Judith Wright.

Unlike Leonard Mann and Jack McKinney, who presented their disenchanted perspectives of the Great War beneath the veil of fiction, Edgar Morrow chose the more transparent form of memoir. The sensitivity and sincerity of *Iron in the Fire*, published by Angus & Robertson in 1934, met with the approval of Nettie Palmer who contrasted this rather artless book favourably with 'such roaring accounts of happy warriors as *Hell's Bells and Mademoiselles* and *The Fighting Cameliers*'. She also compared the book (very generously) with 'some of the sensitive English books, like those of Sassoon and Robert Graves'. Morrow was trapped by his war experience when he returned to civilian life, unable to talk about it because 'it had become bad form to discuss the war', yet unable to forget. 'There seemed no way out to forgetfulness, or consolation.' He finished the book with a description of what came to be described after the Vietnam War as post-traumatic stress disorder:

Only at night now – when I am alone and quiet – do I allow myself to remember. I sometimes think it helps me to readjust my balance. But ... I don't know. For it is then that I quiver again with the shock of explosions, and fear. I duck at the sound of a shell, and stand like a statue while a flare dies down. I smell the gas again; I feel the tiring strain of the facial muscles in the effort to keep them steady. I itch with lice, and shiver again with the wet and cold. I feel the weight of wet mud on my boots. In the silent safety of my cosy room I see again the pale faces of the freshly dead, and the pathetically still, silent forms hanging on barbed wire. I feel the unutterable weariness of work and sleeplessness and

prolonged fear … And late at night, before I go to bed, I turn
on the radio and let its noise blare into the room – as a safety
measure.[46]

General J Talbot Hobbs, wartime commander of the AIF's 5th
Division, wrote the foreword to *Iron in the Fire*, just as he had done
for HR Williams' *The Gallant Company*. Hobbs had praised Williams for not exaggerating the horrors of the war, unlike some of
those 'so-called war books', but for enlightening Australians as
to the 'gallantry, determination and endurance of the Australian
soldier'. *The Gallant Company* was 'the best soldier's story [Hobbs
had] yet read in Australia'. The general's endorsement of Edgar
Morrow's book was less fulsome: the author 'was apparently an
extremely sensitive youngster … [thus] some things seared his
soul which had little effect on older and more sophisticated men'.
Seeking something positive to say about a book that was clearly
not to his taste, Hobbs noted that it was important to present the
view of 'the sensitive type [who] was fairly numerous and formed
an important, if not very articulate cross section of an army that
was made up of all types'.[47]

General Hobbs' qualified praise of Morrow's memoir is indicative of the dilemma faced by literary-minded veterans. In order
to write an intellectually and emotionally satisfying version of the
war – one that would satisfy cultural nationalists such as Nettie
Palmer – a soldier was obliged to betray the cause of martial
nationalists such as Hobbs when describing the idiocy and trauma
of his experience. The tastes of the Australian public were firmly
in Hobbs' camp. While very large numbers of Australians read
*All Quiet on the Western Front*, they showed little interest in local
writers with troubled memories of the war. If writers like McK-
inney, Mann and Morrow were lucky enough to find publishers,
their books sold poorly, while more mainstream records such as
*The Wells of Beersheba, The Desert Column, Hell's Bells and Mademoiselles,*

*The Gallant Company* and *Backs to the Wall* went into reprints and new editions. The theme of the tragic but ennobling war was being remembered in soldier literature, while memory of the unremittingly awful war was left largely unexamined.

The reluctance of Australian novelists of the inter-war years to write about the Great War has been noted often by literary critics: 'It is as if a whole generation of writers by tacit agreement declined to incorporate the Great War into their imaginative fiction', the literary scholar Harry Heseltine observed in 1964.[48] Though critics lamented the lack of an Australian Remarque, Graves or Owen, the literary silence is not entirely surprising. The bulk of creative writers in inter-war Australia sat to the left of the political centre. They were interested in nationalism only in as much as it facilitated the development of a vernacular culture that would engage on an equal footing with other independent cultures. What creative grist could these artists derive from an event that was grafted so strongly to nineteenth-century notions of martial baptism? Heseltine listed two important exceptions to the creative silence: Vance Palmer and Katharine Susannah Prichard. Both novelists chose to write about

> *The theme of the tragic but ennobling war was being remembered in soldier literature, while memory of the unremittingly awful war was left largely unexamined.*

the psychological effect of trauma experienced by men in the Great War, an issue familiar to many families of returned soldiers, though one rarely discussed in public.

The extremity of the trench warfare experience and the number of men caught in its psychological wash-up challenged long-held conceptions of bravery and cowardice. The official medical historian, AG Butler, estimated that mental troubles accounted for about 80 per cent of postwar health problems among returned Australian soldiers; these could not all be men of questionable moral fibre. The 'mental soldier' was a phenomenon well recognised anecdotally in postwar society, yet the psychiatric infrastructure that would begin to explain the condition was still being assembled. Former soldiers who bore physical wounds were seen as heroes, but those who were 'shell-shocked', 'nervy' or 'not normal' were subjects of stigma and shame. When Katharine Prichard's husband, Hugo Throssell, killed himself in 1933, the coroner concluded his suicide was an indirect result of physical injuries sustained during the war, despite evidence that he 'used to dread going to bed, saying he had the most horrible thoughts whenever he lay down'. The Victoria Cross winner had acquired meningitis at Gallipoli and, according to the coroner's report, his apprehension about a recurrence precipitated the 'brain storms and depression' that drove him to this drastic act.[49] A physical explanation, however tenuous and disingenuous, would lessen the shame for Throssell's wife and family.

Katharine Prichard conceived her novel *Intimate Strangers* as 'a study of the married relation, urban and as close in as possible'. The intensely psychological narrative is structured around Elodie and Greg Blackman. Elodie is a musician who has surrendered her talent to domesticity and Greg is an unsettled war veteran, haunted by images of 'decomposing bodies, arms, legs and faces'. Each spouse seeks intimacy and solace outside the disintegrating marriage, as the economic depression worsens and Greg struggles to earn an income. As Prichard originally drafted the novel, Greg kills himself after being rejected by a young woman he believes himself to be in love with. The author was in the final stages of an overseas trip when she learned that her husband had shot himself at the couple's Greenmount home in the Perth Hills. He had left a note on his will that read: 'I have never recovered from my 1914–18 experiences'.[50] Prichard was forever troubled by the idea that Throssell had found her as yet unpublished manuscript and been spurred to suicide. Whether or not this was true, she changed the ending of *Intimate Strangers* to effect a rather unconvincing reconciliation between Elodie and Greg on the basis of their mutual devotion to internationalism socialism.

The damaged war veteran appeared in the work of another left-wing novelist and cultural nationalist, Vance Palmer, though Palmer's socialism stopped far short of the Soviet communism to which Prichard was dedicated. Palmer was a pacifist and active anti-conscriptionist who, after much vacillation, enlisted in the AIF when he became concerned that Germany might win the war during its great offensive of March 1918. Despite arriving in France after the Armistice was signed, Palmer chose the Great War, or more precisely 'the psychological malaise induced by participation in the war', as a recurrent theme in his writing. His collection of poetry, *The Camp*, includes what the literary critic HM Green regarded as 'one of Australia's finest war poems'. 'The Farmer Remembers the Somme' describes a soldier's return to an Australian landscape untouched by war:

> But all that my mind sees,
> Is a quaking bog in a mist – stark, snapped trees,
> And the dark Somme flowing.[51]

Vance Palmer revisited the theme of psychological trauma in his novel *Daybreak*, published in 1932. The book, which Palmer preferred above all his other work, is set in a small town in the Dandenong Ranges outside Melbourne. It charts the journey of Bob Rossiter, a former soldier in the AIF and now a fruit farmer, from submissiveness to self-assertion. It also describes the final disintegration of Rossiter's former commanding officer, Sievright, a character based partly on a retired colonel and Military Cross winner Palmer had known when he lived in the Dandenongs, and who had committed suicide. The author describes how Rossiter used to be 'haunted by the need for a hero' when he was younger, and had found one in Sievright. But now it is Rossiter, married and expecting his first child, who feels an increasingly grudging responsibility to look after his depressed and delusional former commanding officer. When Sievright kills himself accidentally, it seems the inevitable outcome for a man wrecked by the war. Rossiter feels liberated by the death of his former hero; he discovers a new-found 'faith in the fixity of his own inner being'.[52]

Though well received by critics who were always keen to encourage works of Australian literary fiction, *Daybreak* and *Intimate Strangers* failed to find favour with readers. Among other things, the indifference of the public probably reflected the ambivalence of the authors. Personal tragedy compelled Prichard to rewrite the ending to her novel and, given the circumstances, it is hardly surprising that it failed to ring true. In both *Intimate Strangers* (before the rewrite) and *Daybreak*, there is no concept of catharsis through remembering. Rossiter achieves release from Sievright's psychological imperialism because he is able to forget the war and get on with civilian life. That Vance Palmer stopped just short of giving Sievright the self-inflicted death his characterisation warranted points to the taboos that shrouded both suicide and the 'mental soldier' in inter-war Australia.

⊷⊜⊜⊶

A great deal has been written by academics about the soldier literature produced in Britain after the Great War. Paul Fussell claimed famously in *The Great War and Modern Memory* (1975) that writers such as Wilfred Owen, Siegfried Sassoon and Robert Graves created a new, 'ironic' style, which served to distance the traumatised artist from his subject. The heroic figure of prewar literature was replaced by the emasculated and passive anti-hero. Fussell's claims have been substantially revised by scholars such as Rosa Maria Bracco, Jay Winter and Dan Todman, who have shown that traditional forms of memory and commemoration not only survived, but thrived after the war. Bracco recovered a mass of mostly forgotten middlebrow writing, which neither perpetuated prewar forms nor employed the modernist style. These writers, she argued, were 'merchants of hope'. They did not shirk from the horror of the war but offered redemption through camaraderie, links with home and family, and traditional Christian customs. And it was their writing that the bulk of inter-war Britons were reading.

The major Australian work on war literature was written by the literary academic Robin Gerster. *Big-Noting* (1987) claimed that Australian war literature was untouched by the modernist revolution documented in *The Great War and Modern Memory*: 'Owen and Rosenberg, Ford and Barbusse and Remarque might as well have never written a word'. Australians eschewed the medium of irony and its message of futility in favour of a traditional heroic literary style and a propaganda campaign about the 'heroic racial characteristics' of the digger.[53] The academics Christina Spittel, Clare Rhoden and Claire Woods have shown that Gerster's case was overstated; in his rush to find the grandiose digger, he failed to hear his expressions of fear, doubt and loneliness.[54] Australian war literature of the 1930s is more properly classified as middlebrow. Though it stopped well short of glorifying war, the bulk of Australian war writing, and certainly the most popular of it, presented a war that was terrible, but not entirely without redemption.

While Gerster overreached in his characterisation of Australian war writing as pre-modern and heroic, there is a kernel of truth in his argument. Australians produced few books of lasting literary merit and very little poetry of quality from the Great War. Books such as *Hell's Bells and Mademoiselles* and *The Gallant Company* presented Australians with, in the words of the historian Alistair Thomson, 'a past they could live with'.[55] They salved people's grief and soothed Australians' anxious nationalism, but they lacked the sensitivity and truthfulness that mark classic literature. Why does there exist no Australian version of *All Quiet on the Western Front*, *Goodbye to All That* or Owen's 'Anthem to Doomed Youth'? What can explain this literary dearth?

In chapter 2 we saw how Professor Ernest Scott's imperial history of the war was overshadowed by the Beanian version, which presented a far more flattering version of Australian nationhood. Soldier literature differed in many respects from Bean's *Official History*: the diggers did not boast about their victories (to big-note was un-Australian), nor claim that the Australian nation was born at Gallipoli. However, the themes of the *Official History* and soldier literature were aligned in one crucial respect: both answered the lingering question about Australians' racial integrity with a resounding 'yes'. The war had measured the worth of Australian manhood and found it more than satisfactory.

Of course, there was writing that did present a more complex and profound version of the war experience – *Flesh in Armour* is the best example. If accounts in which Australian soldiers sought gratuitous sex, swore, occasionally drank too much and were not universally subscribed to the code of mateship were lucky enough to a find publisher, they did not find a readership. The Australian public was eager to read European representations of the war in the modernist style, but wanted to remember the *Australian* war as something different – an event that was dreadful but not entirely without meaning.

The explanation for this need to remember a war that was tragic but ultimately ennobling can be found in the history of Australian nationalism. Unlike the nations of Western Europe, settler countries such as Australia went into the Great War with an unresolved nationalist question. The war not only gave Australian soldiers pride in their martial prowess, but pride in the kind of country they were creating. Raised in an era of frenzied imperialism, the generation who fought in the Great War had a chance to measure Britain and Britons against the childhood propaganda of the *Royal Readers* and *Deeds that Won the Empire*. Much to their delight, these soldiers frequently found themselves better educated and bigger and stronger than the 'narrow-chested runts' of industrial Britain. Australian memoirists often remarked that the English class system had rendered the average British soldier impassive and unresourceful.[56] Despite its devastating consequences, the Great War was also the occasion of Australia's nationalist epiphany.

The ideology of nationalism decreed that its adherents celebrate their first experience of warfare. The mediums best suited to this propaganda task traditionally were literary history and Romantic prose. By the time that Australia had fought its nation-making war, the literary form had been infiltrated by modernism and could no longer do the bidding of an eighteenth-century ideology. Literary memory of the Great War in Australia fell into the gap between the heroic nationalism of *Deeds that Won the Empire* and the ironic modernism of *All Quiet on the Western Front*.

In 1932 John Treloar, the director of the Australian War Museum, sought Charles Bean's advice as to whether he should endeavour to accumulate the war books that were being written by former soldiers. Bean thought the exercise would be futile: 'Novels etc. with a war flavour [...] would simply be collected to be stacked in cellars and eaten by silverfish'.[57] The official historian was characteristically prescient.

# 4

# 1940s–1960s: MARXISM AND MEMORY OF THE GREAT WAR

A S WE HAVE SEEN, THE IDEOLOGY OF nationalism shaped early ways of remembering the Great
War in Australia. This nationalism came in different
shades: there was the imperial nationalism of Ernest Scott,
the triumphal Australian nationalism of Charles Bean, and
the more muted nationalist pride of the soldier-writers.
The dominance of the Beanian nationalist version of the
war in contemporary Australia tends to obscure the fact
that there was always a part of the population that did
not subscribe to the view that the nation was born on 25
April 1915. How did memory of the Great War change
in the hands of people who were more interested in class
than nation?

The near-unanimity with which communism is now
perceived to be a discredited ideology could equally have
applied to capitalism during the 1930s. The laissez-faire
capitalism that produced the 'war to end wars' and the
Great Depression had proved incapable of preventing the
death and suffering of hundreds of millions of people. It
is hardly surprising that many children of the inter-war
generation were impelled by their experience of war and
poverty towards the ideas of Karl Marx. This chapter
shows how memory of the Great War fared during the

years after the Second World War, when a group of influential scholars proposed a radical new interpretation of Australian history. It tells the story of the radical historiography of the war through the lives and work of three historians: Russel Ward, Ian Turner and Geoffrey Serle. These men were influenced profoundly by the pioneer of radical nationalist historiography, Brian Fitzpatrick.

Radical nationalism had its first flowering in Australia in the 1880s and 1890s when it was expressed primarily in the literature and journalism of a group of writers based in Sydney. Through their fiction and journalism, men such as Henry Lawson, Joseph Furphy and JF Archibald at the *Bulletin* magazine expressed their wish to make Australia a haven for ordinary men, free from the class structure and inequity of Britain. Their working-class creed was typically paired with an aggressive, anti-British Australian nationalism. These radicals created an idol for their utopian religion, the noble bushman, who was fiercely independent, egalitarian, irreverent and, above all, loyal to his mates. The radical nationalists were heavily influenced by pervasive socialist utopian attitudes and were also rebelling against the aggressively minded new imperialism, which sought to boost imperial solidarity through rituals such as the school flag-raising ceremony mentioned in chapter 1. The radical nationalists and their emblematic bushman reached the peak of their influence in the mid-1890s before being swamped by the rising tide of jingo-imperialism, which Australians embraced in response to their service in South Africa, and concerns about Japanese, Russian and German activity in the Pacific Ocean. By the time of the Great War, Henry Lawson was calling for German blood and the *Bulletin* magazine was making the case for conscription.

A small group of Australian writers that included Nettie and

Vance Palmer, Katharine Susannah Prichard and Frank Wilmot continued to advocate a left-wing, nationalist program, both before and after the Great War, but their effort did not grow into a widespread, popular movement. When radical national-ism re-emerged as a cultural force in the late 1930s, it primarily described an *historical* rather than a *literary* sensibility.

The pioneer of radical nationalist historiography was Brian Fitzpatrick, an activist-intellectual who remained forever on the fringes of Australian academia. Born in 1905, Fitzpatrick was raised in a cultivated lower middle-class family and spent his childhood in far western Victoria, Ballarat and Moonee Ponds, a western suburb of Melbourne. He became radicalised after win-ning a scholarship to the University of Melbourne in 1922, where he co-founded the university Labour Club and the campus mag-azine *Farrago*, and sought companionship among the university's small bohemian set. Fitzpatrick was unimpressed by his encoun-ter with the famous Professor Ernest Scott; he resented Scott's unconsidered repudiation of Marx and his dismissal of the gold miners' Eureka uprising as 'a riot got up by a lot of troublesome foreigners'.[1]

While working as a journalist, first in Sydney and then in Melbourne in the late 1920s, Fitzpatrick wrote feature articles on the gathering economic crisis, taking issue with the analysis of academic experts such as Douglas Copland, Lyndhurst Giblin and Edward Shann. In 1935, he resigned from his job at the Mel-bourne *Herald* and devoted himself to historical research and civil libertarianism, becoming one of the founders of the Australian Council for Civil Liberties. In 1936 he began researching an eco-nomic history of Australia 'that would confound the academics and challenge their standard story'.[2]

The 'standard story' that Brian Fitzpatrick sought to over-turn presented the economic relationship between Australia and Great Britain as one of mutual benefit. This interpretation fitted within a prevailing historiographical tradition wherein liberal British values and institutions had been grafted successfully onto local stock. This imperial 'Whiggery' was proclaimed with varying degrees of sophistication and flair by a small and interconnected group of historians of Australia, which included Ernest Scott, Keith Hancock, Stephen Roberts, GV Portus, Fred Alexander and Edward Shann. These men, the majority of whom were members of the Round Table group, which promoted closer ties with Britain, collaborated under Scott's editorship to produce the Australian volume of the *Cambridge History of the British Empire*, published in 1933. HV Evatt, then a High Court judge, sounded a rare note of dissent when he complained that the 'patrician tone' of the *Cambridge History* implied that 'every important event in our history must, in some mysterious way, have revealed its true importance to a Melbourne coterie exclusively'.[3]

Evatt provided the Introduction for Fitzpatrick's first book, *British Imperialism and Australia*, published in 1939. The sequel, *The British Empire in Australia*, appeared in 1941. In these and subsequent publications, Fitzpatrick argued that the development of Australian capitalism was driven by British imperial exigencies, such as the exploitation of Australian resources by British capital and the supply of primary goods for British industry. He described an unequal relationship, wherein the 'reservoir of Australian labour and industry has never failed to provide a stream tributary to the broader river of English wealth', and sought to show how the hostile relationship between British capitalism and Australian labour had shaped Australia's class system and political structure.[4] Whereas standard interpretations of Australian history cast Britain in the role of noble benefactor, Fitzpatrick dared to portray the mother country as a manipulative and self-serving colonial master.

The Great War was largely absent from Brian Fitzpatrick's analysis of Australian history, a fact that reflected his interest in economic relations between labour and capital and his disdain for the conventional narrative of national awakening. On the rare occasion that Fitzpatrick did mention the '1914–8 European war', as he called it, it was only to describe its impact on Australian workers, which was invariably negative. Measures such as the banning of the Industrial Workers of the World, the passing of the War Precautions Act, and legislation directed against trade unions characterised 'a time when democratic experimenting came to a standstill and the Australian democratic system itself was badly damaged by wartime and post-war authoritarianism'.[5] There was no call in Fitzpatrick's version of the war for recounting the deeds of 25 April 1915, the fighting reputation that the Anzacs had earned in France, or Prime Minister Hughes' strong showing at the signing of the peace treaty in Versailles in 1919. This new version of Australian history did carry a nationalist message, but that message derived not from military heroics or the diplomatic grandstanding of national leaders, but from the heroic battle of the working class against bourgeois and British oppression.

The impact of Fitzpatrick's books on Australian historical scholarship was profound. The radical nationalists of the 1880s and 1890s had expressed anti-British attitudes in their ballads, poems and journalism, but rarely had this sentiment been presented in the authoritative medium of history. Writing in the Foreword to the 1969 edition of *The British Empire in Australia*, the historian Geoffrey Blainey declared it was the most influential book on Australian history yet written: it made the subject 'seem relevant to thousands of readers whose schooldays' diet of early explorers, colonial governors, and constitutional crises had persuaded them that history ... was irrelevant to their world'. Fitzpatrick's quasi-Marxist analysis was an intellectual balm to young radicals such as Ian Turner, Noel Ebbels and Stephen Murray-Smith, who crowded into university campuses

in the years after the Second World War. It taught 'my generation to see Australia as a semi-colony, controlled and exploited
by British imperial power', Turner later recalled. The appeal of
Fitzpatrick's analysis lay as much in its nationalist clarion call as
it did in its radicalism. Though they were ostensibly concerned
with class identification, Fitzpatrick's books could also be read as
nationalist polemics. Previous historians tended to 'muffle Australian nationalism with the drum beats of Empire', but Fitzpatrick
promoted a rebellious, working-class nationalism, fattened on a
sense of injustice and mistreatment at the hands of Britain and
Australian loyalists.[6] Fitzpatrick had laid the intellectual foundation upon which a radical historiography of Australia would be
built.

Like the Great War, the Second World War acted as a forc-
ing house for nationalist sentiment. Britain's preoccupation with
the European theatre and the consequent fall of Singapore represented for many Australians the demise of imperial security.
The subsequent mobilisation for war in the Pacific fostered a new
sense of confidence and independence. For all the significance of
these geo-political developments and Australians' pride in their
military performance, the spike in nationalist feeling, especially among fighting men, was
more personal in origin. The
war brought into contact men
whose paths would otherwise
never have crossed: those of

*Fitzpatrick had laid the intellectual
foundation upon which a radical
historiography of Australia would
be built.*

English and Irish descent; working class and middle class; Protestant and Catholic. The historian Russel Ward's first night in camp
as a soldier at the Sydney Showgrounds was spent with an Irish
Catholic: 'Never before had [he] been so close to a person of
the old religion'. Religious and racial prejudices were forgotten,
at least temporarily, as the adversity and suffering of war forged
deep bonds.[7]

Like many sensitive Nonconformists of his generation, Ward had traded the austere, teetotalling Methodism of his childhood for Marxism in the 1930s. He joined the Communist Party in 1941, a year after it was banned by Prime Minister Robert Menzies. Entwined with Ward's childhood Methodism was a deep attachment to Great Britain; no-one could have been 'a more perfervidly loyal Briton than I was at seventeen', he recalled in his autobiography. It was not until his experience as a soldier during the Second World War that Ward's Anglophilia was displaced by an equally zealous Australian nationalism. He recalled his nationalist epiphany as occurring one night in Sydney during the war when he heard some Scottish friends and visiting British submariners singing an old Australian folk song about dingoes, crows and coolibahs in 'bizarrely unsuitable' accents. This unlikely performance hinted at the existence of an authentic and original Australian culture about which this upper middle-class man, raised in the faux-English surrounds of Nonconformist boarding schools, knew nothing.[8]

Ward spent the years immediately after the war as a high school teacher. He left the Communist Party in 1949 to appease his wife, who had suffered a nervous breakdown and was paranoid about government surveillance of the couple's activities, though he never renounced Marxism. When he began writing his doctoral thesis at the Australian National University (ANU) in 1953, it was with the purpose of collating Australian folk songs like the one he had heard during the war. As Ward examined journals, newspapers, magazines, poems and ballads from the nineteenth century, the nature of his inquiry was transformed. *The Australian Legend*, published in 1958, was a study of the emergence of an Australian national type: the noble bushman. It argued that the legend of the itinerant pastoral worker – whose nature owed much to the convicts and currency lads of the past – had been created in the 1880s and 1890s by writers like Henry Lawson,

Joseph Furphy, 'Banjo' Paterson and the journalists of the *Bulletin*. This national mystique embodied a collection of disparate social forces (such as utopian idealism, industrial trade unionism, secularism, belief in material progress and a nationalism that was anti-British, chauvinist and racist) operating at the close of the nineteenth century.[9]

The foundations for Russel Ward's bushman had been laid in the eighteenth and nineteenth centuries, but his legacy was evident in the twentieth. Ward nominated the official war historian Charles Bean as one of the chief propagandists of the noble bushman, and anointed the digger as heir to the bushman legacy. Though soldiers in the Great War came from the city and the country in almost equal numbers, Ward endorsed Bean's claim that 'even city-bred Australians were bush men at heart'. The legendary traits of the Australian soldier – his laconic humour, comradeship, suspicion of authority and reluctance to salute – were all inherited from the bushman. The old diggers' notorious behaviour on Anzac Day, namely their predilections for heavy drinking and illegal gambling, was further evidence of their bushman lineage.[10]

*The Australian Legend* was quickly recognised as a seminal work; it sold 40 000 copies in its first twenty years and has never been out of print. Despite the success of his book, Ward was denied two academic jobs because of his radical politics. He eventually won a position in 1957 at the University of New England in rural New South Wales, where he remained until his retirement. Ward did not produce another significant publication for twenty years, until *A Nation for a Continent* appeared in 1977. The book, which was an attempt to popularise a radical version of the national story, allocated a separate chapter to the Great War, in which Ward portrayed the event as a disaster that shattered dreams of making Australia 'the ideal democratic state of the common man'. Ward did not take comfort from the defeat of conscription in the referenda of 1916 and 1917. Instead, he presented the controversy as the harbinger of catastrophe, splitting the Labor Party, the labour movement and the general population, and setting Australia on the path of political conservatism. With the Labor Party marginalised on the far left, Australians gravitated towards the traditionally imperialist conservative parties. Proud though people were of their 'newly blooded Australian identity', the war had only emphasised Australia's dependence on Britain and imperial unity for protection from foreign invasion.[11]

In *The Australian Legend* Russel Ward had been silent about the disjunction between Charles Bean's loyal, if undemonstrative, imperialist Australian and his own radical republican model. Nor had he mentioned the political conservatism of the diggers, as he listed the traits they had inherited from the pastoral worker. Despite *A Nation for a Continent*'s despondent analysis of the legacy of the Great War, there was something irresistibly attractive about the soldiers themselves to an aggressive nationalist such as Ward. Sounding more like a late nineteenth-century martial nationalist than a Cold War socialist, Ward declared that the Anzacs' landing at Gallipoli 'had shown the whole world – and themselves – that they could fight as well, or better, than the men of any other nation, including England itself ... they had passed the test of battle with first class honours'. But, Ward admitted, there were important differences between the bushman and the digger. The bushman was a political radical and an anti-British Australian nationalist, while the returned soldier was a conservative, Australian–British imperialist.[12] Ward was drawn to the iconic digger for his overt working-class 'Australianness'; that he was, in reality, a right-wing loyalist was due to forces beyond his control.

The historian Stuart Macintyre has linked the defeat of the bush unions in the great industrial conflicts of the 1890s with the radical nationalists' projection of the bushman legend upon the nation as a whole.[13] The same process was repeated in the mid-twentieth century. As the truth about Soviet communism began to emerge, so did a mighty historiographical effort to establish the radical provenance and revolutionary potential of the Australian working class. Russel Ward's mission to find an historical precedent for his radical political program snagged on the political conservatism of the diggers, who were more likely to be saluting the Union Jack than storming the barricades. It would take another lapsed communist historian to admit just how awkwardly the digger fitted within the radical nationalist tradition, and to begin to dismantle the foundations of his faith.

Ian Turner was the product of a conventional middle-class upbringing. Born in 1922, his early years were spent in the dry Wimmera country of western Victoria, where his father Frank worked as a stock and station agent and his mother belonged to the ladies' auxiliary of the United Australia Party and doted on her talented son. Though Frank Turner had served as an officer during the Great War and was 'sound RSL', his wife was descended from Scots landed gentry and resented the diminution in status that marriage had brought her. Ian won a scholarship to Geelong College where he became passionately concerned about Spain under General Franco and the rise of German fascism. Nina Turner held high hopes for her 'good-looking brilliant little schoolboy', and was dismayed by his rebellion against the respectable and conventional values of his upbringing.[14]

Turner's law studies at Melbourne University were interrupted when he was conscripted into the home militia in 1940 and transferred from there into the Australian Imperial Force (AIF). Though he 'believed strongly – even passionately – in the war', Turner was happy to make his contribution from well behind the lines: 'I was neither a good nor an enthusiastic soldier', he later wrote. He served as a transport driver in Australia and in Papua New Guinea, where he read Brian Fitzpatrick, along with Marx and Engels. Turner's radicalism was rapidly leading him towards the Communist Party, which he joined in 1945. He was far from alone in his radical idealism: 'the times were radical; the Russians were popular, and the dreams of post-war reconstruction were grand', he recalled. Under the patronage of the writer and literary scholar Tom Inglis Moore, Turner transferred to the Army Education Service – which the army brass rightly suspected to be 'riddled with commos' – for the balance of his war service.[15]

Turner resumed university studies in 1945, and set himself to working for the revolution that he now believed was inevitable. He became co-president of the Labour Club, secretary and president of the Students' Representative Council, co-editor of *Farrago* and president of the university branch of the Communist Party. Postwar university campuses were more crowded and cosmopolitan places than they had been before the war. The federal government's Commonwealth Reconstruction Training Scheme gave returning servicemen free university tuition, plus living and book allowances. The war was rarely spoken about. It was 'like families and ethnicity, something you put behind you', according to former student Amirah Inglis.[16] But despite the pact of silence, everybody knew who the ex-servicemen were; with their cars, their flats and their sophisticated ways, they were much admired by younger female students. They were revered and resented in equal measure by young men, such as Ken Inglis, who had arrived at university straight from school and felt gauche and inexperienced by comparison.

Like several other prominent historians of his generation, Ian Turner studied in the Melbourne University history department under the leadership of Max Crawford. The Sydney-born professor led the 'Melbourne School' for thirty-three years and mentored a generation of distinguished historians, such as Manning Clark, Kathleen Fitzpatrick, Geoffrey Blainey, Greg Dening, John Poynter and Margaret Kiddle. Clark's brief turn as a lecturer in Australian history left a profound mark on Turner. Clark's extreme hostility towards 'Yarraside' and the straiteners of the 'Protestant Ascendancy' complemented Turner's division of Australian society into an Anglocentric and greedy bourgeoisie, and a virtuous and radical proletariat. According to Turner, Clark showed him 'the possibilities of an Australia which lived on its own ground, stood on its own feet, and spoke with its own voice'. Clark's course in Australian history terminated at the beginning of the twentieth century, but Ian Turner had no need of the events of 25 April 1915 to stoke his own patriotism: 'it was from the working class that whatever there was of an Australian spirit had come ... radicalism and nationalism seemed natural partners'.[17]

After graduating, Turner dedicated himself to becoming a professional revolutionary, willing to go wherever it pleased the party to direct him. He served as secretary of the Australian Peace Council before being discarded in the fall-out from some undisclosed factional bickering: 'I was a disciplined Communist and I copped it sweet'. Turner was shunted off to clean railway carriages at the Dudley Street workshops in West Melbourne, apparently in order to gain some industrial experience. But the long-haired intellectual struggled to conform to working-class mores. Despite turning up for work each day in his worn army greatcoat and shabby clothes, he was dismayed to realise that 'the cultural gap between me and my colleagues was impossible to bridge'. His expulsion from the party came after he wrote a public letter criticising the Soviet Union's suppression of the Hungarian uprising. Despite its inevitability, the break with communism was traumatic: 'I had lost the movement in which I had lived, for fourteen years, as in an extended family, which had provided me with emotional security, intellectual certainty, and what I thought of as a significant role'.[18] Flailing around for a new direction, he turned to history.

Turner's first book, *Industrial Labour and Politics* (1965), was the result of doctoral research at the ANU. The book was an early contribution to the emerging field of labour history, which was being pioneered in Britain by EP Thompson and in Australia by Robin Gollan, Eric Fry and Bede Nairn. It sought, in the author's words, to introduce 'the concept of masses rather than *élites* as the moving forces in the historical process'. Though *Industrial Labour and Politics* covered the period of the Great War, the conflict was of interest to Turner chiefly for its impact upon Australian workers. Writing in the aftermath of the Labor Party split of 1954–55, Turner also sought to study the actions of Labor politicians and industrial advocates during the split over conscription in 1916. Like Brian Fitzpatrick, Turner had no interest in the martial baptism or the Anzac legend. The issues raised by the war – price-fixing, wage-freezing, conscription – revealed the ideological divisions within the labour movement, but the war's disproportionate toll on the working class also provided a unique opportunity for Marxists to prosecute their case for change. Purged of their moderate political faction after the Labor Party split in 1916 and bolstered by their conscription victories, 'the socialists looked at the post-war world with prophetic eyes'.[19]

Between the writing of *Industrial Labour and Politics* and the publication of an edited collection of writings about Australia's future called *The Australian Dream* in 1968, Turner's utopian dream had become a nightmare. The workers in whom he had invested faith had disappointed him with their willingness to be ruled 'by conservative and incompetent élites', and placated by 'the inanity of plastic culture'. The radicalism that Turner and his peers had attributed to the working class, and been building an historical precedent for, had been replaced by apathy: 'the clenched fist, shaken in the face of injustice, has abdicated to the indifferent shrug'. Anybody who still dared to dream, he declared with Clarkian grandiloquence, 'was filled with dark foreboding'.[20]

*The Australian Dream* and various articles that Ian Turner produced subsequently show how his loss of faith in socialist revolution was influenced by Australia's Great War experience. After
all, the men who wore khaki were the men who would make
the revolution. That the digger shared so many character traits
with the nineteenth-century bushman initially excited Turner;
it 'seemed to reinforce the claim for something unusual ... and
valuable in the Australian culture'. If these values could be relia-
bly traced over time, they offered the 'hope of realisation in the
modern working class movement'. The soldiers' imperial loyalty
and political conservatism were certainly stumbling blocks, but
they did not negate the importance of the digger within the radical nationalist tradition. The Anzacs may have been 'deluded by
imperial or national sentiment', but what they 'fought for was not
as important as what they were'.[21]

Like Russel Ward, Turner retained his affection for the digger,
despite his increasing acknowledgment that he was not the gulli-
ble victim of a false consciousness inculcated by bourgeois propagandising. In 1974, Frank Crowley, professor of history at the
University of New South Wales, edited a *New History of Australia*,
which sought to incorporate into the national story the advances
in research and changes in interpretation and approach that had
occurred in Australian historical scholarship over the preceding
two decades. The book included a chapter by Ian Turner on the
period of the Great War. Turner had no qualms about sifting the
diggers' achievements from the capitalist–imperialist detritus of
the Great War. His words could conceivably have been written
by the official historian Charles Bean fifty years earlier. The Australian soldiers' efforts at Gallipoli were 'a personal and national
triumph ... They had reinforced the established values of the
Australian bush. A man was judged by his performance, not by
his birth, and by how he stood with his mates ... They had come
to know their own manhood and that of their fellows'.[22]

Unlike Ernest Scott in his domestic volume of the *Official History*, Turner did not pull any punches about a home-front that was becoming increasingly fractious as the war dragged on.[23] Trade union revolt over the Labor government's inadequate efforts at price control was followed by a series of strikes by maritime workers, coal and metal miners and shearers during 1916. Radical elements of the labour movement, such as the Industrial Workers of the World, which were opposed to the war from the outset, were joined by the labour movement and a good portion of the parliamentary wing as the war ground on. The industrial unrest of 1916 foreshadowed the even greater strife that soon erupted over the question of compulsory military enlistment, which was fervently advocated by the Labor Prime Minister WM Hughes. The conscription debate split the parliamentary Labor Party and forced the industrial wing, which was increasingly influenced by communist and socialist elements, over to the hard left. By the end of the war, Turner concluded, the nation was divided: 'capital against labour, government against the unions, ex-servicemen against civilians, the war generation against their children, the traditional modes of behaviour against the new'.[24]

*Ian Turner, like Russel Ward, had come to consider the Great War to be portent of doom for progressive forces in Australia.*

Turner, like Russel Ward, had come to consider the Great War to be the portent of doom for progressive forces in Australia. The hopes expressed by Charles Bean's *In Your Hands, Australians* and by Leonard Mann in *Flesh in Armour* – that postwar Australia might somehow by its brilliance compensate for 60 000 dead – were disappointed. If the public backlash against the introduction of conscription for the Vietnam War had renewed Turner's faith in Australian radicalism, that hope was short-lived. In resignation, Turner closed his chapter in Crowley's *New History* with the words of CJ Dennis' eponymous protagonist, Digger Smith. The soldiers of the Great War did not want revolution. They just wanted 'The chance to live a clean, straight life' and 'A dinkum deal for kids an' wife'.[25]

Ian Turner died of a heart attack in late 1978 during a game of beach cricket on Erith Island off the coast of Tasmania. He was fifty-six years old. Despite his premature death, Turner lived long enough to relinquish his belief that the digger was fashioned in the image of Russel Ward's radical working-class male. In an article published posthumously, the man whose ideological trajectory had taken him from revolutionary communism to the Unity faction of the Victorian Labor Party acknowledged that the radical nationalists had been wrong to make 'assumptions about the inherent tendency of the Australian working class to adopt radical positions'. 'Comrade' did not have as much in common with 'mate' as this disillusioned utopian nationalist had once dared to hope.[26]

The radical nationalist historians were used to being criticised by the political right. In the early 1960s, the journalist Peter Coleman had endorsed Manning Clark as the leader of a conservative counter-revolution in Australian historiography, having mistaken Clark's mystical dissatisfaction with Marxist materialism as an endorsement of its opposite. But it must have come as some surprise to the radical nationalists when their interpretation of the Great War was questioned by someone who was not a warrior of the right. In an article published in the cultural and literary journal Meanjin in 1965, the historian Ken Inglis claimed that the majority of his peers neglected to study the history of the Great War because they found no ideological succour in its events; those who had embraced Marxist ideology were 'unlikely to see much point in studying the actual course of a war between nations which is not a class war', he wrote. Instead, Inglis argued, scholars such as Brian Fitzpatrick, Ian Turner, Robin Gollan and Geoffrey Serle preferred to seek historical legitimacy for their left-wing-nationalist ideology. This ideology led them to see the defeat of the conscription referenda in 1916 and 1917 as a great victory for the working class, despite the fact that the victories were narrow and compulsion was supported by many Catholics and workers. Inglis did not seek to challenge radical historiography of the Great War on political grounds, though his arguments lay challenge to its fundamental assumptions. Rather, he wanted to shift the entire basis for thinking about the war from the realm of politics to those of ritual and commemoration: 'A study of the ceremonies of life and death performed on Anzac Day should tell much about our society; and a national history which does not explore the meaning of these ceremonies is too thin'.[27]

Born in 1929, Ken Inglis was too young to fight in the Second World War, and too old to be swept up in the campus radicalism of the 1960s. Despite being only a couple of years behind radical intellectuals like Ian Turner, Stephen Murray-Smith and Geoffrey Serle at Melbourne University, once they returned from war service, Inglis was not tempted to join the Marxist cause. Inglis agreed with his teacher Manning Clark that materialist philosophy alone could not account for the human condition. His experience of growing up in a downwardly mobile family in the Melbourne suburb of Preston had left him suspicious of the idea of the working class as a singular and constant entity – it was insufficiently accommodating of the experience of families such as his own. After the ritual pilgrimage to England for doctoral work, Inglis returned to Australia with plans to study the social history of religion in Australia. Ruminating about the decline of religion and the sense of the sacred in Australia, Inglis began to think about Anzac Day as a quasi-religious event, a 'civic religion'.[28]

One of the few historians to respond directly to Ken Inglis' essay about 'The Anzac Tradition' was Geoffrey Serle. Though Serle is inevitably grouped with the likes of Ian Turner, Stephen Murray-Smith, Russel Ward, Robin Gollan, Edgar Waters, Eric

Fry and Ken Gott as a radical nationalist intellectual, he walked
a pace apart. Serle was Ian Turner's exact contemporary and their
lives followed similar paths. Both men were born in Victoria, one
in rural Nhill, the other in the middle-class Melbourne suburb
of Hawthorn. Both served in the Second World War and traded
their conservative, middle-class childhoods for left-wing politics
at the University of Melbourne. Both became prominent historians of Australia and colleagues at the newly established Monash
University in outer-suburban Melbourne. But while Ian Turner
was the charismatic rebel who broke with his parents and was
written out of his father's will, Serle was possessed of a milder,
more subtle temperament. He had been raised in the typically
bicultural fashion of cultivated Australians of the inter-war years,
where local artistic endeavour was encouraged, but considered
inferior to that produced in the mother country. Despite joining
the Left Book Club and being exposed to class discussions about
the Spanish Civil War at Scotch College in the 1930s, Serle left
school as an acquiescent member of a generation that had 'hearts
and minds centred on England'.[29]

The Second World War functioned as a patriotic growth
hormone for Geoffrey Serle, as it did for so many others. The
exigencies of wartime rubbed out state and regional loyalties, as
well as sectarian ones, and trained men's minds upon their membership of the national tribe. Serle's nationalisation went hand in
glove with his move to the left, which was always less drastic and
emphatic than that of other soldier-historians, such as Ian Turner,
Russel Ward and Robin Gollan. Serle may have become a socialist during the war, but his socialism was more in the style of the
Christian socialist intellectual and survivor of the first day on the
Somme, RH Tawney, than of Stalinist communism.[30]

Geoffrey Serle's war service was more dramatic and traumatic than that of Ian Turner. He was severely injured while serving in Papua New Guinea, and almost died during a painful and

protracted evacuation to Port Moresby. He used his long recov-
ery to keep reading – 'practically the whole corpus of Australian
history, such as it was' – and was ripe for the nationalist injunc-
tions of Manning Clark when he resumed his studies at the University of Melbourne in 1944. Like Turner, Serle was profoundly
affected by Clark's instruction in Australian history. Clark, for his
part, thought Serle an enviable combination of Apollonian ration-
ality and Dionysian passion. While Ian Turner was 'the Moses
leading his people to the promised land', Serle was a 'a dinky-di
straight-down-the-centre social democrat, a sweetness-and-light
man, who wanted middle-class Hawthorn to spread its beneficent
influence over the whole world'. Serle was active in the university
Labour Club and helped to establish the Victorian Fabian Society, but never joined the Communist Party. After a doctorate at
Oxford University, he returned to Melbourne University, where
he set about 'revelling in [the] virgin fields' of Australian historiography.[31] Serle's early academic work was on the history of
colonial Victoria. *The Golden Age* (1963) covered the gold rushes
of the 1850s, while *The Rush to be Rich* (1971) examined the boom
of the 1880s. His commitment to the development of a mature
and distinctive Australian culture led to Serle's close association
with the literary and cultural magazines, *Meanjin* and *Overland*.
In addition to making regular contributions to each, he edited
*Meanjin* in 1957 and served on the board of both magazines.

In his response to Inglis, Serle congratulated his colleague
for opening up 'the first serious modern discussion of Anzac and
the digger legend'. In most respects, he argued, the digger was
an updated version of the bushman – independent, scornful of
pretension, self-reliant and egalitarian – and he soon joined the
bushman as a 'second national stereotype or idealised Australian
type'. Serle's reply to Inglis was concerned mostly with explaining
how the digger legend was appropriated by the middle class in
the inter-war years, and why digger idealism was channelled into

conservative causes. He offered several reasons for the break-down of the traditional nexus between Australian nationalism and radical politics, and the concomitant rise of a right-wing nationalism, 'based on the new patriotism and pride of race of the Protestant middle class'. Many old soldiers were alienated by the Labor Party's leftwards momentum during and after the war. Those who were inclined towards radicalism resumed their class and trade union affiliations, thus exacerbating the Returned Services League's (RSL) conservative bias. The diggers were expertly courted by the conservative side of politics and any utopian ideals they may have possessed were extinguished by the Great Depression. The digger legend received a boost from the Second World War, Serle argued, but had been in decline ever since. Writing in 1965, its future did not look promising: 'The natural tendency of the young is to regard a military legend as sorry stuff on which to build a tradition'. Serle saw more longevity in Russel Ward's work: 'The bush legend is more romantically attractive'.[32]

Geoffrey Serle reiterated this analysis of the digger legend in his cultural history of Australia, *From Deserts the Prophets Come*. Like the earlier Victorian histories, *From Deserts* was propelled by a social-democratic nationalism, whereby the past was weighed according to its success in achieving social justice and a national voice that

*The diggers were expertly courted by the conservative side of politics.*

was neither an echo of Great Britain's, nor shrill and jingoistic. Just as the idealism of the nineteenth-century bush workers had been snuffed out by depression, drought, jingo-imperialism and national security threats, so the idealism of the diggers had been dampened by class division, depression and the connivances of cynical conservative politicians. This explanation of the disconnection between radicalism and nationalism foreshadowed that provided by Ian Turner in the Crowley history and by Russel Ward in *A Nation for a Continent*.

Serle's next major project after the cultural history required him to consider the history of the Great War directly. In 1975 he was approached by the descendants of John Monash to write a biography of the general who had led the Australian Corps in 1918. A biography of a war hero was an interesting choice for a radical historian, even more so because of the atmosphere of cynicism and disillusion that existed about the Anzac legend during the 1970s. Pre-empting the direction that military historiography would take a decade later, *John Monash: A Biography*, published in 1982, subverted the Anzac legend's emphasis on bush virtues and natural gifts by suggesting that Monash's success derived from his experience as a civil engineer, his administrative ability and his willingness to employ advanced technologies in innovative ways. Serle avoided the aggrandisement that Monash himself had been guilty of in *The Australian Victories in France in 1918*, but still concluded that the general deserved his reputation as a great Australian, a judgment no doubt more easily made because Monash was an engineer of German–Jewish heritage who had risen through the militia and succeeded, despite his lack of social and racial pedigrees. John Monash's success said as much about the egalitarian nature of Australia as it did about his own capacity: 'it was no ordinary nation which allowed Monash to lead in a time of uncommon stress'.[33]

Over the course of his career, Geoffrey Serle offered plausible explanations for the failure of the Anzacs to uphold the radical tenets of the Australian legend. What he did not do was to engage with Ken Inglis' endeavour to map out a new field of historiography on the intellectual borders between labour history and religious history, a field of research that used as its primary evidence the commemorative rituals of Anzac. Despite being only seven years apart in age, Ken Inglis and Geoffrey Serle were separated by a huge gulf in history. For the radical nationalists, the Great War was their fathers', brothers' and uncles' war. The second war belonged to them and their peers. War was personal, and often something best forgotten. The fact that Inglis' father was too young to fight in the first war and old enough *not* to fight in the second, and that Inglis himself was too young to enlist in 1939–45, afforded him the perspective from which to ask new questions about the Great War. In Ken Inglis, the war had begun its transition from personal experience to memory. While Geoffrey Serle was tilling 'the virgin fields of Australian historiography' with his radical nationalist plough, Ken Inglis was weighing the yield of fields already harvested. He would go on to write the seminal book, *Sacred Places*, documenting the history of war memorials in the Australian landscape, and to be acknowledged internationally as the pioneer of the scholarship of war, memory and commemoration.[34]

⊷⧟⧠⧠⊷

The radical nationalists' reluctance to subject the Great War and its official historian to close scrutiny was shared by their less radical peers and was arguably as much about their psychological proximity to its events and a general distaste for war as it was about the undesirability of the war's historical lessons.[35] Still, it is true to say that historians such as Russel Ward, Ian Turner and Geoffrey Serle had a relationship with the Great War that was more complex and vexed than that of their liberal and conservative colleagues. The radical historians demanded more from Australian history than their conservative peers; they were mining it for the evidence to build their case for proletarian revolution. The working-class male upon whose shoulders Russel Ward had balanced an historical case for Australian radicalism was manifest in the latter half of the nineteenth century as an itinerant bush worker. This radical template did not fit neatly over the working-class soldier who enlisted enthusiastically to fight for the imperial cause in the Great War.

As their hopes for a new social order faded, radical nationalists began to search for explanations and to address some of the questions that Inglis had asked of them in 1965. Yes, they had wrongly assigned radical sentiment to a working class that had proved itself complacent and easily seduced by the temptations of 'plastic culture'. The finger of blame was pointed at the conservative leaders who had dominated Australian politics since the Great War. These 'incompetent élites' had extinguished the reforming sentiment of the late nineteenth and early twentieth centuries, and welded Australian nationalism to conservative values and the British heritage. This characterisation of the Great War as the wrecking ball of progressive sentiment in Australia would be controversially revived by the former prime minister Paul Keating and a group of academic historians in the early twenty-first century.[36]

By drawing attention to the gulf between the left's claim of a radical working class and the conservatism and imperial loyalty of the diggers, Ken Inglis hastened the demise of their enterprise. But the most telling blow to radical nationalism came, not from Inglis, nor from the right, but from the far left. In 1970, the young Marxist historian Humphrey McQueen published a polemical and highly influential critique of radical nationalism. *A New Britannia* argued that the bush worker, upon whom contemporary radical nationalists built their faith, was racist, chauvinist and militaristic. A few years later, the former communist Miriam Dixson, who had studied history at the University of Melbourne in the years after the Second World War, wrote a pioneering feminist book called *The Real Matilda*. In it, she argued that the bush ethos articulated most famously in *The Australian Legend* was virulently misogynistic. A group of radical young historians, soon labelled the 'New Left', claimed, among other things, that the radical nationalists' definition of the working class had been too mechanistic.

With its idol, and unifying force, exposed as racist, sexist, violent and irresponsible, the radical nationalists' project was terminally compromised. The 'disasters of 1975 and 1977', as Ian Turner referred to Malcolm Fraser's election victories, were devastating confirmation of the spuriousness of the assumptions that underlay radical nationalism.[37] Once the homogenous, working-class male was removed from the centre of the historical enterprise, historiography spun in several directions: feminist history, social history and eventually cultural history, all of them to the ideological left of centre. As they shed their Marxist skins, men such as Ian Turner, Russel Ward and Geoffrey Serle looked increasingly like the European nation-making historians of the nineteenth century. Unlike their New Left successors, they held, at least initially, a coherent vision of the nation, and they chose history as their means of proselytising it. That theirs was a socialist nation, as opposed to the pre-industrial nations of earlier European historians, was an accident of Australia's late arrival on the nation-making scene.

The radical nationalist historians grew to adulthood during an especially destructive age. They bore the aftermath of the 'war to end wars', the Great Depression and the rise of communism and fascism. They fought in the Second World War to defeat fascism and endured the Cold War against communism that followed. They were drawn to what they believed to be the authentic Australianness of the diggers of both world wars, yet ultimately were disappointed that these men did not share their dream of socialist revolution. History has laid bare the flaws in the radical nationalist response to what the late historian Eric Hobsbawm called 'the age of extremes'.[38] But we should admire these people's idealism as much as we decry their naivety. As Ian Turner wrote of the radical nationalists of the late nineteenth century:

> We may well wonder, with Manning Clark, at the naiveté of
> men whose belief in material progress and mateship was 'their
> only comforter against earth and sky, man and beast'. But we
> still admire the nobility of their bearing.[39]

# 5

# 1965–1985: THE FALL AND RISE OF MEMORY OF THE GREAT WAR

B Y THE LATE 1960s, THE ANZAC LEGEND was in clear decline. The triumphant nationalism of the Anzac myth had been primed by a belief in the superiority of the British race. This belief could no longer be sustained in the face of the atrocities committed by the Nazis in the name of racial science. Deprived of its sustaining ideology, commemoration of the Great War began a long and seemingly inexorable decline. This chapter traces the waning of Anzac commemoration and its unexpected revival in the early 1980s. It shows how the race-based nationalism that had once powered the Anzac legend was replaced by a gentler brand, one that prized mateship, loyalty and sacrifice. This new version of Anzac placed less emphasis on the circumstances under which the nation was conceived – war being repugnant to much of its audience – and more emphasis on the tragedy and sacrifice of its birth.

In 1953 a dispute broke out in the Victorian Returned Services League (RSL) about the observance of Anzac Day between members of the Thirtyniners' Association, who had enlisted for service during the first year of the Second World War, and veterans of the Great War. The younger men were pushing for 'a brighter Anzac afternoon', which might include sports meetings, in addition to, or in place of, the traditional pursuits of drinking and gambling.[1] The apathy of the younger men mirrored that of the Great War veterans in the 1920s and 1930s, and probably reflected a similar desire to forget about the war and get on with everyday life. But the ageing soldiers, forgetful of their earlier desire to forget, were fiercely protective of Anzac Day and sensitive to any indication that younger Australians placed insufficient store in the observance of its rituals. They were particularly loud in their opposition to anything that might hint of the commercialisation of what they considered to be a sacred day. The old diggers were supported in the dispute by the War Widows and Widowed Mothers' Association, whose spokeswoman believed that businessmen who wanted to hold sports events were only looking for an opportunity to do away with Anzac Day altogether.[2]

It is a common misconception to attribute the beginning of the decline of Anzac Day commemoration to the Vietnam protest movement and the baby boomer generation. The diggers of the first war had been concerned long before Vietnam that their legacy was not being sufficiently honoured by those who came after them. In 1950 a returned soldier wrote to the local paper expressing alarm that fellow veterans were not paying proper respect to their fallen comrades. Mates who fought and died would not begrudge the diggers a good time, but 'they would be astounded to know that they were being remembered by the quaffing of beer', he wrote. In 1954 an old digger warned readers of the *Argus* that Anzac Day would die in ten years, unless the men who had fought in the Second World War took more interest. His concern must have been exacerbated a few days later when the paper reported that Melbourne's Anzac Day march had been attended by the smallest crowd for years.[3]

As the Great War generation slipped away, those who were left clung more tightly to their commemorative traditions. By the late 1950s, the apathy of the thirty-niners towards Anzac remembrance had begun to yield to the hostility of their children, whose liberal values clashed with the diggers' moral and political conservatism. The antipathy ran both ways. The RSL, a long-time and strident advocate for the needs of returned men, became an even more influential conservative voice in political and cultural debate. The hostility expressed towards feminists, communists, homosexuals and non-white migrants, also extended to young people with their modern ideas. Australian youth was complacent about the defence of the nation, complained Queensland RSL branch president Sir Raymond Huish in 1951. Only the introduction of compulsory military training would safeguard the country and secure 'equality of sacrifice'. The vice-chancellor of Adelaide University warned in 1957 that the Anzac spirit was being displaced by 'the standard of living'. Young Australians were becoming soft and complacent. They enjoyed a 'comfort and convenience unknown to kings and emperors of not long ago. At the flick of a finger we have heat, light, cold, transportation, conversation with friends, news and music: all this and crooners too'.[4]

It is significant that the playwright Alan Seymour chose to set his drama about the generation gap, *The One Day of the Year*, around the commemoration of Anzac Day. The play's protagonist, university student Hughie Cook, is among the baby boomers to benefit from the postwar economic boom and the consequent expansion of tertiary education. Hughie feels ashamed of his father's xenophobic philistinism, and questions his adherence to the legend of Anzac: 'Do you know what that Gallipoli campaign meant? Bugger all … A face-saving device. An expensive shambles. The biggest fiasco of the war'. For his part, Alf thinks his son is a spoiled, 'jumped up little twerp' who is filling his head with fancy ideas at university. The meaning of Anzac Day had been distorted in its transmission from Alf's generation to Hughie's. The occasion on which Australia became a nation, according to Alf, was in Hughie's eyes a day of 'bloody wastefulness' perpetuated year after year by a 'screaming tribe of great, stupid, drunken, vicious, *bigoted* no-hopers'.[5]

The extent of the widening cultural divide between the Great War generation and young Australians was clearly demonstrated by the fall-out from an episode of *Four Corners* broadcast on ABC television in 1964. The report on the RSL by the prominent left-wing journalist Allan Ashbolt noted the organisation's opposition to communism and non-European immigration, and revealed it for the powerful political lobby that it undoubtedly was. Ashbolt alleged a split between the highly politicised leadership and the rank and file, and showed footage suggesting, in the words of the historian Ken Inglis, 'that beer was important to the community of RSL members'. Branch officials began fielding telephone calls from irate members before the program had even finished going to air – it was 'crude and really got into the gizzards of returned men', was how one man described it. Sir Raymond Huish and other senior officers accused Ashbolt of entrapment and bias, and alleged that there was communist influence within the ABC. Prime Minister Menzies who, according to Inglis, paid the RSL 'the special deference of an imperial patriot who had never been to war', called for a transcript of the report, as well as those of previous episodes made under Ashbolt's supervision.[6] RSL outrage was assuaged when Ashbolt was temporarily removed from his position at *Four Corners*.

When the Menzies government announced in November 1964 that it was introducing military conscription for Vietnam, a public that had been largely apathetic about the war sat up and paid attention. The conservative government was taken aback by the extent of opposition to the war, not just from the usual groups such as the young and radical, but among the middle class

as well. The Melbourne moratorium march in May 1970, for
instance, drew a crowd of more than 100 000 people. Anzac Day
provided an obvious platform for protest groups such as Save
Our Sons to demonstrate their opposition to conscription and to
the war in Vietnam more generally. Hostility towards Vietnam
morphed rapidly into opposition to commemoration of war. Participants in the Anzac Day dawn service at Melbourne's Shrine
of Remembrance in 1971 arrived to find the letters 'P-E-A-C-E'
graffitied in bright white paint across the Doric columns at the
formal entrance to the Shrine. To many, especially the young, the
rituals of Anzac Day became indistinguishable from the glorification of war. The sentiments of a young woman who wrote to the
*Australian Women's Weekly* were typical. She raised the questions
asked every year by the young: 'What is Anzac Day? What does
it stand for?'. While admiring of the Anzacs' bravery in the face
of defeat, she was appalled by the glorification of war. Anzac Day
was 'a day when bigotry is displayed, as well as courage'.[7]

As the furore over Vietnam abated with Australia's final withdrawal in 1972, Anzac Day attracted the ire of other social movements. A Melbourne-based organisation called Women Against
Rape in War claimed that Anzac Day glorified the role men play
in wartime and ignored that fact that 'in war, as in peace, women
have always born [sic] the brunt of male violence'.[8] Dressed in
black robes with the words 'Remember women raped in war'
daubed on their backs in bright red letters, the women laid a
wreath at the Shrine of Remembrance on Anzac Day in 1979.
The response of Bruce Ruxton, head of the Victorian RSL, indicated the distance that separated Anzac traditionalists from
younger Australians. He thought members of Women Against
Rape in War were 'rabble-rousers' who were probably 'commu-
nist-inspired': 'When I look at them on the television, I wonder
how rape would be possible'. Ruxton was even more vexed when
a group of men from the Gay Service Association attempted to

lay a wreath at the Shrine on Anzac Day in 1982. Waving his umbrella like a sword, he blocked the entrance to the Shrine and bellowed for the men to be stopped. He later told a journalist that he did not 'mind poofters in the march, but they must march with their units'. A separate 'poofter' delegation was just a 'denigration of Anzac Day'.[9]

By the 1970s, the gulf between the meaning that the old diggers attributed to the Anzac legend and that imputed by younger people seemed impossible to bridge. A martial nationalist ideology, anchored in ideas of racial supremacy and Empire, had stoked the Anzac legend for half a century. As the pillars of this ideology were dismantled, so the legend itself collapsed. Perhaps it was not surprising that Anzac should last only as long as its custodians lived to preserve it. When commentators, Ken Inglis among them, announced the inevitability of Anzac Day's demise, only the old veterans raised their voices in dissent.

The demise of the Anzac legend coincided with a period of debate about the Australian 'national identity'. This national rumination was prompted in large part by Britain's decision to loosen its economic ties with Commonwealth nations as it increasingly pursued its post-imperial future within Europe. Though the myth of imperial omnipotence had been punctured during the Second World War, Australians were surprised by Britain's actions, and unprepared for the period of communal introspection that was forced upon them. If Australians could not seek comfort and confidence in their Britishness any longer, how could they know themselves and understand the civilisation they had created? The outpouring of artistic, popular and political expression in response to this question came to be known as the 'New Nationalism'.[10]

That the rhetoric of British race patriotism on which Robert Menzies had drawn so deeply during his prime ministership was less available to his successors caused them considerable consternation. At the World Expo in Montreal in 1967, the Prime Minister Harold Holt sought to convey to an international audience what was distinctive about Australia. His invoking of 'our corals, our apples, our gum trees and our kangaroos' would not have commended the nation highly to the rest of the world. Recognising that unique flora and fauna were no substitute for a distinctive culture, Holt established the Australian Council for the Arts in November 1967, with the aim of fostering 'a greater awakening to the Australian people of Australia and its possibilities'.[11]

Holt's successor John Gorton was less instinctively pro-British than his predecessors and more enthusiastic about the new, post-British mood. The new prime minister spoke of the need to develop 'a feeling of real nationalism': 'For a long time we stood not really as a nation in our own right, but as a nation the people of whom spoke of "home" and meant ... Great Britain'.[12] Gorton extended the Arts Council's activities to include film production. The first feature film to be funded by the new Australian Film Development Corporation was Barry Humphries' *Adventures of Barry McKenzie*. Though it appalled some critics and audience members with its satire of Australian cultural aspirations, *Barry McKenzie* was one of the few government-sponsored films of the period to find commercial success. In a sequel, *Barry McKenzie Holds His Own*, the ocker Bazza tells his mate Col: 'An arty-crafty bloke like you would be laughin' back in Australia right now. The government's shelling out piles of bloody moulah for any bastard who reckons he can paint pictures, write pomes or make fillums'.[13]

While the government-subsidised search for what the historian Manning Clark called '*homo Australicus*' left itself open to satire, it was by no means the only kind of nationalist activity in 1960s and 1970s Australia. The historians James Curran and Stuart Ward's claim in *The Unknown Nation* that 'that the drive for cultural renewal was anything but a grassroots movement' is surely too sweeping. The desire among Australian artists and intellectuals for a national

culture that tackled 'complex adventures of the spirit', as Nettie Palmer had put it in 1935, was particularly strong during the New Nationalist period. Writers, painters, poets and historians, such as Patrick White, Sidney Nolan, William Dobell, Arthur Boyd, Judith Wright, James McCauley, AD Hope and Manning Clark, might have benefitted from government grants, but their effort to match Australian subject matter to the universal themes of art, and avoid the traditional deference to Europe, was a separate phenomenon from the state-subsidised search for national symbols. Sidney Nolan described his Ned Kelly series, painted in the years after the

> *By casting timeless themes such as tragedy and love in the mould of European–Australian history, a group of people might begin to feel they belonged in a place.*

Second World War, as an attempt to achieve 'a more universal application of Kelly' (than the traditional anti-British, pro-Irish motif), and thereby 'get through to some sort of sacramental feeling'. Similarly, Patrick White wanted to give his explorer novel *Voss* 'the textures of music [and] the sensuousness of paint, to convey through the theme and characters of *Voss* what Delacroix and Blake might have seen, what Mahler and Liszt might have heard'.[14] This kind of artistic endeavour was not nationalist in the drum-beating nineteenth-century sense. It was a less muscular, more cerebral form of nationalism, which sought to bolster the fragile connection that European Australians felt to their environment. By creating an emotional history of their experience, by casting timeless themes such as tragedy and love in the mould of European–Australian history, a group of people might begin to feel they belonged in a place.

The sharp decline in public regard for the Anzac legend coincided with the dismantling of the White Australia policy, which had reinforced the British–Australian identity and sent the nation's troops to fight for Britain in 1914. Good relations between the RSL and the Coalition endured despite the government taking the first steps to remove the policy in the 1950s and 1960s. The most significant reform was made in 1966, when the Holt government removed race as a category when considering people's suitability for migration to Australia. Non-white migration to Australia consequently rose rapidly. In another sign of shifting social attitudes towards race, the results of referenda held in 1962 and 1967 gave Aboriginal people the vote, allowed them to be counted as Australian citizens and gave the Commonwealth government the power to make specific laws for them.

The consensus between government and the veterans' lobby ended once Labor's Gough Whitlam took office in December 1972. The new prime minister had fought in the Second World War and was no jingoistic nationalist, but he was more determined than his predecessors to push the rhetoric of Australian independence from Britain. Whitlam thrilled his supporters when he spoke of the need 'to move away from the father and son relationship of the past to a more normal bilateral relationship' with Great Britain, and championed the desirability of securing 'our own symbols of our own nationhood'.[15] In pursuit of the latter, he replaced the imperial honours system with the Order of Australia and abolished legal appeals from the High Court to the Privy Council. He substituted the Australia Council for the Coalition's Australian Council for the Arts and continued the state's generous subsidisation of cultural pursuits. In foreign policy, Labor showed a willingness to deal with Asian, African and European nations historically shunned by Australian governments.

Efforts to renovate the symbols of nationhood did not always go smoothly. Barely a month after taking office, Whitlam announced a competition to find a new national anthem. The song that replaced 'God Save the Queen' would be a potent symbol of Australia's new-found maturity and independence from Great Britain: 'The choice of the Australian people, not the musical tastes of George II, should determine Australia's national anthem', Whitlam said.[16] However, a judging panel that included Manning Clark, playwright David Williamson and the Aboriginal poet Kath Walker could not choose a winner from a short list of songs notable for 'the banality of their imagery and the shallowness of the sentiment'. Even the better entries, such as that of the writer Bob Ellis, could find nothing to say about Australia except that it was not British: 'Lift your head Australia; / The hour to stand alone; / Without the Proud regalia; / Of Kingdoms not our own'. Discarding the idea for a newly composed version, Whitlam announced 'Advance Australia Fair' as the national anthem after an indicative plebiscite preferred it to 'Waltzing Matilda' and 'Song of Australia'. But the conservative-led states of Queensland and Western Australia defied Whitlam's decision and continued to play 'God Save the Queen'. When the Liberal leader Malcolm Fraser came to power after Whitlam's dismissal, he restored 'God Save the Queen' as the official anthem for royal and vice-regal occasions. On other occasions when it was 'deemed necessary to denote a separate Australian identity', the government allowed a choice between 'Waltzing Matilda', 'Song of Australia' and 'Advance Australia Fair'. The *Age*'s response to this revealing debacle was to declare the national anthem 'God Save Australia's Fair Matilda'.[17]

Veterans of the Great War were inclined to see Whitlam's modernising measures as a betrayal of their legacy. Queensland's RSL branch president feared that Labor's move to change the national anthem was symptomatic of an 'evil philosophy' designed to 'brainwash our children to forget our old ideals, cut ourselves off from the past'. He also attacked the 'vandals' who sought to 'tear down the flag Australians had carried into battle' and replace it with 'something depicting a kangaroo or a gum tree'. The old diggers shed no tears when the Governor-General John Kerr sacked Gough Whitlam on 11 November

1975, after the latter had attended a ceremony at the Australian War Memorial for Remembrance Day. Commentary noted the warm welcome Sir John Kerr received at the War Memorial on Anzac Day the following year, and how it contrasted with the jeers he had been receiving in other parts of Canberra since the dismissal of the Whitlam government.[18]

The business of finding new national symbols was proving unexpectedly difficult. The suburban ocker in the form of characters such as Barry McKenzie, the comedian Paul Hogan and Norm from the 'Life Be In It' health campaign had become a potent symbol of Australianness, an anti-Briton who was, in his larrikinism, anti-intellectualism and demotic status, a contemporary reworking of Russel Ward's noble bushman and poet CJ Dennis' Ginger Mick and Digger Smith. But like the noble bushman and the Anzac, the ocker was not a sufficiently consensual substitute for the British embrace; its exaggeration of the mores of working-class males left a large proportion of the population cringing. Moreover, as feminist scholars like Anne Summers, Carmel Shute and Adrian Howe noted with growing indignation, men seemed to have an exclusive hold over human incarnations of the national identity.[19] Despite the government's best efforts, Barry Humphries' early suspicion that a national culture could not be bought with a bureaucrat's chequebook seemed prophetic. Nothing or no-one had appeared to fill the void left by British race patriotism.

When Bill Gammage arrived at the Australian National University (ANU) in 1961 as an eighteen-year-old, the subject of the Great War was neither taught nor researched by academic staff. The Australian history course was run either by Manning Clark, who nursed great private shame about his psychological and physical incapacity to serve in the second war, or Eric Fry, a former RAAF officer. According to Gammage, Australian history 'stopped in 1914 and re-started in 1918, stopped in 1939 and re-started in 1945'. The subject of war was of academic interest to the radical historians Eric Fry and Robin Gollan only in as much as it pertained to issues of class, while the metaphysically preoccupied Clark shared the left's disinterest in matters of a martial nature. Anybody who professed an interest in studying war was likely to be perceived as militaristic, Gammage recalled in a speech he made in 2002.[20] Military history remained a discrete sub-discipline of history, concerned with generals and politicians, campaign strategy and weapons. It was practised outside the academy by military historians and enthusiastic amateurs. As Ken Inglis wrote in the literary journal *Meanjin* in 1965, it was as if Charles Bean's *Official History*, with its groundbreaking effort to encompass broader themes of national development within a history of war, had not been written.

Bill Gammage's seminal book about the Great War, *The Broken Years*, is based upon several hundred letters and diaries held mostly in the Australian War Memorial, as well as the author's correspondence with returned servicemen. Gammage became aware of the archives during a social visit to the War Memorial in 1960. When a librarian friend of his mother's 'pulled open the grey cabinet that he was leaning on, and took out two or three letters written by an Australian soldier of the Great War', Gammage was intrigued.[21] The letters, along with scores of diaries, memoirs and private papers, had been procured by Charles Bean's assistant Arthur Bazley in the 1920s and 1930s to assist in the writing of the *Official History*. In the event, Bean had barely consulted the material, which had lain dormant ever since. Gammage surprised not just his teachers at the ANU, but also the staff at the War Memorial, when he undertook to use the letters and diaries for his honours and postgraduate theses: 'Choosing to work in the Memorial [whose staff were used to being ignored by the academy] was as eccentric as choosing to do what seemed military history at university', Gammage recalled. When he wrote around the world in 1967 looking for precedents for using personal records to write about war, he found none.[22]

It is possible to conceive Bill Gammage's Great War project as another cog in the social history wheel, which was gathering momentum in the 1960s. His desire to explore 'the experience of individuals, to get across what had happened to people' certainly resonated with the aspirations of social historians.[23] Lloyd Robson at the University of Melbourne was the first of the growing band of social historians to turn their attention to the Great War. Robson's doctoral thesis had analysed convict records to reach conclusions about the social origins of the transportees and their experience once in Australia. He subsequently applied these same quantitative methods to another vast body of data, the personnel records of the 1st Australian Imperial Force (AIF). Robson shared the view of more radical colleagues, such as Russel Ward and Ian Turner, that the conscription controversy shattered 'the spirit of optimism' and 'cocky pride with which the new Commonwealth entered the war'. His statistical analysis challenged the Anzac legend by contradicting the tenet that Australians made great soldiers by virtue of their bushman backgrounds. Robson's analysis proved that the majority of soldiers came in fact from urban rather than rural backgrounds.[24] Robson's influence went beyond his research. He established

*Gammage's desire to explore 'the experience of individuals, to get across what had happened to people' certainly resonated with the aspirations of social historians.*

a course at the University of Melbourne on the social history of Australians at war, and was instrumental in moving historical inquiry away from a Beanian-style focus on Australian military performance and national awakening and towards the war's impact on Australian society. Robson supervised the doctoral thesis of another historian who would make a major contribution to Great War historiography in Australia: Alistair Thomson.

Despite the parallels between Gammage's inquiry into the Great War and that of Lloyd Robson, Gammage stood apart from the social historians who sought to write history 'from the bottom up'. Though he was active in left-wing university politics at the ANU, Gammage was too independent and idiosyncratic by nature to settle on the radical left, where many historians of his vintage had found an ideological home. His university peers might have been wary of Gammage's interest in war, but he was equally suspicious of the value of their endeavour. While satisfying his intellectual curiosity about the Great War, Gammage kept one eye on his country boyhood, berating himself about 'what someone with rural instincts such as mine was doing at university'. His own democratic convictions stemmed not from an internationalist philosophy that was built around the urban proletariat and expected ideological conformity, but from his empathy with the old bush lifestyle in Australia, where 'individual freedom' was prized and authority and bureaucracy resented. Gammage shared Russel Ward's belief in the nexus between the bush and the development of an Australian ethos of manhood – he had experienced an intellectual epiphany upon reading Ward's *Australian Legend* in his second year at university: 'the characteristics [of the noble bushman] really staggered me. I just thought "This is me he's describing"'. Yet Ward's radical socialism was not to Gammage's liberal tastes. The 'boy from the bush', as Manning Clark characterised him, is best understood as the ideological heir to another war historian who believed in the legend of the Australian bushman: Charles Bean.[25]

Charles Bean and Bill Gammage were born barely 50 kilometres apart in western New South Wales, the former in Bathurst in 1879 and the latter in Orange in 1942. Gammage was the oldest of three sons of schoolteacher parents; Bean the oldest of three sons of a schoolmaster father. Bean's family moved to England when Charles was ten, and he did not return to Australia until he was twenty-five. Gammage's family moved from

Orange to Sydney during his childhood, before settling on the rural fringe of Wagga Wagga in southern New South Wales. Bill relished the country lifestyle, 'working on farms and walking in paddocks. It was a rural consciousness; the radio was full of stock prices'. Unlike the erudite Bean family who were steeped in British learning, 'there was no intellectual tradition' among the Gammages: 'Book-learning was not big, and I didn't think much of academics'. Like most boys of his generation, Gammage read classic English stories such as *Billy Bunter* and *William*, but the books had little resonance with his experience in country Australia: 'British culture seemed remote from my life, but I was not hostile to it'.[26] As he emerged from his own British chrysalis, Charles Bean devoted his life's work to documenting the ways in which Australian men were different from Britons. But the differences were obvious to Gammage, who wore his nationality with the ease of someone deeply settled in his physical surroundings.

Upon first approaching Charles Bean's *Official History* in the mid-1960s, Bill Gammage was primed to disapprove. Immersed in the politics of Vietnam, he expected Bean to be 'pro-war' and to find his books 'militaristic'; he planned in his own postgraduate research to 'take [Bean] on as a conservative'. But, in the course of writing *The Broken Years*, Gammage came to admire Bean for his 'wonderfully sympathetic detail' and to believe that he was 'correct in most respects'.[27] As some Australian military historians have noted (in disparaging terms), *The Broken Years* affirmed key themes of the *Official History*, in particular, Bean's assertion that the characteristics of the Australian soldier were derived from the bushman's code of behaviour.[28] Gammage also agreed with Bean that an important aspect of the digger's character was the democratic ethos that he brought with him from civilian life.[29]

The language with which Gammage described the Light Horse, the qualities he ascribed to them and the nostalgic admiration that seeped through his descriptions are all distinctly reminiscent of Charles Bean. He believed that 'bush types' persist in an army and that their influence was particularly strong among the men of the Australian Light Horse:

> The fierce individualism with which he fought Turks, Arabs, and English staff officers lay close to the heart of the Australian light horseman. He lived under few restraints, and was equally careless of man, God and nature. Yet, he stood by his own standards firmly, remaining brave in battle, loyal to his mates, generous to the Turks, and pledged to his King and country. His speech betrayed few of his enthusiasms, and he accepted success and failure equally without demonstration, but the confident dash of the horseman combined with the practical resource and equanimity of the bushman in him, and moved him alike over the wilderness of Sinai and the hills of the Holy Land. Probably his kind will not be seen again, for the conditions of war and peace and romance that produced him have almost entirely disappeared.[30]

Gammage endorsed Bean's belief that mateship was what sustained the Australian soldiers during the war: it was 'by far the firmest tenet in their creed', he wrote. For the sake (and the approval) of their friends, men strove to live up to an ideal of manhood that existed 'among bushmen before the war, on Gallipoli, and in France'. This kind of manliness prized physical toughness, emotional stoicism, wry humour and loyalty. 'The best Australians were loyal to their mates in every circumstance', Gammage wrote, citing examples of a soldier who died after giving his gas mask to a friend, and another who walked 28 miles to tend his friend's grave.[31] Gammage has spoken often since he wrote *The Broken Years* about his esteem for the soldiers of the 1st AIF. Of the men he interviewed while writing the book, he said: 'Their very being showed what Australia once was ... Many had those distinctive strine accents you hear rarely now, and almost never in a city, and many came out with neat, witty phrases and comparisons. What and how they spoke let me glimpse an Australia even then vanishing'.[32]

These distinctive Australian traits have been drained away by the homogenising influences of bureaucracy and modern communications, according to Gammage. City-bred Australians are no longer 'bushmen at heart', and the remaining glimpses of nineteenth-century Australia can now only be found in the countryside: 'Most years now I go with an old mate to drovers' reunions, where the contrast between then and now, us and them, is transparent'.[33] If The Broken Years reads like an elegy for the soldiers of the Great War and their values, it is because Gammage believed those men were 'the most adventurous, the most enterprising, the most resolute ... the fittest, of their generation'. He thought wistfully 'of what such men might have done had they lived, and how different Australia might have been'.[34]

The temper of the times in which Charles Bean wrote the Official History prevented him from being as outspoken about instances of British incompetence in the Great War as he would have liked. Bill Gammage, however, writing in the midst of the New Nationalism, had licence to be frank about British deficiencies. The Broken Years is not reflexively anti-British, but it does argue forcefully that interaction with British soldiers, and their experience of British command, did much to strengthen Australians' national pride: 'Though they continued to admire much in the Imperial system, Australian soldiers learnt their own worth, which formerly they doubted, and saw faults and cankers at the heart of their Empire, which formerly they had imagined great above every imperfection', Gammage wrote. He described the Australians' distaste for the British class system – 'few could accept the barrier between British officers and their men' – and their belief that it was this unbending system that had rendered the Tommies passive, inefficient soldiers. Gammage was particularly taken with soldier-turned-writer George Mitchell's description that the Tommies 'all bore the hall mark of the Cog'.[35]

While Gammage vindicated much of Charles Bean's praise of the diggers, he was also prepared to write about their less heroic traits and activities.[36] He was frank about the high incidence of venereal disease and the dark side of the larrikin digger. The Wasser riot in Cairo in early April 1915, and another in July that year, 'betrayed some of the worst aspects of the Australian character'. Bloodthirstiness was not censored for contemporary tastes: Gammage recorded the 'gorgeous time' one soldier at Gallipoli had while picking off Turks during the May offensive. Another Anzac described collecting a souvenir from his 'first kill with the rifle', and 'driving the bayonet into the body of one fellow ... when I drew the bayonet out, the blood spurted from his body'. Most damning of the Australians to contemporary readers was Gammage's evidence of their habit of shooting surrendering enemy troops rather than taking them prisoner.[37]

The most significant difference between Charles Bean and Bill Gammage, and one that the latter's critics have failed to note, lies in their attitudes to nationalism. The *Official History* was immersed in the ideology of martial nationalism, the notion that war 'affords a plain trial of national character'. Its greatest theme was that 'the consciousness of Australian nationhood' was born through the fine military performance of its citizens in arms. *The Broken Years* lacked entirely Bean's war-centred nationalism, a point that Ken Inglis made when he described the *Official History* as an epic and *The Broken Years* as a tragedy. Bean's distress was marshalled into the service of his great nation-making theme: the flower of its youth was sacrificed so that Australia could build a great outpost of British civilisation. The utopian nationalism that sustained Bean's theme was on plaintive and poignant display in his two books, *In*

*Your Hands, Australians* and *War Aims of a Plain Australian*. Though he appeared to uphold a similar ideal of Australian manhood to Charles Bean, Gammage did not share the official historian's optimism about Australian nation-building. The Broken Years rejected the concept of martial baptism and reads instead as a lament for the egalitarian utopia that Charles Bean had envisaged. It blended a Beanian concept of manhood with contemporary notions about the futility of war.[38]

*The Broken Years* defied the general spirit of hostility and apathy towards the Great War when it was published in 1974. Reviewers marvelled at the book's pioneering perspective and the poignancy of its content. One critic thought that *The Broken Years* made '*All Quiet on the Western Front* or any other artistic contrivance tame', while another described it as 'a compelling and accurate account of what the most terrible war in history was really like'.[39] Since its initial release *The Broken Years* has been reprinted and republished several times, most recently in 2010. To date, it has sold well in excess of 30000 copies in its various editions and become a widely acknowledged classic of Australian historiography. Manning Clark came closest to describing the essence of its appeal when he told Gammage, in characteristically grandiloquent style, that it contained 'such grandeur that it is now on my very short list of books that would tell people "what we are" and "the way we are"'.[40]

That the sensibility Bill Gammage brought to Great War history facilitated its revival in Australia was more good luck than good management. Independent by nature, Gammage dared to study the war when his peers were repelled by any subject with military associations. He brought to the subject an unusual blend of nostalgia for nineteenth-century rural Australia, contemporary distaste for war, and the desire to write emotive, narrative history in the manner of his teacher Manning Clark. History should 'comment on the human condition', he believed. 'No less than literature, art and music, it should end by having significance arching above your topic.'[41] The ornate language of *The Broken Years*, written to be spoken aloud, heightened its sense of foreboding and tragedy. Frequently, Gammage's prose recalls the nineteenth-century romantic rhetoric of war, to which the American literary scholar Paul Fussell ascribed the term 'high diction'. *Boy's Own Paper*–style descriptions of 'chivalrous feats', spirits that 'refused to yield' and 'dash and determination' are supplanted at other times by Clarkian notes of melodramatic pessimism. Despite the trials of the dreadful winter of 1916–17, the Australians:

> never doubted that they would fight on: they could not deny
> their manhood, nor by failing in their duty permit the ruin
> of their world. But they realised that they were assigning
> themselves to apparently endless agony, and were sacrificing
> their hopes and probably their lives to defend others. They
> had chained themselves to an odious necessity. They had
> come to Armageddon.[42]

By distilling military content from his book and allowing the soldiers to speak directly through their letters and diaries, Gammage laid the foundation for a new consensus of Great War memory. The emphasis was no longer on the belligerent RSL and its outdated attitudes, but on the tragic experience of the young soldiers. The martial nationalism of Charles Bean had become, in the hands of Bill Gammage, a gentler version evoked through empathy and sadness rather than warrior pride. *The Broken Years'* psychological perspective on the Anzac experience presaged the rise of 'trauma culture' in the 1980s, and the growing tendency to perceive soldiers as victims rather than warriors.[43] Gammage sought to do in history what others had done in art and literature: to elevate Australia's Great War experience above the clamour of Cold War political debate, so that it might address 'complex adventures of the spirit'.[44] By redrawing the boundaries inside which it might be remembered, *The Broken Years* had unknowingly rescued Great War memory from its own Armageddon.

The success of Patsy Adam-Smith's book, *The Anzacs*, confirmed the new public interest in the war. Released four years after *The Broken Years*, *The Anzacs* was a joint winner of the *Age* Book of the Year award in 1978, and underwent eleven reprints or new editions between 1978 and 1991.[45] Like Gammage, Adam-Smith based her book on the diaries and letters of front-line soldiers: 'In the almost epicless land that is Australia the diaries of these men became our Homeric *Iliad*', she wrote. *The Anzacs* steered a course between hostility towards the war itself and admiration for the men who fought, a distinction that Gammage also made. As if the Vietnam generation needed reminding, Adam-Smith pronounced that 'War *is* hell', but in our desire to denigrate and even outlaw it, 'we must remember not to castigate the victims of war – and every man who fights is a victim'. Notwithstanding her sympathetic eye, the author was puzzled by the diggers' devotion to Empire and frank about the high incidence of venereal disease among Australian troops. Other silences were broken also; for example, John Simpson Kirkpatrick , the fabled 'man with the donkey', was shown as 'a boozer, a brawler, a rowdy stoker-type larrikin', not 'the delicate aesthetic visionary the artists and visionaries have recorded'. Despite their feet of clay, Adam-Smith believed these men were destined to be remembered for thousands of years, just like the three hundred Spartans at Thermopylae in 480 BC.[46]

Patsy Adam-Smith was bewildered by the depth of pride that the old diggers felt about their war service, especially 'seeing they lost most battles except the last'. After her self-described 'Odyssey' through the letters and diaries of Australian soldiers and across the battlefields they had fought upon, she concluded that their emotion derived from the archetypal rite of ritual killing: 'tattooed on the folk-memory of these men was an urgent drive as old as pre-history, the blood-sacrifice of a nation'.[47] Despite its outdated connotations, a story of human sacrifice begetting national birth held immense appeal for a country bereft of homogenising symbolism. But was it possible to revive the blood sacrifice myth, so potent among the 1914 generation, and yet condemn the war that had demanded it? Bill Gammage, who conceived the Great War in the role of abortionist rather than midwife, pulled back from such a distinction. The film director Peter Weir did not.

By the time he made his film *Gallipoli* in 1981, Weir had become a leading member of the 'New Wave' of Australian film-makers. Directors such as Weir, Phillip Noyce, Gillian Armstrong, Bruce Beresford and Fred Schepisi had benefitted from the financial 'wetnursing' of a sympathetic conservative government, which encouraged them to bring depictions of Australian culture to the screen.[48] Weir had been interested in making a film about Australians in the Great War since he had finished *Picnic at Hanging Rock* in 1975. He admired Lewis Milestone's 1930 film of Erich Maria Remarque's *All Quiet on the Western Front* and Stanley Kubrick's 1957 version of Eric Cobb's *Paths of Glory*. Both films were angry in their condemnation of the injustice and futility of the Great War, and sought to puncture romantic misconceptions about it. Weir intended initially to focus upon the Australian experience in France. He seems to have been immune, even hostile, to the Gallipoli story – it 'was too redolent of memories and those parades, as a kid you thought it was a defeat' – until his conversion during a trip to the abandoned battlefields of the Dardanelles Peninsula in 1976.[49]

Weir enlisted the playwright David Williamson to help him write the script for his war movie. Williamson had established his reputation in Melbourne's fringe theatre scene in the early 1970s and was a prominent artistic voice for the New Nationalism. He believed that the local theatre ought to explore Australian themes and was contemptuous of 'Australia-hating, European-oriented, sensitive, state-subsidised, upper-middle class audiences' who were offended by the overt 'Australianness' of plays such as *The Removalists*, *The Club* and *Don's Party*.[50] Williamson and Weir took most of the historical information for the film from Bean's *Official History* and *The Broken Years* (Gammage acted as historical adviser), but they also spoke to men who had been on the Peninsula. Their preliminary plans for an epic, encyclopaedic retelling of the Gallipoli campaign were quickly scuttled by their producer on the grounds of prohibitive cost. It took three and a half years of haggling and rewriting to produce the final script. According to Weir, 'it wasn't until we stopped trying to penetrate the myth that things began to fall into place'. The charge of the light horse at The Nek became the climax of a story about two young men that was 'more about the journey than the destination'.[51] Of the film's 111 minutes, 44 minutes are spent on the lead-up to enlistment in the Kimberley district of Western Australia and in Perth; 28 minutes are spent on training in Egypt and 32 minutes on the Gallipoli Peninsula.

The film, which cost $2.8 million to make (a huge amount at the time), took an estimated $11.7 million at the Australian box office, making it the country's highest-ever grossing film at the time.[52] *Gallipoli* was a critical as well as a commercial success. It dominated the Australian Film Industry awards, taking nine out of thirteen major honours, including best film, best director, best screenplay and best actor for Mel Gibson. Like *The Chant of Jimmie Blacksmith* and *Breaker Morant* before it, the film found favour in the United States. *Gallipoli* was the first Australian movie to be given a full commercial roll-out in American cinemas, and was nominated for best foreign film at the 1982 Golden Globe awards.

*Gallipoli* audaciously and brilliantly shifted the foundations of the Anzac legend from military prowess and British race patriotism to values more appealing to contemporary Australians.

Displays of the diggers' once-legendary fighting ability were absent from Weir's film; the only depiction of battle occurred at the end of the film, when Archy charges, unarmed, into a wall of Turkish machine-gun fire. Nor were the diggers white supremacists in Weir's reimagining. The fact that Australians believed, almost to a (white) person, in the superiority of the 'white races', did not stop Archy defending an Aboriginal stockman against a racist insult. In the climate of the New Nationalism, Weir and Williamson had licence to excise the imperial

*As Australians compared themselves increasingly favourably with Britons during the course of the war, so the legend grew.*

loyalty that sent many men to fight. In this new version of the Anzac legend, the Australian nation was born by the blood sacrifice of its peace-loving, anti-racist youth. But that sacrifice was not at the hands of the Turks so much as the incompetent British command.[53]

Not surprisingly, *Gallipoli* ruffled British feathers at the time of its release. *The Times* described it as 'a monstrous travesty of what actually happened' and commissioned the British military historian Martin Gilbert to write a corrective response.[54] An argument ensued about the accuracy of the film and the detail of the military campaign. What was never acknowledged in the controversy was that Australian war memory had always had an anti-British strain. The very genesis of the Anzac legend, apparent in the first headlines after news of the landing reached Australia, lay in a comparison between Australians and Britons. As Australians compared themselves increasingly favourably with Britons during the course of the war, so the legend grew. Motifs of the stuffy, incompetent, upper-class British officer and the ineffective, undergrown British Tommy may not have appeared in official Anzac Day rhetoric, Bean's *Official History* or Charles Chauvel's film *Forty Thousand Horsemen*, but they were alive in vernacular culture. As *The Broken Years* amply demonstrated, the diggers were always ready to mock and denigrate the British while at the same time cherishing the imperial connection. Only Ernest Scott, the first historian in Australia to write about the Great War, failed to distinguish Australians favourably from their British counterparts. Charles Bean's admiration for the diggers was linked to his increasing disenchantment with British society; he believed that Australia's democratic ethos partly explained the superior capability of its fighting men. The soldier-memoirists and novelists of the 1930s noted the inefficacy of the British Tommies, psychologically shackled by an unjust class system, and physically stunted by poor living conditions. The anti-British strain in Australian memory of the Great War became more explicit in the 1970s and 1980s, but it was not new.

*Gallipoli*'s success in foreign markets suggests that it was more than a parochial tale of goodies and baddies. Weir was not principally concerned with comparing Britons with Australians, though the pompous British officer and incompetent British soldier stereotypes certainly lent dramatic momentum to his story. Rather, it was the mythological potential of Gallipoli that inspired Weir creatively – the themes of sacrifice and birth that the event suggested. There are numerous mythological and religious allusions in the film. Early on, a Trojan horse is pushed into an athletics meet as part of a recruitment drive for the Light Horse. A spruiker implores the men to 'Come and find out how to get into the greatest game of them all', and a young boy climbs onto the wooden horse and feebly blows his bugle. There are echoes of the explorers Burke and Wills as Archy and Frank trek across the desert on their way to Perth. Weir mocks the bushman myth, when Archy's navigational skills fail and the boys become lost. They are saved by a camel driver who has never heard of the war, and is puzzled that Archy would travel to Turkey to fight. In a later scene, Frank (the archetypal Australian philistine) brushes off his friend Billy's attempts to philosophise about immortality while gazing at the pyramids: 'They were man's first attempt to beat death'. Weir was fascinated by the concept of the Anzacs as members of 'a kind of warrior class' that stretched back to antiquity; he has Frank and Archy carve their names on a pyramid alongside those of soldiers who fought in Napoleon's *Grande Armée*.[55] The most dramatic scene in the film is the final one, in which Archy drops his bayonet and charges towards the Turkish trenches and certain death. Christian imagery has already been invoked in an early scene where Archy's uncle bandages his feet after the boy has cut them by racing barefoot. At the end of the film, as Archy breasts an imaginary tape and his chest is pitted with machine-gun fire, he becomes Jesus in khaki, a specimen of beautiful manhood sacrificed for his mate Frank (whose place he took in the charge), and for the birth of Australian national consciousness.

International reviewers less attuned to the film's nationalist themes noted its allegorical aspirations, though not all believed that Weir succeeded in achieving them. American *Newsweek* considered that the film dealt with 'the horrors of World War I with something of the same blend of power and lyricism that marked the work of the soldier-poets like Wilfred Owen and Siegfried Sassoon', but Toronto's *Globe and Mail* thought that the film was overly 'self-conscious' in its pursuit of 'epic status with its precise division into three symphonic parts'. Its stylised sequences, its 'sentimental impressionism' and lack of characterisation caused the film to reek of 'the falsely elegiac'. The *Manchester Guardian Weekly*'s Derek Malcolm believed the film was insufficiently condemnatory of war, and compared it unfavourably with *All Quiet on the Western Front* and *Paths of Glory*: 'It never gets angry, and its politics are almost non-existent'. The Australian academic Sylvia Lawson thought the film was a disappointing rehash of the 'demi-official State religion' of Anzac – 'as with some new and idiomatic Life of Jesus, reverence is assumed'.[56]

Lawson was correct in her assertion that an acceptance of the

Anzac legend lay at the heart of *Gallipoli*. Swimming against the New Left tide that was sceptical of nationalist ideology in any form, Peter Weir sought to restore Anzac to its former status as the central myth of Australian nationhood, albeit in an altered form. He had untethered Great War memory from the martial nationalism of the Beanian era; these men were no longer blood-thirsty white supremacists, but conspicuously handsome, tolerant and loyal warriors (who did no actual fighting). In decoupling the Anzac story from the values of militarism, Weir sought to connect it with contemporary nationalist sentiment. While patriotic feeling in *The Broken Years* is engendered indirectly through the reader's empathy with the tragic fate of the Australian soldiers, *Gallipoli* is less subtle. Weir and Williamson wrote an adolescent coming-of-age story for Archy and Frank that was also meant to function as an allegory for the coming of age (or birth into adulthood) of the Australian nation. In their desire to inject metaphysical meaning into the Anzac story, the writers revived a myth that was not so very different from Charles Bean's myth of the martial baptism, the pre-Christian legend of the blood sacrifice of a young male. Given prevailing sensitivities about war, the film's focus was very tightly on the sacrifice and not the blood. It was a performance worthy of a contortionist.

⊹≡◉≡⊹

The years from 1965 to 1985 cover the most dramatic fluctuation in Great War memory in Australian history. If memory of the war had proved unable to regenerate itself in a form that provided nationalist sustenance to post-1945 generations of Australians, then it would almost certainly have expired with the last of the old diggers. Bill Gammage's *The Broken Years* and Peter Weir's *Gallipoli* succeeded so profoundly in influencing public memory of the Great War because they caught the New Nationalist mood.

This was not the state-driven search for 'homo Australicus' pilloried by Barry Humphries and illustrated so well in the fiasco over a new national anthem, but a more cautious nationalism, wary of its 'chest-thumping' variant. Given the stench that had surrounded nationalism since Hitler and the revulsion that the Vietnam generation felt towards war in general, it is extraordinary that the Anzac story re-emerged as strongly as it did. Only hindsight has revealed that predictions of the demise of Anzac Day underestimated both the appetite of Australians for tales of their communal provenance, and their willingness to satisfy that hunger with what is served up to them as history. Themes of tragedy and sacrifice proved to be as effective in the service of Australian nationalism in the 1980s as the theme of martial baptism had been fifty years earlier.

# 6

# 1980s–PRESENT: THE GREAT WAR AS FAMILY HISTORY

'TIME TO PULL OUT THE FAMILY ALBUMS!' announced news.com.au on Facebook in the prelude to Anzac Day in 2012: 'We are seeking personal family stories from past conflicts, to show how we as a nation evolved, how former enemies became new Australians and how their descendants keep the Anzac spirit relevant for each successive generation'. This emphasis on family connections has become a common feature of public discussion of the Great War in Australia. Family links also feature increasingly in commemorative ritual. In preparation for the Anzac Centenary in 2015, Melbourne's Greater Metropolitan Cemeteries Trust is 'encouraging families to renew their links' with their soldier-ancestors. The trust has produced commemorative tiles, each decorated with a brilliant red Flanders poppy, which can be fixed to the gravestones or cremation niches of deceased servicemen.[1]

Over the past thirty years, there has been a profound shift in the way that memory of the Great War is transmitted in Australia (and, indeed, internationally). With the passing of the Great War generation and the declining influence of the Returned and Services League (RSL), family historians have become significant custodians of Great War memory. This chapter considers how war memory has fared in the hands of these family historians. It shows how their work complements the deeply personal perspectives on the war pioneered during the 1970s and 1980s by the historian Bill Gammage and the film-maker Peter Weir. Like Gammage and Weir, family historians have helped to untangle the Great War from the connotations of militarism, racism and imperialism that became so repellent in the decades after the Second World War.

The catalogue of the National Library of Australia (NLA) records that during the 1970s just 51 personal narratives of the Great War were published. That number grew to 98 during the 1980s; there were 153 published during the 1990s and 215 during the first decade of the twenty-first century. Why did the daughters and sons of old soldiers suddenly begin to attach importance to letters and diaries that had gathered dust underneath beds and in backyard sheds for sixty years? Certainly, the film *Gallipoli* had a significant effect on people's attitudes, but there were broader changes afoot that prompted descendants into print – changes in attitudes about who could write history and about what topics were suitable for historical scrutiny.

During the latter half of the nineteenth century, history became consolidated within universities as a discipline with aspirations to scientific objectivity. It was written mostly by professionally trained historians who focused their efforts on political and economic events and consulted documentary records that were inaccessible to non-experts. The events of the Second World War, particularly the systematic killing of the Jews, had a profound effect on the understanding of what constituted history and by whom it might be recorded. The new value accorded to the experience of ordinary people rather than that of the 'great men' of history can be traced to the determination of survivors of the Holocaust to place their individual testimony on the historical record. The desire of the Jewish diaspora for knowledge about family members killed or dispersed during the Holocaust spawned an international boom in genealogy and family history. From the 1960s, Jews began in earnest the process of recording their histories.[2] In the absence of archival records and state sanction, personal testimony, or 'memory', assumed momentous significance for its ability to provide evidence of the travesty of their ordeal. The French historian Pierre Nora's observation that 'Whoever says memory, says Shoah' is a pithy acknowledgment of the roots of the memory boom.[3]

Another significant factor in the democratisation of history has been the rise of oral history. The ready availability of tape-recorders from the 1960s enabled the collection of historical evidence from people who were unlikely to be represented adequately in written records. Oral history became widely associated with radical and progressive causes, such as the labour and civil rights movements. While some historians decried (and continue to decry) the unreliability and subjectivity of oral history, advocates countered that the subjectivity of oral evidence was an opportunity to extend the parameters of historical inquiry. In a perspective that borrowed from psychoanalysis, pioneers of oral history, such as the Italian historian Luisa Passerini, argued that human memories were ripe with meaning and significance, regardless of their factual accuracy.[4]

The new taste for genealogy, family history, oral history and personal testimony exhibited particular characteristics in its Australian form. In a dramatic expression of the prevailing New Nationalist mood of the 1970s, Anglo-Australians began revising their traditional reluctance to discuss the convict phase of their history: the success of contemporary society could be submitted as evidence that the 'convict stain' was no more than a temporary blot. Family historians consulted transportation records and announced proudly the discovery of convict ancestors. This burgeoning Australian interest in family identity was manifest in the booming memberships of historical and genealogical societies and has been encouraged more recently by the ready availability of digital resources.[5] In 2007 the National Archives of Australia (NAA) made available digitally the entire collection of enlistment records for the Great War, as well as the records of official artists, photographers and the official historian Charles Bean. The NAA has also created a website called 'Mapping our Anzacs', which encourages people to use enlistment records to digitally locate service men and women in their prewar communities.[6]

Jay Winter, arguably the foremost cultural historian of the Great War, has made the point that traditional modes of commemoration, for example middlebrow literature, served a vital purpose in the aftermath of the war. Unlike ironic forms, such as the poetry of Wilfred Owen, traditional modes enabled 'the bereaved to live with their losses and perhaps to leave them behind'.[7] The same cathartic assumption has become attached to the recording of personal testimony since the 1960s. Thus, it is not surprising that historians who have revisited the history of the Great War armed with the insights gained from memory studies have tended to direct their research to the psychological effects of the war on its participants. Both academic and popular research into the Great War is frequently underwritten by the belief that 'the voicing of pain and outrage is ... "empowering" as well as therapeutic', that there are psychic benefits to be gained by recalling and historicising traumatic events.[8]

Historical memory had been wrested away from the 'great men' in history and put into the hands of the masses. While the Second World War may have led people to look back at the first war with fresh eyes, the meanings that family historians have discovered in their ancestors' letters and diaries have necessarily been bound by the nature of those documents. Letters to and from home provided a crucial psychological support for soldiers during the Great War; they were a 'life-line to a better and secure world' to which the men hoped to return one day.[9] 'Home' was often an idealised place of respite from the war, and soldiers delighted in being regaled with the trivial details of domestic life. While links with the home-front played a vital role in keeping men in the trenches, they also reflected the general truth that men sought refuge from their war experience in euphemism, humour and silence. Soldier-authors typically spared readers the blatant propagandising of official press reports, but their communications were affected, nevertheless, by their own biases and omissions.

Family historians note frequently that the letters and diaries lack detail and introspection. In examining her uncle's letters, Eunice Laidler wrote that it was 'necessary to read between the lines of Walter's letters ... to discern that the Battalion was actually at war. The letters themselves tell us very little, complaining all the time of "no news", and being filled up with messages of love and good health to those at home'.[10] Ron Sinclair's description in a letter to his sweetheart of being under heavy shell fire revealed nothing of the nervous strain and fear he likely felt, but instead uses humour and understatement: 'Things are still plodding away in the same old groove here. We're supplying Fritz with "Iron rations" free of charge. But he doesn't seem to appreciate them so he returns them with thanks'.[11]

Soldiers' reluctance to describe their experience candidly in letters served to protect not just themselves but their families, particularly their mothers. Following his initial exposure to the frontline, Eunice Laidler's Uncle Walter wrote frankly and intimately to his mother of two nights enduring an intense German bombardment: 'it was the most awful experience I have ever been through'. The poignant candidness of Walter's confessions of shock and fear, mixed with veiled pride at having been tested and proved capable, is substituted in subsequent letters for a carefree tone, which is more typical of soldier letters. 'Walter must have realised how much his letter ... upset his mother, and never again mentions anything but the easy times', surmised his niece.[12] Soldiers filled the gaps left by their reluctance to write about the traumatic aspects of their experience with lighthearted banter and questions about home.

Diaries, on the other hand, presumably written for no audience but the author, reveal a preoccupation with routine. Private Max Laidlaw is meticulous in noting down weather conditions each day:

Saturday 4 May – In the line. Very quiet.
Sunday 5 May – Fine day, very wet night.
Monday 6 May – In the line, still very quiet. Showery morning. Fine afternoon.[13]

Private Archie Kirk's single-line entries focus on drill and parade:

8th September Drilling
9th September Military church parade
10th September Drill in morning. Sports parade in afternoon.
11th September Shooting on range
12th September Platoon drill, bathing parade
13th September Drilling and throwing bombs
14th September Company stunt
15th September Went for a walk with B Trott.[14]

The inclination to avoid self-revelation and discussion of the violence of warfare was common, though not universal. Letters to girlfriends and wives were more likely to be emotionally honest than correspondence with mothers and siblings. As the war ground on and his nerves unravelled, Lewis Nott confided in his wife: 'I'm not feeling over fit today, been getting a bit too much work I think, and not enough sleep ... The mud begins to get on one's nerves ... it is pretty hard to have a wife and a son, Pettie, and be at this game. It is tough turkey but has to be digested'.[15] Chaplain TC Rintoul confided his emotional distress to his sweetheart, though he could not bring himself to describe the detail of his experience: 'Oh my angel girl, it is *war* and it is *hell*. I will in future never refer to burials or deaths. There are always some. But it is sickening and vile'.[16]

Apart from their tendency towards the prosaic, the other defining feature of soldiers' letters and diaries is their idiosyncratic perspective. Though they were documents written in wartime, the letters and diaries contain very little military history. Censorship, as well as the emotional predilections of the soldiers, demanded that the letters include scant information about where soldiers were stationed, what action they were involved in and how the war was progressing. To the traditional military historian, the letters and diaries are often of little scholarly value. To the historian interested in social history, genealogy, family history and cultural history, the letters and diaries are a trove of information. Their elevation as historical sources perpetuates and accentuates the trend, begun by Bill Gammage in *The Broken Years*, towards a social and cultural history of Australians in the Great War. The power of the letters and diaries, like that of the film *Gallipoli*, is not to be found in the evidence they provide of what fine fighting men the Australians were, nor what marvellous victories they achieved, but in their ability to forge an empathic connection between the diggers and their contemporary audience.

The majority of men who wrote letters and kept diaries during the Great War had no pretensions to literary greatness and never intended their words for public scrutiny. Their outpourings helped them and their families to survive psychologically in extraordinarily trying circumstances. Once the war was over, the documents were either discarded or packed away and forgotten as returned soldiers resumed their civilian lives. That so many of these papers have subsequently found their way into publication says more about the status of Great War memory in contemporary Australia than it does about the content of the letters and diaries themselves. The family historians who have published the words of their fathers, uncles and grandfathers have typically devoted years to their task. Compilations are almost universally self-published; some editors have tried and failed to find a commercial publisher, others have not bothered. The costly and dedicated labour of bringing the letters and diaries to publication has a history of its own, which can be discovered through oral interviews, as well as close attention to the forewords, prologues and intra-textual commentaries of family historians.

Eleven years after his grandmother died, Fraser Gregg made a 'most remarkable discovery'. He was clearing up his grandparents' house when he chanced upon a small military kit-bag tucked away beneath a bed: 'To my great surprise it contained various medals, scrolls and certificates, along with fourteen small weather-beaten … diaries. Little did I know that they would turn out to be one of the most significant records to survive the Great War of 1914–18'. Gregg's moment of discovery is echoed time and again. Letters and diaries have been found in old shoeboxes in a garage, 'littered with sawdust from bench work'; bundles of letters have been left unread in wardrobes, pantries, sheds and chests for decades.[17] That so many of the letters and diaries of the Great War were lost or neglected for years indicates two things: the silence that remained veterans' best defence against traumatic memories, and the lack of historical significance that was attached by families to the documents, until recently. The growing wave of popular interest in the Great War, evident in films such as *Gallipoli* and *The Lighthorsemen*, and the post-Holocaust conviction that personal stories are of historical significance, transformed forgotten family papers into historical relics.

On the night that Monica Sinclair came home from seeing *Gallipoli*, she pulled out a bundle of old letters that her soldier-father had written to her mother during their courtship seventy years earlier. The film had revived memories from Sinclair's child-hood and made her newly curious about her father's experience of the war. Sinclair eventually fashioned her father's war letters into a book, which was published in 1996 as *Dear Ad...Love Ron*. 'I do not know if my Dad's letters will be of interest to you', she told readers in the Introduction. 'You did not know him, and cannot hear his voice as we who knew him hear it echoing in every word he wrote.' Sinclair worried that the letters were trivial and of little interest to general readers. 'Yet the letters are not trivial. They are part of our historic literature. Their story is part of our story as a young nation concerned about values of justice, freedom and independence.'[18]

There is no doubt that the increasing attention given to the Great War by politicians and the media reassured family histor-ians that their projects were important. John Duffell discovered his father's war correspond-ence on the eve of Anzac Day in 1990. It was the sev-enty-fifth anniversary of the Gallipoli landing, and 'There was considerable euphoria about the occasion throughout Australia'. The Prime Minister Bob Hawke had accompanied a group of original Anzacs on a well-publicised trip to Gallipoli, an event that signalled the begin-ning of the modern relationship between politicians and memory of the Great War. A spate of books, articles, films, and radio and television programs about the Anzac legend spurred discussion about 'the meaning of it all. How and why did it happen? Who

*The increasing attention given to the Great War by politicians and the media reassured family historians that their projects were important.*

was to blame?'. In light of this increased public debate, Duffell felt 'it was proper' for him to make the letters public.[19] As the historian Joy Damousi has shown, the state is increasingly inclined to court family historians. Through the resources of the Department of Veterans' Affairs, the Australian War Memorial (AWM) and the National Archives, it encourages Australians to place their personal stories within the larger story of national Anzac commemoration.[20]

Many family historians make no explicit claim about the public significance of their books, but they do mention their desire to leave a record for their families. Claire Skelton believed her grandfather's war diary would be 'a family treasure and a lasting gift to his descendants'. For Narelle Wynn, the record of her grandfather's war stories would 'be handed down from one generation to the next, and the memory of these courageous men will never die'.[21]

Lynette Oates was conscious that she was adding her uncle's record to an already crowded field when she published *With the Big Guns* in 2006: 'It is with some hesitation, over-ridden by a sense of compulsion, that I present yet another account of Gallipoli and the Western Front'. Oates' compulsion stemmed from her strong response to the content of the material. In a sign of the increasing tendency for authors to conceive their family history projects in the language of psychology, Oates felt that she now had 'a greater understanding of who I am, and sometimes, why I am as I am'.[22] Winsome McDowell Paul also combined family history with the language of personal exploration that emerged in the 1980s. She described her book, *Blessed with a Cheerful Nature*, as the result of 'my journey in search of the young man who later became my father ... It has been an amazing journey in search of Stanley; it has also been a journey of self-discovery'.[23]

Some family historians regard the publication of the letters and diaries as the settlement of a moral debt to their forebear, one that can only be paid in full by the publication of the entirety of the record, no matter its intrinsic interest. Thus, Janette Rogers resolved to transcribe her uncle's entire diary because 'it should be remembered that the diarist possibly found some days quiet or uninteresting, and the inclusion of these seemingly insignificant entries will serve to give a truer representation of all daily activities'.[24] Eunice Laidler agonised over whether to 'weed out the dull and boring letters, and the repetitive greetings to all and sundry' from her uncle's letters. In the end, she decided that the drudgery of reading dull and repetitive letters was trivial in comparison to the suffering of men such as Uncle Walter: 'Someone has said that war is moments of sheer terror in between days and weeks of utter boredom. If we want to share in the terror of Walter's War I think it is up to us to share the boredom with him'.[25]

The notion that succeeding generations of Australians owe a debt of gratitude to the men who fought in the Great War is less apparent in the second generation of descendants than in the first. However, even second-generation family historians are reluctant to tinker with their relatives' words, no matter the inaccuracy of their spelling or the unseemliness of their attitudes measured against contemporary sensibilities. John Davidson believed it was important that his grandfather's language in *The Dinkum Oil of Light Horse and Camel Corps* was left untouched: 'Some words (such as abo, gypo, buck nigger and dago) are not acceptable today but that is how he and others of his day spoke and we decided not to alter his words'.[26]

That family historians attach great significance to their ancestors' war diaries and letters is unsurprising given the labour they have expended in bringing them to publication. What is perhaps more surprising is the fact that the sacralisation of these documents does not equate with unthinking reverence for the event that led to their production. Nor does an emotional attachment to war diaries and letters suggest an uncritical relationship with

Australian nationalism or an adherence to traditional or official versions of the Anzac legend. Rather, the attitudes of family historians reveal a complex and nuanced memory of the Great War.

Unlike the brief boom in books about the war in the early 1930s, the family history phenomenon has continued for more than thirty years and has begun to acquire a history of its own. Those who initiated the trend in the 1980s were typically the daughters and (less often) the sons of men who had fought in the Great War. Born in the 1920s and 1930s, it was not until they were in their fifties and sixties that these women and men began to discover or rediscover their fathers' war writings and contemplate circulating them to a public readership. The lives of the children of the war generation were shaped not only by their fathers' war service, but by the ongoing grief of parents and grandparents for brothers, sons and fathers lost. The generation that followed and has perpetuated the family history boom was born mostly in the economically prosperous Australia of the 1950s and 1960s. These men and women were spared the first-hand encounters with death and grief that informed their parents' war memories, but were greatly influenced in their views of the Great War by Australian military involvement in Vietnam.

While the antipathy of the Vietnam generation towards war is well remembered, the more gently expressed pacifism of the inter-war generation tends to be forgotten. Patsy Adam-Smith's *The Anzacs*, for which she read nearly 8000 soldier letters, was born of her desire to understand why men had gone to war and why they stayed. As we saw in chapter 4, Adam-Smith drew a distinction between the soldiers and their cause: 'War *is* hell', she wrote, 'But in our rush to condemn war, we must not denigrate the men who fought'.[27] This tendency to condemn the Great War, but to venerate the men who fought in it is typical of the family historians of the inter-war generation.

Like Patsy Adam-Smith, Monica Sinclair was full of admiration for the soldiers of the 1st Australian Imperial Force (AIF) and willing to cast them as 'heroes in a very real way, because they were prepared to take on what they perceived to be a serious responsibility, the defence of their country, and to live with the consequences of their decisions'. Yet Sinclair's characterisation of Great War soldiers as heroes did not equate to a belief that the cause they fought for was worthwhile. She explicitly distinguished between the men and the cause, and between contemporary views about the war (her book was published in 1996) and what young men believed at the time:

> History may condemn the 'Great War' as the greatest and most expensive blunder of the century. Some of those who enlisted formed this opinion for themselves as they witnessed the senseless deaths of their friends on front after front. Be that as it may, I believe that this in no way detracts from the greatness of the young Australians, like Dad, who believed they acted for a noble cause and were prepared to risk their life in its pursuit.[28]

Mary Reddrop published her father's war letters in 1982 as *Jim's Story* and had no doubt about how the inter-war generation remembered the Great War: '"What a waste!" is our generation's frequent response to a record of suffering and death of Australian soldiers in the war of 1914–1918'. But Reddrop was concerned that subsequent generations of Australians might focus too much upon the tragedy of the war – by turning on it 'the lasers of an imagined modern enlightenment' – and lose sight of the role it played in forging a sense of Australianness. Despite the 'waste', she felt that the war's role in the development of Australian nationalism ought to be recognised and celebrated. During the war, 'our nation established its identity in the eyes of the western

world. The fabric of this identity is more than the tragic roman-
ticism of devil-may-care ockers, though that may be one strand.
Mateship, loyalty and sheer fighting courage are some of the
other strands'.[29]

Winsome McDowell Paul, another of the female family historians born between the wars, confessed to feeling ambivalent
about the Great War. The author of *Blessed with a Cheerful Nature*
wrote of being stirred by stories of war, by 'the exploits of those
involved in battles, their courage, determination, resilience, cre-
ativity and comradeship as they face enormous challenges and
the possibility of death and injury'. McDowell Paul reported her
highly emotional response to a trip she and her husband took
in 1990 to Gallipoli and northern France, two years before she
first read her father's war letters. She felt her family identity, her
national identity and a broader 'human identity' strongly at different moments during the journey. At a ceremony held at Cape
Helles on 25 April with British, Turkish, French, German, Australian and New Zealand troops present, McDowell Paul felt
'Australian, but also part of a world community that longed for
peace in our time'. When she and her husband were given a smile
and a wave by the Prime Minister Bob Hawke and his wife Hazel
as the official party arrived at Cape Helles, McDowell Paul 'had a
sense of being represented by them ... a sense of national identity I suppose'. Later that day, in the more intimate environment of
a wreath-laying ceremony at Lone Pine, she found herself saying,
'I'm here for you today, Dad, and I'm here for all the family'.[30]

As a counter to her fascination with the Great War and its
emotional resonance with her family and national identities,
Winsome McDowell Paul admitted to feelings of unease and dissatisfaction about her father's experience as a soldier. She recorded the revulsion and shock she felt at reading a letter in which her
pious, teetotalling father boasted to his sister of killing Turkish
soldiers: 'This day last year I shot my first Turk, the first I was sure

of, he was only the first of many poor unfortunates, the privilege was mine and the misfortune theirs; it might have been the other way'. McDowell Paul wondered how her aunt reacted to this sentence: 'it pulled me up short when I read it nearly eighty years later. I did not like to think of my father expressing these feelings about killing other men'. McDowell Paul was equally troubled when her father described himself in a subsequent letter as having been 'pronounced fit for killing'. She struggled to understand how her father survived and even seemed to prosper at war:

> There is something about his life in France that he likes. To
> be *back amongst the boys again*, to be beside his mates, whatever
> the hardships, was a central component, perhaps the central
> component, of his *in the grain* life; the friendships he formed
> during his war service seemed to surpass in their nature and
> depth friendships formed in civilian life.

Stanley McDowell was a successful soldier. He entered the 1st AIF as a private and retired as a lieutenant with a Military Cross. His identity as a proud and effective member of the 13th Battalion endured long after the war. For his coffin, McDowell's wife chose flowers in the light and dark blue colours of his 'beloved fighting Thirteenth'.[31]

Like most returned soldiers, Stanley McDowell rarely spoke about the difficult aspects of his experience. Yet his daughter wondered what psychological scars the war left on her father: 'there were reports of "shell shock" in the First World War, these days we hear about "post-traumatic stress disorder"'. Stanley seemed to emerge from the war with his nerves intact, though McDowell Paul perceived 'signs of postwar stress in later years'. She recalled occasions during her childhood when her father would become 'withdrawn and silent; I can't recall how frequent they were, or how long they lasted, but these times cast a shadow over the household'. She wondered whether Stanley confided in his wife: 'What did Dad tell her of his war experience? What part did she play in helping him live with these memories? ... Were they able to talk about it? I can only guess the answers to these questions'.[32]

Winsome McDowell Paul raised sophisticated and distinctly contemporary questions about the Great War in *Blessed with a Cheerful Nature*. She did not seek to evaluate the martial ability of Australian soldiers, nor did she conceive of the war using the conventional templates of nationalism and national identity, though those elements did not escape her contemplation. She was not content to merely place her father's war letters on the public record for her children or future generations; nor did she wish to 'argue' with her father in the book.[33] McDowell Paul wanted to come to a personal accommodation of how Stanley coped with, and indeed seemed to thrive upon, his war service. The 'cheerful nature' that her father ascribed to himself in a letter to his family, is as close as she comes to an answer: Stanley seemed to be temperamentally inclined to survive the trauma of the war, in a way that many of his fellow soldiers were not. Just as McDowell Paul was both fascinated and appalled by the Great War, she believed that the traumatising impact of trench warfare, about which her father rarely spoke, had to be measured against the friendships he made that stayed with him throughout the rest of his life and the sense of purpose and achievement that his war service provided. In McDowell Paul's reading, the Great War becomes a morally complex event, upon which contemporary observers transpose and seek resolution of their own psychological and moral dilemmas.

The psychological tone of *Blessed with a Cheerful Nature* was echoed in Lynette Oates' *With the Big Guns*, published in 2006. Oates' view of the Great War incorporated understandings drawn from the post–Vietnam War era, wherein post-traumatic stress disorder replaced shell shock and combat fatigue as the diagnosis for psychologically distressed soldiers. Hence her dramatic

conclusion that death was perhaps Uncle Ernest's best destiny, 'When one considers all that is now known about Post
Traumatic Stress Disorder'. In her book, Oates probed not only
her uncle's psyche, but also her own. She felt that a reading of
her uncle's diaries and letters had 'made me realise my identity
far more deeply than I could have imagined possible'. Lynette
Oates grafted post-Holocaust and post-Vietnam insights about
trauma onto more traditional, nationalism-based understandings
about Australian involvement in the Great War. She concluded
that the story of her uncle's 'life has given me enormous pride in
my nation and the values that have come down to me through my
Australian family'.[34] For her, the Great War was both a national
event and a personal and psychological one.

Elizabeth Whiteside is another of the inter-war generation
to integrate newly emerging psychological perspectives into her
understanding of the Great War. *A Valley in France* recorded her
regret that she did not read her father's letters while he was alive:
'There may have been a better understanding of him as a person.
It may have been beneficial, perhaps even therapeutic for both of
us, to have talked of those times'. Before the 1980s, when insights
drawn from psychological investigations into the function of
trauma began to filter into popular culture, Australians might
have understood that returned soldiers 'bottled up' their feelings;
they may even have believed that repression had negative impli-
cations for ex-soldiers' mental health. However, they would not
have expressed these beliefs as Elizabeth Whiteside did in 1999,
when describing her father:

> Like most others he had returned a changed man, tense and
> highly strung. The disturbing effect of war on sensitive men
> was very great, and the hardships and horrors experienced
> in the extreme cold, the mud and slush of the trenches as
> bloody battles raged, could not be shared with loved ones

at home. They did not speak of these traumas but instead suppressed them.

Whiteside's observations about the psychological effects of the Great War on its participants are coupled with an emphatic opinion about the war itself: 'The absolute futility of war comes home when research is made into the period of the 1914–1918 Great War. It has been called the world's greatest disaster'.[35]

George Bevan, author of *Jum's War*, is one of the comparatively few male family historians in a field that is dominated by women. He is of the same inter-war generation as Elizabeth Whiteside and expressed a similar view of the war. Initially, he found the research into his father's experience 'exciting; but then I began to feel annoyed, then angry and finally disgusted as a picture of criminal waste of human life on a scale of unprecedented proportion unfolded. The suffering of the men was unimaginable, the devastation beyond belief'. Written in the style of an historical novel, and drawing on material from his father's diaries, official records and a large dose of the author's own memories and imaginings, the principal theme of *Jum's War* is the psychological disintegration of Jum Bevan, which his son attributes to the trauma he suffered in the Great War. Jum became an alcoholic who abused his wife and children over a long period, until his wife eventually left him. He died a sad and isolated man, estranged from his family and haunted by his experience of war.[36]

In *Jum's War*, George Bevan told the story of a war that exacted an immense psychological toll on its participants. The war was not a story of military prowess or national identity in the making, but of trauma: 'Alcoholism, violence, depression, broken marriages and, in many cases, suicide were rampant among returned soldiers who had been cheered as winners and heroes after the Great War'. The Foreword to *Jum's War*, written by the former head of the Australian Defence Force and current Governor-

General, Peter Cosgrove, illustrates the extent to which per-
ceptions of the Great War have shifted to incorporate, and frequently be dominated by, the language and concepts of trauma
psychology. Bevan's book is not the usual story of inspirational
courage and heroism with which military leaders are associated.
Indeed, it is damning of war. Cosgrove describes the damage the
Great War 'wrought to the psyche' of men such as Jum Bevan and
the way in which it inflicted not only death, but deep physical
and emotional scars upon the youth of a generation.[37]

The taste for psychological readings of the Great War is discernible among family historians of all ages, but it is by no means
universal. As the post–Second World War generation replaced
their parents as the principal custodians of family memory of the
Great War, they brought to bear a new set of biases and preoc-
cupations. The anti-war attitudes expressed by people such as
Elizabeth Whiteside, Monica Sinclair and Mary Reddrop were
often tempered by observations about the heroism of the soldiers or the boon that the war gave to Australian national identity. The uncompromising hostility of the Vietnam generation
to the Great War has mellowed over the years and now allows
for empathy and sympathy for the men who fought, but it stops
short of embracing the nation-making rhetoric that the previous
generation allowed, even in its condemnation of the war.

David Noonan's maternal and paternal grandfathers both
fought in the Great War and returned to Australia. While Isaac
Miller, the subject of Noonan's book *Dearest Violet*, seemed to adjust
well to civilian life, Noonan's paternal grandfather suffered severe
shell shock after the battle of Bullecourt and never fully recovered.
As an engineering student at the University of Melbourne during
the Vietnam War, Noonan was conscripted for national service.
His intention to become a conscientious objector was rendered
unnecessary when conscription was abolished in 1972. Noonan
feels immense empathy for Isaac Miller and is moved by the

stoicism and gentleness of spirit conveyed in his letters, but remains disgusted by contemporary attitudes to war commemoration, by 'how falsely war is presented, the gut-churning jingoism of it'.[38]

Julie Cattlin, born a few years before David Noonan, in 1946, was similarly initiated into Great War memory through the experience of Vietnam. As a student, Cattlin marched in protest against the war and, in common with many of her generation, broadened her opposition to Vietnam into a condemnation of war in general: 'I was incredibly anti-war', she recalls. Cattlin began transcribing Jim Osborn's war diaries for her cousin and quickly became convinced of their historical significance: 'I felt that he was such an extraordinary man, his diary is full of such beautiful descriptions and he is so non-judgemental. I really felt that it was my duty to have his story out there'. The intense admiration that Julie Cattlin developed for Jim Osborn caused her to reconsider her attitude to the Great War. She now believes that the hostile attitude to all aspects of war and soldiering that she held as a young woman was ignorant and arrogant: 'I didn't think too deeply about it. I think we were just brainwashed to hate war'. Though her father had fought in the Second World War, she knew little about that conflict and very little about the Great War, 'especially the Western Front, because all we heard about was Gallipoli'.[39]

Cattlin's attitude to the Great War now is more subtle and complex than it was forty years ago. The emotional bond that she formed with Jim Osborn, years after his death, brought her view about the war closer to that of the children of old soldiers, such as Monica Sinclair and Mary Reddrop. Cattlin makes a distinction between the war itself and the men who fought, a distinction that the Vietnam generation did not previously make. 'Now I have thought so much more about it', she says. 'I'm still incredibly anti-war, but I just have an extraordinary sympathy for the ordinary soldier.'[40]

The woman who once marched in protest against the Vietnam War now marches on Anzac Day. She believes that the Anzac Day march strikes a good balance between commemoration of Australian achievement and recognition of the suffering of ordinary soldiers: 'It's not so much about allies and enemies, but more about human beings who have been destroyed by war'. Her participation in the march is a reflection of her fondness for the memory of Jim Osborn and other ordinary soldiers like him, more than any nationalistic impulse. Cattlin recoils from overt displays of nationalism, such as have become common among young Australians. 'I don't have an Australian flag and I don't like Australia Day', she says. She grants that her strong connection to Osborn 'must have something to do with him being family and Australian. But somehow my love for him was due to him being an outstanding human being. His qualities really impressed me ... The smaller our world gets, the more I think of people belonging to "the world" more than I do to a country'.[41]

⋯⋯

The majority of family historians of the Great War in Australia conceive the significance of their projects within the boundaries of national history: the stories of their fathers and grandfathers are worth preserving because they are 'part of our historic literature'.[42] Apart from succinct assertions such as this, most family historians feel no need to justify the value of their projects or mount an interpretative scaffold for the documents they present. This unself-conscious belief that ordinary soldiers' letters and diaries are historically significant originates from the same source that has led the family history phenomenon to be expressed more keenly in Australia than in other countries and causes Australians to make so much of 25 April 1915 – the vacuum that exists in the national mythology. However, the willingness of family historians to remember the Great War as a crucial phase in the story of Australian nationalism is not evidence of an uncritical relationship with either the war or with nationalist sentiment.

The monopoly that nationalist memory of the Great War has held among Australian family historians has been challenged in the last decade as the insights and perspectives gained from memory studies suggest new ways of reading soldiers' letters and diaries. Family historians are now likely to read their ancestors' writings with questions in their minds about trauma, shell shock and psychological well-being, questions that Australians would never have asked half a century or even quarter of a century earlier. As the historian Christina Twomey has argued, these new psychological readings have helped to rehabilitate the Anzac legend through their portrayal of the diggers as traumatised victims worthy of our sympathy, rather than as bloodthirsty warriors or (in their later years) elderly men with antiquated ideas.[43] The rise of the concept of the traumatised digger does not, however, signal the demise of the traditional nationalist script. Indeed, the Great War is proving that it can be a servant to both nationalism and the Holocaust. In a testament to the elasticity and utility of human memory, the Great War is traumatic and tragic, yet still comprises a pivotal and proud moment in the history of Australia.

# 7

# SINCE 1990: POLITICIANS AND COMMEMORATION OF THE GREAT WAR

THOUGH HE RETIRED FROM POLITICS IN 1996, the former Labor prime minister Paul Keating has never lost his capacity to grab the headlines. In 2008 he told a Sydney audience:

> I have never been to Gallipoli and never will ... The truth is that Gallipoli was shocking for us. Dragged into service by the imperial government in an ill conceived and poorly executed campaign, we were cut to ribbons and dispatched ... [yet] we still go on as though the nation was born again, or even, was redeemed there. An utter and complete nonsense.[1]

Condemnation of Keating's comments came not just on talkback radio and from conservative politicians, but from his own side of politics. The Labor Prime Minister Kevin Rudd declared that 'Paul is completely wrong on that, completely and utterly, absolutely 100 per cent wrong'. Rudd grasped at sentiments that would distance him from Keating: 'On the question of Gallipoli, can I say, for me, it is absolutely fundamental to the Australian identity ... [It's] part of our national consciousness. It's part of our national psyche, it is part of our national identity ...

I, for one, as prime minister of the country am absolutely proud of it'.[2]

The reaction provoked by Keating's speech shows how significant Gallipoli is in the national psyche, nearly one hundred years after the landing. Indeed, the reverence accorded to Gallipoli and the scorn reserved for unbelievers resemble religious worship, an observation that the historian Ken Inglis made five decades ago when he characterised the Anzac legend as a 'civic religion'.[3] The response to Keating's declaration is also evidence of the leading role that prime ministers are expected to play in the stoking of the Anzac legend. Many Australians born in the 1980s and after are unaware that the intimate relationship between politicians and war commemoration is a recent phenomenon. Little more than twenty years ago, political leaders were participants in acts of remembrance, but they were not instigators of them. Today, prime ministers are not only the high priests of Anzac, but its chief benefactors as well. Both Labor and Coalition governments provide millions of dollars annually to promote the Australian experience of war, principally through funding of the Australian War Memorial (AWM) and the educational activities of the Department of Veterans' Affairs.[4] Why have Australian prime ministers become our commemorators-in-chief over the last twenty years? And what impact has the growth of political commemoration had on the way that the Great War is imagined?

Until frailty and death defeated them, commemoration of the Great War was organised by the returned men and guided by their grief. Almost from the outset, the men argued about the form that commemoration should take. To what extent should religion feature in services? Should there be a representative of each of the Protestant and Catholic churches? What kinds of recreational activities were appropriate to this sacred day? Still, there was no argument about the fundamental purpose of commemoration, given the legacy of 60 000 killed and 167 000 counted officially as wounded from a population of less than five million.[5]

The Labor Party split in 1916 had increased the proportion of its members who were hostile to Britain and sympathetic to Archbishop Daniel Mannix's reported view of the Great War as 'a sordid trade war'. Hostility towards Britain and the cause of the war were also widespread in the industrial movement and among the left-wing press. Despite the acrimonious nature of politics in the postwar years, however, there was no dispute about commemoration of the dead. Traces of bipartisanship also endured in the repatriation system that was established after the war, though the issue of provision for former soldiers became increasingly contested as Labor struggled to re-establish itself as a viable alternative to the Nationalist Party.[6]

Though cost prohibited most Australians from visiting battlefields and cemeteries in Turkey, France and Belgium, a trickle of Australians did undertake the long and expensive journey almost as soon as the war ended. In 1923, Australia House in London received 850 inquiries from Australians who were planning to visit soldiers' graves in the United Kingdom, France and Belgium.[7] Intermittently, there was talk among veterans about a mass return to Gallipoli or the Western Front, but cost always proved an insurmountable barrier. The government was usually approached for funding on these occasions, as it often was by grieving mothers seeking financial assistance to visit their sons' gravesites. Its answer was invariably 'no'.

The prime ministers who held office in the years after the Great War were concerned with its immediate legacies: the burial of the dead, the raising of memorials, the reassurance of a traumatised population. The first postwar Australian prime minister to visit the battlefields was Stanley Melbourne Bruce, who had served as an officer in the British army, where he saw action at Gallipoli. On his way home from an Imperial Conference in London in 1924, Bruce visited France and the Dardanelles Peninsula. After inspecting the construction of cemeteries and memorials, he was able to 'assure relatives that the graves of their loved ones are being tended with due and reverent care'.[8]

The prime ministerial role in commemoration also extended to the preparation of an Anzac Day message: a ritual exercise that called for extravagant language and an acknowledgment of Anzac's behemothian status within the national history. Stanley Bruce's effort in 1924 eschewed Australia's convict phase in favour of its pioneer beginnings. It skirted Federation to declare that the nation was not made until its soldiers went to the Great War:

> Today – the ninth anniversary of the momentous landing
> on April 25th 1915 – we pay homage to the memory of
> our glorious dead, and we repeat expressions of faith in our
> country – a country founded by pioneers of British stock.
> Those early settlers took the first step in the moulding of
> Australian ideals, but it was left to Australian soldiers to make
> Australia a nation. This day nine years ago, followed by the
> glorious history of the Australian Imperial Force in France,
> in Palestine and in other sections of the war zone, led to
> the recognition of the peace of Australia – not of Australia a
> dependent colony, but of Australia a nation.[9]

Bruce's successors continued to oversee the construction of memorials and graveyards. Given the time and expense involved in a journey to the northern hemisphere, trips to battle sites and war graves were combined with other government business. In February 1935, Prime Minister Joseph Lyons (who had opposed conscription as a Tasmanian Labor parliamentarian during the war) embarked for Britain with a travelling party that included his wife Enid, and the Attorney-General Robert Menzies and his wife Pattie. It was the first time any of the quartet had been overseas. The Menzies paid their own fares, so that they might witness the Silver Jubilee celebrations of King George V. After attending the jubilee and a Commonwealth prime ministers' conference, Joseph and Enid Lyons crossed to the Continent, where they 'swiftly toured the war graves, covering 150 miles, from Ypres to Amiens, visiting over twenty British, Australian, French and German cemeteries'. The year after his visit to the war graves, Lyons approved the raising of an Australian war monument at Villers-Bretonneux in northern France. Lyons inspected the construction site on a flying visit in June 1937, and was 'convinced the complete structure will be a wonderful memorial to our men'.[10]

Prime Minister Lyons did not attend the unveiling of the completed monument in 1938 by King George VI. Instead, the Australian government was represented by three ministerial members of a trade delegation to Britain: deputy prime minister Earle Page, Attorney-General Robert Menzies and the Minister for Customs Thomas White. The Returned Sailors' and Soldiers' Imperial League of Australia (RSSILA) was aggrieved at the presence of the 'shirker', Robert Menzies: 'it would be the wish of the fallen, whose services and sacrifice the memorial commemorates, that those who come from their home country to pay tribute in an official capacity should be men who responded with them to the call to service in 1914–1918'.[11] Consternation also surrounded the selection of returned Australian servicemen to attend the ceremony at Villers-Bretonneux. The government had rebuffed, on the basis of cost, the RSSILA's request that it fund the attendance of a returned man from each of the Australian states, agreeing instead to pay all the expenses of one delegate. Eventually, the government consented to fund the travel of returned Austral-ian servicemen who were residing in Britain. About four hundred veterans of the Australian Imperial Force (AIF), a 'motley crowd' according to an observer, constituted a guard of honour for the King.[12] The ceremony was attended by the French president and broadcast throughout Britain, Australia and New Zealand.

When Prime Minister John Curtin opened the AWM on Armistice Day in 1941, the Pacific phase of the Second World War had not yet begun. Like the previous prime minister but one, Robert Menzies, Curtin had not enlisted in the Great War. While Menzies' parents had prevented him from enlisting because his two older brothers were already serving, Curtin had been a pac-ifist and an outspoken opponent of conscription. Yet, in opening the memorial, he drew upon the legend that had, in Australian eyes, confirmed the nation as a legitimate member of the British race. The building was symbolic of 'the very basic ways of life of the people of Australia and of the whole British race'. It enshrined the story of 'the deeds that helped to make the nation'.[13]

If Curtin's civilian status during the Great War left him uncomfortable with its commemoration, the same could also be said of Robert Menzies, who was in the penultimate year of his second, long prime ministership when the fiftieth anniversary of the Gallipoli landing was celebrated in 1965. In recognition of the significance of the occasion, the government authorised the construction of a road in the national capital to be named 'Anzac Parade' to run south from the War Memorial towards the recent-ly filled Lake Burley Griffin.[14] The road was officially opened on Anzac Day 1965 by the Duke of Gloucester in front of a large crowd that included members of the 1st AIF.

The fiftieth anniversary also saw a group of three hundred people from Australia and New Zealand, about half of them Great War veterans, travel to Gallipoli. The trip was organised and subsidised by the Returned and Services League of Australia

(RSL) and its equivalent in New Zealand. The historian Ken Inglis accompanied the old soldiers and wrote despatches for the Australian press. Inglis does not remember any Australian political involvement in the event: 'I don't recall any government patronage, or any talk of its possibility: it was all organised by the RSL's national secretary, Bill Keys. Certainly there were no politicians on board. If any messages from politicians were received (e.g. by cable to the ship), I don't remember. There were certainly no politicians there'.[15]

A pilgrimage to Villers-Bretonneux in 1968 for the fiftieth anniversary of the battle in which Australians turned back the German advance had greater success in attracting the patronage of governments both at home and abroad. The trip was organised by two returned soldiers, Les Irwin and Fred Cahill. Both men had entered politics after the Great War and were able use their connections to navigate around the government's reluctance to fund commemorative activities. In addition to managing to extract some subsidies and concessions, the party was received by British royalty and honoured at about twenty civic receptions. According to the historian Bruce Scates, 'Though their journey was organised as a private undertaking, the group behaved and were treated like Australian ambassadors'.[16]

The fiftieth anniversary of the Gallipoli landing coincided with Australia's entry into the Vietnam War. Hostility towards the announcement in March 1966 that conscripts would be sent to Vietnam and anger at the conduct of the conflict let loose an anti-war sentiment that leached into Anzac commemoration. But Vietnam was not the catalyst for a process that can be traced back to the late 1950s. Alan Seymour's play, *The One Day of the Year*, first performed in 1961, captured a mood of cynicism and hostility among young Australians towards the Great War generation.

Politicians responded to the new public mood by muting the rhetoric of commemoration; they lauded the courage and

sacrifice of the Anzacs, but the martial baptism was largely forgotten. Joseph Lyons' visit to Villers-Bretonneux in 1937 was the
last official trip to the Great War battlefields by an Australian
prime minister for more than fifty years. There was no electoral
advantage for leaders such as Robert Menzies, Gough Whitlam
and Malcolm Fraser in associating themselves too closely with
memory of the Great War. Though he made official statements
on Anzac Day and Remembrance Day, Fraser never contemplat-
ed a visit to the battlefields: 'In my time as prime minister if I'd
gone to Anzac Cove for Anzac Day, people would have said
"What on earth is Fraser doing?"'.[17]

By the time Bob Hawke travelled to Gallipoli in 1990, the
Anzac revival was in full swing. The legend had been reworked
by the historians Bill Gammage and Patsy Adam-Smith (as we
saw in chapter 6) to reveal the tragic stories of individual soldiers.
This work was complemented by that of family historians, who
forged empathic connections with their soldier-forebears. Peter
Weir's extraordinarily influential film *Gallipoli* also introduced new
generations to a sympathetic version of the Anzac story. Only a
handful of the old diggers, whose views about race, Empire and
women so offended younger generations, survived. The demise
of the Great War generation had left a hole at the centre of
Anzac commemoration. Reassured by the new popular regard for
Anzac, Bob Hawke prepared to step into the breach.

The Gallipoli 'pilgrimage', as it became known, was first
proposed by Bill Hall, a veteran of the Second World War and
patron of the New South Wales World War One Veterans' Association. Late in 1988, Hall suggested to the defence minister Kim
Beazley the idea of a trip to Gallipoli with a group of old diggers
on the occasion of the seventy-fifth anniversary of the landing.[18]
Beazley liked the idea and took it to Prime Minister Bob Hawke.
For seven decades, Australian governments had resisted calls
from soldiers of the Great War to provide financial and logistical

support for their return to the battlefields. In 1990, when the few hundred surviving soldiers of the 1st AIF were in their nineties, the federal government finally agreed.

Born in 1929, Bob Hawke was too young to serve in the Second World War, but old enough to experience its immediate legacy, as well as the more distant legacy of the Great War. Hawke spent most of his childhood in suburban Perth, where his father was a Congregational minister. At the University of Western Australia in the late 1940s, he studied with returned soldiers from the Second World War who received free university tuition under the Commonwealth Reconstruction Training Scheme. Unlike Ken Inglis, who had felt intimidated by the older, worldlier men, Hawke recalled that he enjoyed their company: 'They were good men. They didn't talk about the war, unless you asked them about it. If you asked them, they were happy to talk about it'.[19] After a period at Oxford University as a Rhodes scholar, Hawke began doctoral work on industrial arbitration at the Australian National University (ANU), but abandoned his study when he was offered the position of research officer at the Australian Council of Trade Unions (ACTU) in Melbourne. As the president of the ACTU between 1969 and 1980, Hawke became known for his pragmatism and ability to settle heated industrial conflicts. He had opposed the Vietnam War but remained a strong supporter of the American alliance. Unlike those whose opposition to Vietnam was extrapolated into an opposition to Anzac commemoration, Hawke retained a conventional and uncomplicated attitude towards the Anzac legend. The former prime minister has rejected the historian James Curran's suggestion that the lessons of the Second World War left him with a wariness of nationalism:

> I wasn't sceptical about nationalism, I believed that
> Australians ought to be very proud of their history, that we as
> Australians had set standards for the world in many ways and

we had every reason to be proud of that ... What I always feel strongly about is nationalism going mad and going from nationalism to jingoism to not recognising the virtues of others. But I was very much an Australian nationalist in the sense that I believed we had an enormous amount of which to be proud.[20]

Bob Hawke's speechwriter, Graham Freudenberg, had a personal connection to the Great War. Freudenberg's father had been a stretcher-bearer at Gallipoli and, like many on the left with a family link, he did not share the hostility of his comrades about the Anzac legend. In a speech in 2010, Freudenberg recalled that he encouraged Hawke to 'associate himself closely with the 75th anniversary'. He believed that Hawke's Bicentenary speeches 'had failed to resonate' with the public, paralysed as they were by Aboriginal resentment and the desire to avoid offending non-British Australians. Here was an opportunity to grasp a significant national occasion and turn it to the advantage of the Labor Party. If handled well, the Gallipoli visit could 'break the conservative monopoly on the interpretation of Australian military history'. Freudenberg's candour afforded a rare glimpse of the political machinations of war commemoration. 'I thought like [the Methodist preacher Charles] Wesley about hymns: "Why should the Devil have all the best tunes?", so I myself had political motives in urging Hawke to go to Gallipoli'.[21] Despite the political conniving, it was important to lend the endeavour an appearance of bipartisanship; the newly elected leader of the Coalition Opposition, John Hewson, was invited to accompany the prime minister to Turkey.

The government's decision to support the 1990 trip was weighed against the risk of upsetting the generation of Australians that had opposed the Vietnam War and was reflexively hostile to war commemoration. Kim Beazley, who served as Hawke's defence minister from 1984 to 1990, felt confident that community attitudes were sufficiently transformed. He believed that the 'emotional outpouring' of the Australian public when veterans of the Vietnam War were formally welcomed home in 1987 was a strong indication that people would be well disposed towards a trip that would cost $10 million of public money:

> There was a feeling that [the Vietnam veterans] had
> been very harshly handled as a result of the controversy
> surrounding the war and that political dispute had been
> unfairly imposed on the fighting men and women. Honouring
> them gave the government a sense of the scale of these sorts
> of enterprises which, again, contributed to a willingness to
> go big on the 75th anniversary of the landing.[22]

Like Hawke, Beazley felt no misgivings about absorbing the Anzac legend into Labor's progressive and reformist policy program. That program included a 'strong reassertion of Australian nationalism', which was evident in initiatives 'such as the South Pacific Nuclear-Free Zone, APEC [Asia-Pacific Economic Cooperation], the peace settlement in Cambodia [and] defence self-reliance as a fundamental strategy of government'. To Beazley's mind, Anzac echoed the independent nationalist tone of these initiatives: 'We turned our attention to the national icons that we traditionally felt made us distinctive and Gallipoli fell into that category'.[23]

The government's willingness to fund the Gallipoli visit was enhanced by 'a feeling that this would be the last chance', recalled Kim Beazley. 'There would be no other commemorative services related to Gallipoli that could be attended by our obviously ageing veterans.' Graham Freudenberg also recognised that the dying off of the original Anzacs would lend 'a special significance' to the seventy-fifth commemoration.[24] The fifty-two men who embarked on the trip were born in the last two decades of the nineteenth century; the youngest was 93 and the oldest was 104. They may have held attitudes that younger Australians found anachronistic and offensive, but their frailty and proximity to death made them inappropriate targets for scorn and political spite. The government had judged correctly that old age had granted to the diggers the near-universal affection of the Australian public.

Bob Hawke's rapport with the old soldiers set the tone of the trip. Freudenberg recalled the prime minister's emotional response to reading the war diary of Freudenberg's stretcher-bearer father Norman: 'Bob Hawke was deeply moved when he read these pages on the RAAF plane taking us to Turkey ... where he delivered the best speech I ever wrote for him'. Twenty-two years after the visit, Hawke recalled it as 'one of the most moving experiences of my prime ministership'. His fondest memory was of the camaraderie between the old diggers and young Australians, several thousand of whom had travelled to Turkey for the dawn service:

> We really got to like the old boys very much as we got to
> know them ... We were all seated there and ... As the old
> blokes came up, the young people expressed their enthusiasm
> and they embraced this great generational gap, enthusing
> with one another. It was very, very moving.[25]

As the government had foreseen, nationalist sentiment proved highly compatible with this wrinkled, wheelchair-bound version of the Australian digger. Bob Hawke's invocation of the Anzac legend, which was televised live to Australian audiences, could trace its lineage all the way back to the official historian CEW Bean. Hawke spoke of the courage, devotion to duty, ingenuity, good humour and comradeship of the Australian soldiers, whose exploits defined 'the very character of the nation'. Because 'of the bravery and bloodshed of the Anzacs ... because these hills rang with their voices and ran with their blood, this place Gallipoli is, in one sense, a part of Australia'. Later in the morning, the prime minister told an audience at the Lone Pine memorial that it was incumbent upon each generation 'to breathe ... new life into the old story: and, in separating the truth from the legend, realise its relevance to a nation and a people experiencing immense change over the past three-quarters of a century'. Leaving aside the exhortation to sort truth from legend, Hawke breathed new life into the Anzac myth. In his retelling, the commitment of the diggers towards maintaining the purity of the British race became a shared commitment to Australia between people of different cultures and races: 'it is that commitment to Australia, which defines and alone defines what it is to be an Australian. The commitment is all'.[26] The multicultural revision of Anzac contained no trace of hostile sentiment towards Britons or Turks or, indeed, anybody from anywhere. Despite its martial origins, Anzac was a legend devoid of military content. By the late twentieth century, the myth whose beginnings lay in the fighting skill, humour, stoicism, pragmatism and mateship of the Anzacs had morphed into the inspiration for a nation of universal mateship.

The 1990 pilgrimage was a popular and political success. Coverage was beamed live by satellite to ABC television audiences for five hours, and relayed to commercial television channels. Domestic press reports remarked upon the revival of Anzac Day and its superiority over Australia Day as the national day of celebration. The Sydney Morning Herald noted that the Anzac spirit was 'more to do with mateship and sacrifice than conquest and power'.[27] The trip is rightly seen as the beginning of the mass Australian 'pilgrimage' to Gallipoli; every year since 1990, thousands of Australians, sometimes upwards of 15 000, gather at Anzac Cove for the dawn service on 25 April. The decline of

the RSL created an opportunity for leadership and patronage of
Anzac remembrance that governments, now free of the wariness
with which they had regarded the commemoration of war since
Vietnam, rushed to fill. By portraying the experience of soldiers
through their letters and diaries, Bill Gammage's book *The Broken
Years* and Patsy Adam-Smith's *The Anzacs* had done much to promote a new understanding of the Great War. That personalised
and largely sympathetic portrait of the digger was given massive
impetus by the success of Peter Weir's film *Gallipoli*. When the men
of 1915 spoke of the war in 1990 they remembered mateship, fear
and horror. They did not think that war was glorious. They were
bemused by their late celebrity, though generally appreciative of
it. Whether they recognised the war that was being remembered
as the one they had fought in, they did not say.

Bob Hawke shared with Kim Beazley an understanding of the
Anzac legend that accepted elements of its original form and discarded others. While they did not subscribe to the imperial or
racist aspects of the original legend, both men agreed that the
experience of war made Australians feel their nationality more
intensely than before. To these men, Gallipoli complemented a
version of Australian nationalism that was progressive and independent, yet far from jingoistic. When Hawke's successor as
prime minister, Paul Keating, looked at Gallipoli, he drew entirely different conclusions.

Paul Keating took the prime ministership from Bob Hawke in
December 1991 after a period of acrimonious wrangling within
the Labor Party. The extent of Keating's low regard for Gallipoli
did not become apparent until several years after his retirement
from politics; even the self-described political 'maddie' pulled up
short of condemning the Anzac legend while in office.[28] During
his four-and-a-half-year prime ministership, Keating sought to
impress upon Australians the significance of the Pacific battles
of the Second World War and to relocate the axis of the Anzac

legend from Gallipoli to Kokoda. This second, radical undertaking was inspired by an equally radical reading of Australian
history.

Paul Keating's speechwriter, the historian Don Watson, has
described how the circumstances of Keating's term in office
contrived to impose a series of military anniversaries that were
greeted with resignation rather than relish. The Second World
War 'washed through Keating's prime ministership like reflux ...
there is scarcely a country between Australia and Japan that does
not have a cemetery with Australian graves in it, or a monument
to the sacrifice of Australian servicemen and women'. Watson
argued that much of the controversy attached to Keating's war
speeches was derived not from design but from his desire to avoid
'the platitudes with which such occasions are generally observed
... Insofar as we avoided [platitudes] it made for better speeches, but also for controversy sometimes. [Keating] was on sacred
ground: any departure from the customary words and gestures
would always offend someone'. Watson has also written that it
was 'silly to imagine that there might be an art' to what Paul
Keating was thinking when he spoke about important issues.[29]
While it is true that historians tend to impose order and reason
where they do not exist, it is difficult to imagine that Watson
and Keating failed to understand that their desire to renovate the
most sacred symbol of Australian nationhood was an exceptional
and controversial undertaking.

Keating chose to travel to Papua New Guinea for his first
Anzac Day as prime minister. In doing so he became the first
Australian leader to visit the battlefields since 1942. He began his
speech in the sweltering tropical heat at Ela Beach by affirming
the importance of the Anzac legend to 'a nation born at Gallipoli', sentiments that he would later describe as 'deeply flawed
and wrong'. 'The spirit of Anzac became the canon of Australian life: the ideals to which we aspired, the values by which we

lived', he continued. After carefully noting that 'Legends bind nations together [and] define us to ourselves', Keating edged into sensitive territory. These legends, he told the audience, 'should not stifle us. They should not constrain our growth or restrict us when we have to change'. The Anzac legend 'does not confer on us a duty to see that the world stands still'. John Curtin understood this when he defied Churchill and turned to the United States in December 1941, and Keating hoped that contemporary Australians might understand it too:

> [Curtin] took the Anzac legend to mean that Australia came first – that whatever the claims of Empire on the loyalty of those who died in the Great War, the pre-eminent claim had been Australia's. The Australians who served here in Papua New Guinea fought and died not in defence of the old world, but the new world. Their world. They died in defence of Australia, and the civilisation and values which had grown up there. That is why it might be said that, for Australians, the battles in Papua New Guinea were the most important ever fought.[30]

Don Watson described Keating's Port Moresby speech as 'mildly inflammatory'. The political journalist and commentator Paul Kelly called it 'the most contentious Anzac Day speech ever given by an Australian prime minister'. Keating himself admitted to Kelly that the aim of the speech was to 'break the conservative hold on Australian nationalism'.[31]

Veterans of both world wars complained that Keating was assigning greater significance to one battle over others, and were especially bothered by his implied disdain for Gallipoli and the cause for which the 1st AIF had fought. They didn't know whether to be more alarmed by Keating's speech at Ela Beach or his act of kissing the ground as he approached the Australian

182 ⊧ ANZAC, THE UNAUTHORISED BIOGRAPHY

memorial at Kokoda later in the day. Two decades later, Keating described his gesture as an act of homage to Bruce Kingsbury, the posthumous winner of the Victoria Cross who led a charge against the Japanese at Kokoda, and those men who had fought alongside him. 'Rather than some well-meaning, politely filtered speech', Keating hoped to indicate by his action 'that there was a new weighting, another view of these events, which might more appropriately befit the history and importance of what happened in Papua New Guinea'. Watson reflected in his memoir that Keating had wanted to 'indelibly mark Kokoda in Australia's collective memory, as perhaps Gettysburg was marked in the American mind by Lincoln'.[32]

And if Keating's provocative Anzac speech and impromptu papal-like kiss were not confronting enough for cultural traditionalists, an unnoticed boom microphone picked up the prime minister making a derogatory remark about the Australian flag to a young boy. The Victorian RSL president Bruce Ruxton told the media that if the Australian soldiers buried at Bomana cemetery knew of Keating's disparagement of the national flag they 'would have got up and pulled him down one of those holes'. The contempt was mutual; 'to inflame the reactionary parts of the RSL would be to lift one's social standing', Keating has said. 'You would not want to inflame them; you would rather burn them out.'[33]

Paul Keating's unshakeable conviction about the significance of the Pacific War to Australian history was formed during his childhood. He was born into an upwardly mobile, working-class Catholic family of Irish descent in western Sydney in 1944. The family suffered a tragedy when Keating's paternal uncle, William Keating, died on one of the brutal Sandakan–Ranau death marches in Borneo in 1945. Don Watson considers that Keating's interpretation of Australian military history draws from his need to find purpose for his uncle's death. 'How could the sacrifice of his parents' generation be understood if he did not attempt to invest it with contemporary meaning?' Keating found contemporary meaning in the fact that his uncle and others like him had 'fought for all we had created here and had become, not for some notion of a ruling class or people's community, let alone an empire'.[34] The authentic nationalism that had flowered briefly in the 1890s, before being 'cast to the winds' by the Australian response to the Great War, had again bloomed in the Second World War at the hands of people like Keating's uncle. The folly of relying on Britain to protect Australia was laid bare when the Japanese moved down the Malay Peninsula and occupied Singapore. With the imperial blinkers removed, Australia faced its reckoning at Kokoda, where it halted the Japanese advance southwards (with help from the Americans in the battles of the Coral Sea and Midway). For Keating, Kokoda was the place at which Australia had proved its mettle as an independent nation. Kokoda, not Gallipoli, was the sacred site of Australian nationalism.

Keating's determination to register the experience of men like his uncle in the national consciousness was combined with a profound resentment about their anonymity. He told the television journalist Kerry O'Brien in 2013 that the lack of recognition given to prisoners of war 'drove me nuts ... the RSL wouldn't ... say this but the implication was that they were cowards'. The airbrushing of prisoners of war out of the story was part of a broader pattern of preferencing the Great War over the Second World War:

> the whole body language of the RSL, the Liberal acolytes
> and Anzac Day through the fifties and sixties and into the
> seventies was always about the First World War. That is
> not to say that returned service men and women from the
> Second World War did not march there, they did. But the
> complexion of the event was always shaped by the events of
> the First World War.[35]

Keating allowed that there was 'a naturalness' about Australia fighting for Britain in the Great War, given the ties of blood and culture, but he resented the fact that the experience had metastasised into a national foundation myth. Somehow:

> the notion got about that there was something missing in
> us that required some kind of redemption; a redemption
> we could only find at Gallipoli ... Well, there was nothing
> wrong with us and we needed no redemption at Gallipoli
> or anywhere else. The whole notion of us requiring rebirth,
> going through the hell-fire of Gallipoli to become a
> legitimised, redemptive unitary whole should be so shocking
> a concept that no Australian should ever subscribe to it.
> Then, or now.[36]

Australia did not require the Gallipoli midwife, in Keating's judgment, because a thriving nation had been born on 1 January 1901. Evidence of the young nation's robust health could be found in the 'progressive institutions sprouting all over the place'. There was the Arbitration Court 'making decisions about a living wage, social security beginning to become a concept, early Labor governments – all nation-defining things'. On the conservative side of politics, 'the Deakinesque view of the world [was] giving the country a fine start'. Ever the aesthete, Keating noted that the Australian spirit was also evident in the Federation style of housing and decoration.[37] This new nation did not suffer overly from anxiety about its convict origins or its status as a European culture in a foreign, potentially hostile region. Australia had 'a great sense of itself', according to Keating. To the extent that there was a desire for Australian men to be tested in the fires of battle in order to prove the nation's mettle, it came from 'the hard-hatted imperialist militarists. It was not from the thinking people, the people who had the measure of the nation's heartbeat'.[38]

In this radical nationalist reading of Australian history, Gallipoli is relegated to the status of a small and catastrophically bungled episode in a war that was an unmitigated tragedy:

I do not think Gallipoli should be credited as being of such significance that we should go out of our way to replace it. There is but one beacon of our resistance to an invader and that is the one which shines from Kokoda. No similar light can ever glow from Gallipoli because Australia was never under threat at Gallipoli. At Gallipoli we were fighting an imperial war in a fatally flawed campaign.[39]

Paul Keating has argued that the belief that Australia was born at Gallipoli flourished after the Great War because it was championed by a succession of conservative political leaders. The imperial myopia of these 'classic Austral-Britons' caused them to be obsessed with Gallipoli: 'They could never leave off the whole British heritage thing. This was true of a whole gaggle of them, from Hughes to Stanley Melbourne Bruce to Menzies'. Keating felt strongly enough about this issue to raise it in his maiden speech to Parliament in 1970: 'It was the Labor Party that dragged the Liberal Party out of the excesses in which it was indulging [during the Second World War]. At that stage it was all Britain and all the Empire. To the Liberal Party it was a terrible thing when John Curtin ... turned to the Americans to help us get out of the predicament we were in in South East Asia'. As prime minister, Keating saved some of his fiercest rhetoric for British loyalists. These 'hat-doffers', 'lickspittles', 'crawlers', 'snivellers' and 'tin-tookies' had stunted the nation's economic and cultural growth. The Liberal Party was the custodian of a derivative, imperial nationalism; only the Labor Party understood and encouraged an expression of authentic Australian nationalism.[40]

Despite his low regard for the Great War, Paul Keating has

recalled that he felt 'very happy' to support a proposal from the AWM to inter the remains of an unknown Australian soldier at the memorial. Though they belonged to a soldier of the Great War, these anonymous remains did not represent to Keating the deferential attitude to Britain that he found so galling. The soldier 'came home as a loved Australian person ... We might have found his body at Kokoda and said exactly the same things of him'. The universal admiration for the speech that Keating gave at the interment on Remembrance Day in 1993 was based on its elegant prose and unifying sentiment: 'He is all of them. And he is one of us', Keating said of the Unknown Soldier. The prime minister even allowed for the possibility that the soldier had gone to war 'for no other reason than that he believed it was ... the duty that he owed his country and his king' (though he could not resist reversing the usual order of the incantation). In resorting to the platitudes that he and Watson so despised, Keating achieved a rare moment of bipartisanship. The national president of the RSL Alf Garland and some staff at the AWM had strongly opposed the prime minister delivering the eulogy for the Unknown Soldier; they variously considered the Governor-General, the chief of the Defence Force, or indeed the leader of the RSL, a more suitable candidate. Keating insisted that the role was his, as head of the executive government with responsibility for sending Australian troops to war. His performance left his critics pleasantly surprised. 'For a short while the people who were normally driven to a frenzy whenever the Prime Minister said anything about the country's military history were silent', recalled Don Watson. Michael McKernan, the former deputy director of the War Memorial, was struck by the reaction of John Howard, who was then the Opposition spokesperson for industrial relations. 'He looked at me with tears in his eyes and said "This is not the time for words, but didn't the PM do us well?" It was a highly emotional time.'[41]

On the twentieth anniversary of the Unknown Soldier speech in 2013, at the invitation of the memorial's director Brendan Nelson (the former defence minister and leader of the Liberal Party in Opposition), Paul Keating returned to the AWM to deliver the Remembrance Day commemorative address, His speech acknowledged 'the bravery and sacrifice' and 'latent nobility' of the diggers, yet condemned the Great War as a catastrophe that was 'devoid of any virtue'. This latter characterisation earned him the ire of conservative commentators, one of whom refuted what he called Keating's Leninist-inspired, 'nihilist perspective' of the war, declaring such a perspective was a betrayal of 'the memory of all those who served and died'.[42]

Keating's address coincided with the unveiling of a bronze panel struck with the text of the Unknown Soldier speech. Brendan Nelson had 'fallen in love with Keating's speech' and initially intended to replace the inscription on the soldier's tomb, 'Known unto God', with Keating's 'He is all of them. And he is one of us'. Rudyard Kipling's phrase, 'Known unto God', had been added to the tomb without ceremony in 1999 when Steve Gower, a former army officer, was the director of the memorial.

It is not widely known that the initiative to add a Christian inscription to the tomb of the Unknown Soldier came from the eminent historian Geoffrey Blainey, whom Prime Minister John Howard had appointed to the Council of the AWM in 1997. In April 1998, Blainey wrote to the chairman of the council, the former head of the Defence Force, Peter Gration, claiming that the Unknown Soldier had not been 'treated with quite the respect he deserved' when he was brought home in 1993. Prime Minister Paul Keating's 'eloquent and moving but partisan speech' had claimed that we could not know the religion of the soldier, a claim that was in keeping with the secular nature of the interment ceremony, though not with the weight of historical evidence. Blainey protested that the Unknown Soldier would almost certainly have been a Christian. In the belief that 'we should not shrink from paying respect to our mainstream culture, especially as it was so highly valued during the First World War', Blainey proposed that a Christian symbol or text be placed on or near the grave. He also discovered, some time after writing to Gration, that the grave from which the soldier's body had been removed in northern France was inscribed with 'Known unto God', indicating that its occupant, like all unknown soldiers, was presumed to be a Christian, or at least a believer in God.[43]

Despite the initial hesitation of a couple of members of the council and the entrenched resistance of memorial staff, Blainey's proposal was adopted. In an effort to diffuse the controversy that would surely be generated once the change became public, the council resolved to keep the announcement 'low key', and record that the inscription was merely 'remedying an oversight'. Council members were pleasantly surprised when the announcement created no interest, apart from an enquiry from the Sydney radio station 2KY.[44]

During subsequent visits to the AWM, Blainey noticed that the Christian inscription on the tomb of the Unknown Soldier was often covered by a floral wreath; 'even if there was only one wreath, staff would place it so as to hide the inscription'. The objection of staff to the inscription probably lay in their loyalty to the founder of the AWM, Charles Bean, who had been adamant that the memorial should be a place of secular commemoration. In response to the defiance of memorial staff, Blainey successfully moved a council motion that wreaths should not be placed over the inscription, unless there was a conspicuous absence of space.[45] Blainey's term on the council expired in 2004, but the staff's resentment about the Christian inscription endured. On a visit to the memorial in 2013, Blainey again found that flowers had been carefully placed to obscure the words 'Known unto God'.[46]

Blainey had no role in the move to scuttle Brendan Nelson's plan to remove 'Known unto God' from the tomb of the Unknown Soldier. Nelson was forced to discard his plan after complaints from 'veterans and war buffs' to the newly elected conservative government of Tony Abbott. A compromise was reached in which Keating's phrase was inscribed on the bevelled edge in front of the tomb, while Kipling's Christian sentiment remained undisturbed at the other end.[47]

With the wisdom of hindsight, Keating has come to believe that the political emphasis on war commemoration in Australia has perhaps been overdone, and not by conservative governments alone: 'I hope I have not played too significant a hand in causing it to be overdone. I suspect I might have', he has said. In addition to his championing of the Pacific War, Keating oversaw during his prime ministership the *Australia Remembers, 1939–1945* program, which enjoyed near-universal support. The program ran over the course of 1995, with the purposes of celebrating and commemorating the end of the Second World War. The Department of Veterans' Affairs allocated $12 million to educational resources, the restoration of war memorials and a range of events that included a ceremony to honour the wartime role of women and a major VP (Victory in the Pacific) Day celebration in Brisbane. The scheme was generally lauded for its inclusive, non-political orientation. It was also the moment when government began to invest heavily in the production of educational resources about the Australian experience of war.[48] Keating worries that the distinction between commemoration and celebration of war is not always maintained:

> The commemoration of the bravery of our soldiers past
> and our gratitude to them ought to be both obvious and
> profound. But I would not want to see our respect and deep
> appreciation move from these higher emotions to jingoism,

where we start waving banners to imagined notions rather than what is relevant and real. I have been very happy to have started the debate around the Pacific War in the speeches at Boona and at Kokoda. And also to acknowledge the tremendous contribution and bravery of Australian men and women in the First World War. But we do not want to see an earnest and conscientious commemoration of their brave deeds subsumed into a kind of chanting jingoism.[49]

By the end of Paul Keating's prime ministership in March 1996, Australians were more aware than previously of what had happened at places such as Kokoda, Borneo, Singapore and Thailand, partly because of the prime minister's advocacy and partly due to the success of the *Australia Remembers* program. The growth of interest in the Pacific War continues. The Kokoda Track now ranks second only to Gallipoli as the most famous place in Australian military history; approximately 3000 Australians walk the track each year. Increased public awareness has been reflected in the raising of monuments. Ken Inglis has estimated that more war memorials were built in the years between 1995 and 2005 than at any time since the 1920s, and that many of them commemorate episodes in the Pacific War.[50]

The Liberal Prime Minister John Howard continued his predecessor's effort to lift the status of Kokoda, though without the same intensity and certainly not at the expense of Gallipoli. Howard described Kokoda as being 'of enormous historic and military significance to Australia', and moved to stymie plans to mine sections along the track. Howard's successor, Kevin Rudd, walked the Kokoda Track as the Opposition foreign affairs spokesperson and inaugurated Battle for Australia Day as prime minister in 2008. The first Wednesday in September would be an occasion to recall battles such as the Coral Sea, Milne Bay and Kokoda, in which Allied forces had resisted the Japanese movement southward. Rudd declared that it was time that 'all Australians knew more about 1942 … It's often said, at Gallipoli our nation was born. But at the Battle for Australia, our nation stood up and confirmed that we as a nation would endure'. If not for the inelegance of the language, the speech might have been delivered by Keating himself. For his part, Keating felt resentful that Rudd's Battle for Australia initiative included no acknowledgment of his role in promoting better understanding of the Pacific War. His anger increased several weeks later when Rudd condemned Keating's public denigration of the Gallipoli campaign and the notion that the nation was born there: '[Rudd] quickly picked up my views and lines about the battle for Australia, but ran to distance himself from me [about Gallipoli]. What you do hope for from these people is some breadth of vision and understanding. And, I might add, consistency'.[51]

While Paul Keating lodged the Pacific War more firmly in Australian minds, his attempt to recast the military mythology in the image of his ambition for an independent, republican and reconciled nation was unfulfilled. This failure was due partly to the temper of Keating's rhetoric but mostly to Australians' emotional connection to their British heritage. If Keating had promoted his radical view of Gallipoli and the Great War during the 1960s or 1970s, he would have found a receptive audience among those whose opposition to Vietnam had been diffused into hostility towards all war and its commemoration. By the 1990s, however, his effort was swamped by the incoming tide of Gallipoli nostalgia, a tide generated by forces more profound than politics. Such is the centrality of Gallipoli in the Australian culture of the early twenty-first century, and the timid nature of political debate, that it is difficult to imagine another politician imitating Paul Keating's crazy-brave attempt to recast Anzac.

Keating's interpretation of Australian military history reads more like a lament for an alternative past or a manifesto for the future than an account of 'what really happened'. The difference between Keating's conviction that Gallipoli was an insignificant debacle and the dominant belief that the nation was born on the Dardanelles Peninsula in 1915 is perhaps a leader who could offer an alternative myth with which to bind the nation. Such a leader might have convinced Australians that their thriving young nation had no need of martial baptism, that such bloody notions had no place in a progressive social democracy. It is possible to hear in Keating's claim that he has 'always believed Australia could be a great country' the regret that he was not able to staunch the psychic wound that draws Australians back to Gallipoli.[52]

John Howard watched with growing indignation as Paul Keating sought to rearrange the national iconography during his period as prime minister. Like Keating, Howard was an ideological warrior who took a keen interest in Australian history. Just as Keating's version of the past was patinated by his political ideology, so Howard had developed an interpretation of history that complemented his socially conservative and economically liberal philosophy. While the seeds of Keating's contempt for Gallipoli lay in the death of his uncle in Borneo during the Second World War, the origins of Howard's determination to restore whatever damage his predecessor had done to the traditional Anzac legend lay in his father and grandfather's service in the Great War.

Of the 270 000 men who served overseas in the 1st AIF and survived, none rose to hold the prime ministership of Australia. Though Stanley Bruce fought at Gallipoli, his service was with the British army. It is surprising that John Howard is the only Australian prime minister to claim a father who served and more surprising that this did not happen until 1996. Lyall Howard was eighteen when he enlisted in the war and forty-three when the youngest of his four sons was born: 'I have a perspective in a sense, I suppose, which is atypical', Howard has said. 'When I was at school in the forties and fifties, all my classmates had fathers who fought in World War II. It was a relatively unusual thing to have someone who had a father who had served in World War I.'[53]

John Howard was raised in the lower middle class, inner west of Sydney, where his family had an unquestioning and conventional attitude towards the Anzac legend. Like the majority of veterans, Lyall Howard 'didn't talk a lot' about the war. 'They didn't because the therapy then was to put it behind you, not talk about it ... now, the psychologists would say, "Oh you should have talked and talked and talked about it" ... it was a different attitude then.' Lyall Howard was exposed to mustard gas at Messines, but returned from the war and established a successful service station business in inner western Sydney. He died prematurely at age fifty-nine, when his youngest son was sixteen. John Howard cannot recall whether his father was a member of the RSL, though his paternal grandfather, who also served, certainly was. Lyall Howard 'wore that rather large badge of the 1st AIF [and] marched on every Anzac Day ... until the last year of his life. He wasn't very well that day and he didn't go into the march'.[54]

John Howard inherited his father's uncomplicated attitude to commemorating the Great War. Though the Howards were avowedly Anglophile, their understanding of the Anzac legend did not shy away from criticism of British officers or comparisons between Australia and Britain that favoured Australia. Thus John Howard spoke of the 'feeling of separate identity' that was entrenched in Australians during the Great War by virtue of 'Pride in battlefield successes, the magnitude of our losses, sometime dismay at British High Command decision making and some starkly different attitudes held by Australians and their British cousins in respect to class and discipline'. The war that had shackled Australia to Britain and thwarted its independence in the mind of Paul Keating, had for John Howard (and for Hawke before him) the very opposite connotation. It was the moment at which Australians experienced for the first time their separateness from Britain. The Anzacs 'bequeathed Australia a lasting sense of national identity. They sharpened our democratic temper and our questioning eye towards authority', said the Anglophile John Howard at Gallipoli in 2005.[55]

John Howard was studying law at the University of Sydney in the late 1950s and early 1960s when cynicism about Anzac commemoration and hostility towards the old diggers began to be expressed widely among the young, educated middle class. An article in the student newspaper *Honi Soit* had inspired Alan Seymour's play, *The One Day of the Year*, which dramatised the gen-erational divide through the medium of the Anzac legend. Even as these early expressions of dissent morphed into the more rad-ical and emphatic protest of the Vietnam War era, Howard was unpersuaded, 'because people were so polarised, there was almost a transference of the polarisation over Vietnam onto war remem-brance generally. That was the sense I had'.[56] Howard's under-standing of Anzac remained rooted in the years of his childhood in the 1940s and 1950s and his experience of popular and polit-ical consensus:

> I had relatives, more on my mother's side than my father's;
> my mother's three siblings who I knew well and was very
> close to two of them, they were all Labor voters. And two
> of her brothers had fought in World War II, one of them
> in the air force and one in the army, and they were both
> Labor voters. I'm astonished that anybody would think that
> somehow or other either side of politics was more or less pro
> Australia's involvement in either World War I or World War
> II. I always saw it as something that completely transcended
> party lines.[57]

By the 1980s, John Howard had come to believe that the Great War was one episode in an entire national history that needed rescuing from the radical left. As early as 1985, during his first stint as leader of the Coalition Opposition, Howard decried the historiographical march in the academy towards Indigenous and other minority histories, which reflected negatively, whether implicitly or explicitly, upon the settler society. In his policy document *Future Directions*, Howard claimed that people's 'confidence in their nation's past' was coming 'under attack as the professional purveyors of guilt attacked Australia's heritage and people were told they should apologise for pride in their culture, traditions, institutions and history'. His dismay at this trend grew as Manning Clark's grand, yet maudlin and increasingly radical vision pervaded the national consciousness. On 25 January 1988, Clark – whom Geoffrey Blainey described as 'almost the official historian in 1988' – wrote in *Time Australia* magazine that 'the coming of the British was the occasion of three great evils: the violence against the original inhabitants ...; the violence against ... the convicts; and the violence done to the land itself'. Blainey used the term 'black armband' to describe an interpretation of Australian history put forward by the multicultural lobby, academics and politicians who believed the past was 'largely the story of violence, exploitation, repression, racism, sexism, capitalism, colonialism and a few other isms'. Blainey contrasted this interpretation with the 'Three Cheers view of history', upon which his generation had been reared. Perhaps the pendulum had swung too far, he thought, 'from a position that was too favourable, too self-congratulatory, to an opposite extreme that is even more unreal and decidedly jaundiced'.[58]

John Howard adopted a politically sharpened version of Geoffrey Blainey's analysis of Australian historiography and marshalled the historian's terminology behind an effort to swing the interpretive pendulum back some way towards the 'three cheers' view. Speaking to the Liberal Students Foundation at Sydney University a few months after becoming prime minister, Howard urged that as 'political warriors ... on campuses of Australia, it is very important that all of you understand that winning back of ideas, that winning back of history is tremendously important'. A few days earlier he had told an Adelaide audience that 'One of the more insidious developments in Australian political life over the past decade or so has been the attempt to re-write Australian history in the service of a partisan political cause'. These 'self-appointed cultural dieticians' sought to 'force-feed' to the public their version of Australian history, which had more to do with 'divisive political strategies than respect for the facts of history'.[59]

Howard's advocacy of a more positive view of Australian history was both personal mission and political calculation. He believed that Paul Keating mistakenly considered his promotion of a radical version of Australian history to be an electoral asset:

> emboldened by his victory in '93, [Keating] got more
> strident on this stuff. It probably didn't do him any good
> politically; he thought it did at the time ... he saw some of
> his more strident republicanism and so forth ... as a way of
> consolidating his base ... I remember Max Suich who used to
> be the editorial manager of the *Sydney Morning Herald* and the
> *Age* say that [Keating] saw it as a way of stroking the basket
> weavers.[60]

Howard's famous ('infamous' to many on the left) declaration during the 1996 election campaign that he wanted Australians to feel 'comfortable and relaxed' was intended 'in large part' to appeal to people who felt that Keating's attempt to reorient Australian history was a slight on their heritage. Keating, on the other hand, has professed no surprise at Howard's reversion to a more traditional form of Australian nationalism:

It never surprised me that Howard wanted to reshape the
whole Gallipoli history to psychologically reconnect his
administration with the conservative ones which governed
at the height of the post–First World War immediate
commemorations, the ones that drifted through the twenties
and the thirties. The Liberals think some of their political DNA
resides in Britain's European past and can't imagine themselves
cut off from it. They always yearn for the old world.[61]

While Keating preferred an interpretation of the national history wherein Australians struggled to assert an authentic identity
against the imperial yoke, in Howard's estimation, Britain was a
mostly benevolent power from whom Australians had inherited
many of the best aspects of their national culture: the rule of law,
the Westminster parliamentary system and the Judeo-Christian
system of ethics. Indeed, Howard's assessment of what he called
'the Australian achievement' was not dissimilar to that of Bob
Hawke, though the two might have disagreed on the substance
of that achievement.

I think the Australian achievement is gigantic when you think
about it. Whereas it always seemed to me that people on
the left had a fundamentally pessimistic, negative view, that
Australia had not achieved and that almost until 1972 in the
eyes of some of them our history had been a litany of racism
and prejudice and bigotry and shame and colonial inferiority
… I felt that one of the mistakes that Keating made [was]
that he focused too heavily on the guilt side of it and too
little on the other side of it.[62]

John Howard's effort to reorient Australian historiography was
part of a much broader mission to win back for conservatism the
cultural and social ground that he felt had been ceded to the left

over the past few decades. He has maintained that the left was taken aback by the ferocity with which the cultural battle was joined: 'They thought that you wouldn't really have aggressive conservatism in some of these areas again, they thought it was all finished and they thought they'd won'. Having complained often of the veil of political correctness that had fallen across public debate in Australia during the Keating prime ministership, Howard acted swiftly upon becoming prime minister to shift the axis of discourse about matters such as multiculturalism and Aboriginal affairs. If the voices of the left intelligentsia had been aired regularly during Keating's term, Prime Minister Howard would provide a platform for the populist right. In September 1996, he declared that 'One of the great changes that has come over Australia in the last six months is that people do feel able to speak a little more freely and a little more openly about what they feel ... In a sense the pall of censorship on certain issues has been lifted'. A couple of weeks previously, the newly elected Independent member for Oxley, Pauline Hanson, had delivered her maiden speech in Parliament, expressing contempt for the view that Aboriginal people were the most disadvantaged group in Australian society. She claimed that 'Australia was in danger of being swamped by Asians' and called for the abolition of multiculturalism and a halt to the immigration program.[63] Howard refused for several months to condemn

*In 2006 John Howard redoubled his effort to swing the pendulum of Australian historiography away from the 'black armband' interpretation.*

Hanson's views in the face of extraordinary domestic and growing international pressure to do so, just as he refused to countenance that the bulk of her burgeoning support base was racist. The prime minister was a longstanding critic of multiculturalism and, while opposition leader in 1988, had asserted that the rate of Asian immigration to Australia should be slowed in the interest of social cohesion. To his critics, Howard's reluctance to censure Hanson reiterated the fact that he was prepared to blow the racist dog whistle for political advantage.

In addition to facilitating an environment in which people felt more able to air populist economic views and crudely conceived grievances about Aborigines and Asians, Howard sought to stymie major sources of left-wing ideology, such as the universities, the teachers' unions, the Australia Council, the National Museum, and the broadcasters SBS and the ABC. The first budget of the Howard government announced a 10 per cent funding cut to the ABC and a similar reduction to universities, which Howard had long considered a bastion of left-wing ideology. The short-lived appointment of a conservative managing director and subsequent conservative appointments to the ABC board failed to staunch its left-wing culture. The selection of the freelance historian Keith Windschuttle was a particularly provocative gesture to the intellectual left, given his central role in the 'history wars'. In *The Fabrication of Aboriginal History*, Windschuttle had argued that scholars such as Henry Reynolds, Lyndall Ryan and the late Lloyd Robson had exaggerated greatly the number of Aborigines murdered by British settlers in colonial Tasmania. A subsequent publication challenged the notion that generations of Aboriginal children were systematically and forcibly removed from their parents. Windschuttle's battles against historiographical orthodoxy earned him the public approbation of the prime minister, as well as the ABC appointment. At *Quadrant's* fiftieth anniversary dinner in October 2006, Howard applauded the magazine's willingness to 'defend both Geoffrey Blainey and Keith Windschuttle against the posses of political correctness'.[64]

In 2006 John Howard redoubled his effort to swing the pendulum of Australian historiography away from the 'black armband' interpretation. During his Australia Day speech he called for 'a root and branch renewal of Australian history in our schools', so that children were 'actually taught their national inheritance, a nation like all others with its share of failures and mistakes, but one that has emerged at the start of this millennium as one of the most successful societies on earth'. Howard's view about the content of Australian history was matched with determined opinions about the methodology of historical instruction. The prime minister wanted to see 'a restoration of narrative instead of … the fragmented stew of themes and issues' that was the result of the 'postmodern culture of relativism where any objective record of achievement is questioned or repudiated'.[65]

Howard believed that narrative or chronological history might serve as a means of circumventing the simplistic moralising that was rife in academic history about such issues as race, gender and the removal of Aboriginal children from their families: 'My argument is that you can't properly understand the issue unless you know the narrative … I mean how is it possible for us to understand the context of the conscription debate if you want to talk about World War I without having some understanding of the Anglo-Irish dispute?'.[66] Narrative history would offer context, but Howard's desire for history that told a coherent narrative harked back to an earlier era of professional history writing, when academic historians functioned as 'makers' of the nation-state. The contemporary profession was more concerned with detailing the experience of the disempowered and disadvantaged than with describing the triumphant sowing of British civilisation in Australian soil, in the historiographical tradition of the imperialist historian Ernest Scott.

Suspicion among his critics that Howard's preference for historical narrative reflected his drive for a more conservative version of Australian history was exacerbated when the government linked access to additional school funding to the installation of flagpoles, and sponsored posters proclaiming 'Values for Australian Schooling' with an image of Simpson and his donkey as the background. The increase in displays of patriotism in the first decade of the twenty-first century was seen by the left as an unwelcome legacy of John Howard's populist nationalism. The journalist Bernard Keane complained on the news website Crikey of 'the crass nationalism of which Howard was so proud. You know what I'm talking about – the nationalism of concerts at Anzac Cove, green-and-gold tracksuits and an assumed right to control of any foreign soil on which an Australian may have died in battle'. Howard agrees that there has been a visible increase in displays of patriotism and is 'very happy to plead guilty' to any role he might have played in promoting it: 'It's quite astonishing, my wife often says to me that she could never have imagined herself wandering around a battlefield with an Australian flag on her back and she's quite conservative and supports the Australian flag as I do'. Howard suggests the surge in demonstrative nationalism is partly a legacy of the Australian military involvement in East Timor: 'I think [that] had quite a bit to do with lifting the prestige of the Australian military. Some polls suggest that it's the most respected institution in our society; that probably drives some of the lefties to distraction'.[67]

Integral to John Howard's understanding of the Great War and of national history was his interpretation of the Australian values of mateship and egalitarianism. He variously defined mateship as 'the great capacity to work together in adversity' and 'a concept of treating people according to how you find them and not according to the colour of their skin'. During his unsuccessful attempt to insert a preamble into the Australian constitution, Howard described mateship as the impulse that leads Australians to help people in floods and fires, rescue people buried under the debris of ski lodges and 'work hard to haul bodies out of train wrecks. It's an expression that refers to the willingness, the distinctive willingness of independently minded Australians to help their fellow countrymen and women in times of adversity'.

Howard's critics were sceptical of his enthusiastic embrace of mateship and wondered how it could be squared with his radical economic liberalism and industrial relations policies. Paul Kelly attributed to Howard a 'naked political theft' of 'the mateship brand' from the Labor Party: 'Mateship was the door to patriotism, egalitarianism and civic nationalism. Howard ... rebadged himself as a populist symbol of the nation. It is one of the greatest jokes played on Labor since Federation'.[68]

But Howard does not see the joke. He rejects the suggestion that values such as mateship and egalitarianism are in conflict with the radical individualism of his industrial relations policy: 'Individual effort and egalitarianism are not ... antagonistic. I don't understand that'. Howard professes bewilderment at the suggestion that mateship and egalitarianism might be values that the Australian left traditionally has considered its own, rather than values that belong to all Australians, no matter their politics:

> Egalitarianism and respect for people or their material
> possessions ... was something I was brought up with,
> brought up to believe in ... I never saw mateship as
> belonging to either the left or the right ... My background,
> which was lower middle class, certainly pro-Menzies,
> Anglophile, all of that, but ... I can't remember my parents
> ever sort of saying to me that mateship is something
> that is us or that's not us, it's just sort of something that
> wasn't an issue in my upbringing. Mateship was a natural
> phenomenon, a product of being an Australian, whether you
> were Labor or Liberal.[69]

While the radical nationalist tradition, which Paul Keating invoked frequently, traces the origins of mateship and egalitarianism to the convicts, the itinerant bush workers, the diggers and the unions of the nineteenth and twentieth centuries, John

Howard's explanation of the development of Australian distinctiveness eschews class distinction:

> We were in a new society and in order to survive people had to work together to survive and out of that you develop a respect, just as you do in wartime, irrespective of somebody's background, in order to survive you've got to rely on the bloke next to you and he on you or she on you and the same thing in a new frontier country, whereas they came from societies that had social structures that had developed over hundreds of years and were set and rigid.[70]

John Howard's Australian nationalism found sufficient nourishment in the story of the displacement of a group of Britons of non-specific class to a new environment, the harshness of which united them in unique bonds of mateship. Like the historian John Hirst, Howard did not believe it necessary to find the seeds of Australian egalitarianism within the Irish convict or London criminal class. The opportunities afforded to Howard despite his lower middle-class origin made it easy for him to adopt a nationalism that rejected the social rigidity of Britain for a meritocracy that practised 'an egalitarianism of manners'.[71] Howard's success in seizing the opportunities granted by a meritocratic system consolidated a belief in egalitarianism of opportunity rather than outcome, and confirmed his conviction that mateship meant pulling together in adversity rather than uniting against unjust authority.

Paul Keating looked at the Great War and saw lickspittles and tin-tookies toadying and tugging their forelocks to Great Britain. Bob Hawke, John Howard and Kim Beazley saw something utterly different. To these political leaders, the Great War had shown that Australians were different from Britons. John Howard restored Gallipoli to its place at the centre of political commemoration of the Anzac legend. He accelerated the trend for political leadership and sponsorship of war commemoration that was begun by Hawke and greatly expanded upon during the Keating government under the *Australia Remembers* program. Meanwhile, the ideological battle for Australian history between the left intelligentsia and the political and intellectual right barely registered with a population that remained 'comfortable and relaxed' about a Gallipoli story from which they appeared to draw a religious-like succour.

⁂

Genuflection in the direction of Gallipoli is expected of contemporary Australian prime ministers – its absence provokes sharp condemnation, as Paul Keating learned. John Howard's successors as prime minister – Kevin Rudd, Julia Gillard and Tony Abbott – have all maintained the primacy of Gallipoli in the national iconography, though none has engaged as vigorously with Australian history as did Keating and Howard. When Julia Gillard announced that she would travel to Gallipoli for the ninety-seventh anniversary of the landing in 2012, she said: 'I have never had the opportunity to mark Anzac Day on that sacred soil'. No-one was publicly critical when the Welsh-born prime minister, and former member of the Socialist Left faction of the ALP, said it was a journey she had 'wanted to make all my life'.[72]

The prelude to the centenary of the Gallipoli landing in 1915 has given politicians unprecedented licence to associate themselves with Anzac. The Commonwealth government's leading role in organising the commemorative schedule is bipartisan and undisputed. A committee led by two former prime ministers, Malcolm Fraser and Bob Hawke, was appointed by the first Rudd Labor government in 2010 to recommend how best to commemorate the centenary. Fraser's wish for the establishment of a centre for peace studies did not survive the political process, unlike more conventional recommendations such as the restoration of memorials, mobile exhibitions of Great War memorabilia, and a restaging of the first major convoy carrying troops from Albany, to be televised nationally. Upon becoming prime minister, Tony Abbott added to the list of suggestions the idea of a major interpretive centre focused on the Western Front and the establishment of 'Australia's Arlington', a war cemetery in Canberra, containing the remains of 'significant ex-soldiers'.[73]

The growing political appetite for Anzac has not passed without criticism. The most prominent critique is contained in *What's Wrong with Anzac? The Militarisation of Australian History*, published in 2010. Marilyn Lake, Henry Reynolds, Mark McKenna, Joy Damousi and Carina Donaldson argued that Australian history is overly weighted towards military themes at the expense of subjects such as the dispossession of Aborigines (which ought to be considered a war in the same way as overseas wars), and late nineteenth-century and early twentieth-century achievements in social welfare and industrial arbitration. The authors claimed that the government determined this emphasis, principally through increased funding to the Department of Veterans' Affairs for educational materials that served to indoctrinate in young Australians a militaristic and politically conservative view of the past. They argued that the most disturbing aspect of this emphasis was the way in which the Anzac tradition had been used by politicians to justify Australian military incursions in Iraq and Afghanistan.

The left-wing academic authors of *What's Wrong with Anzac?* found an unexpected ally in James Brown, a former captain in the Australian army and now a defence analyst at the independently funded research centre, the Lowy Institute. Brown's book, *Anzac's Long Shadow*, published in February 2014, is highly critical of Australians' 'obsession with Anzac', claiming that much of the estimated $325 million will be spent on centenary commemoration would be better directed towards the welfare of returned soldiers. Brown also decries the contemporary commodification of Anzac, particularly by RSL clubs, which derive great financial gain from their association with the Anzac brand, but contribute little to the cause of the Australian military.[74]

In a settler nation that is conspicuously short of unifying mythologies, the Anzac legend is uniquely powerful. It is not surprising that politicians seek to harness that power to their own ends – by adjusting the legend for political emphasis, by connecting the Anzac legend with current foreign policies and even with military missions, and by being photographed and filmed in the company of Australian soldiers. Politicians make an obvious target for the derision of people who are disturbed by the Anzac glut, and certainly they have contributed to it, but politicians did not initiate the Anzac revival and their influence over its quantum expansion can be overstated. The limits of political power over war commemoration are best illustrated by the failure of Paul Keating to entice Australians to relinquish their attachment to events on 25 April 1915 on an isolated peninsula in Turkey.

# EPILOGUE

When I gave a lecture to third-year students at the University of Melbourne in 2013 about the history of Anzac, they were amazed to discover that the legend was not always as ubiquitous as it has been during their lifetimes. They were especially surprised to learn that commemoration of the Great War had nearly become extinct in the 1960s and 1970s, before its unexpected revival during the 1980s. One student approached me after the class to say that she felt she had been 'brainwashed' by Australia's Anzac obsession.

I have drawn short in this book of arguing that young Australians have been brainwashed about Anzac. However, I have certainly sought to demonstrate that memory of the Great War is, in the words of the British historian EP Thompson, 'a relationship and not a thing', an ever-changing phenomenon whose form is shaped by the society in which it operates.[1] *Anzac, the Unauthorised Biography* shows how various ideological movements, intellectual fashions and moral beliefs have influenced how we remember and imagine the Great War: racialism, social Darwinism, militarism, socialism, pacifism, the memory boom, trauma psychology and, above all others, nationalism.

Before 1914, Australians subscribed to the ideology of martial nationalism. This ideology purported that war was the truest test of nationhood and that Australia's official status as a nation would not be ratified psychologically until 'her' men had been blooded in war. This muscular nationalism was given legitimacy by social Darwinism, which concocted a hierarchy of races in which the fittest and most morally courageous sat at the apex. The competitive

ethos of social Darwinism raised a vexed question for colonial settler societies such as Australia: was the transplanted race
thriving or degenerating in its new environment? The question
was especially pertinent in a country that was founded as a penal
colony.

Upon the outbreak of war between Britain and the Boers in
South Africa in 1899, the Australian colonies sent contingents
that were merged into British units. Commentators were hopeful
that the war against the Boers might provide an opportunity for
the sacrificial bloodletting of young warriors that was requisite
to authentic nationhood. Among the public there was hope that
the soldiers' prowess in battle might answer affirmatively the lingering question about the integrity of the Australian race. Alas,
the nature of warfare on the South African veldt proved inadequate to the conventions of martial nationalism. The accretion
of indeterminate engagements against an enemy that employed
guerilla tactics to great effect was incompatible with an ideal of
war inspired by Waterloo, in which battle was frequently compared with the sports of cricket and rugby. Returned soldiers and
bereaved families sought to perpetuate memory of the war chiefly
through the raising of monuments and the formation of returned
soldiers' organisations. However, the new Commonwealth government and the wider public were content to let the war slip
from memory. The disappointment of South Africa left the desire
for martial initiation unsated.

Australians responded with enthusiasm to Britain's declaration
of war against Germany in August 1914. There was unqualified
bipartisan political support for the decision to commit Australian troops to the Allied war effort and no shortage (initially) of
volunteers. The dawn landing of Australian troops at Gallipoli
on 25 April 1915, as part of an Allied plan to force Turkey out of
the war, was sufficient for Australians to consider themselves to
have passed 'that transcendent test' of nationhood. The British

journalist Ellis Ashmead Bartlett celebrated the qualities of the Anzacs with extravagant phrases that rang loudly in Australian ears. Despite the reticence of the Minister for Defence, George Pearce, who thought that a later battle might prove to be 'more worthy of remembering', the failure of the Dardanelles campaign proved to be no barrier to what the historian Marilyn Lake has described as the 'new awakening of Australian national consciousness'.[2]

Ernest Scott was the first person to write the history of Australians in the Great War. Scott was an Englishman who had risen from lowly beginnings to become a professor of history at the University of Melbourne. Along the path from Fabianism and theosophy to liberalism, Scott had become an ardent advocate of the British imperial project. His *Short History of Australia*, first published in 1916, conspicuously lacked the nationalist rhetoric that pervaded the press and thrilled the public after the Gallipoli landing. In Scott's imagining, Australia was a dutiful member of the Empire, whose interest in defeating Germany and its allies could not be distinguished from that of Great Britain. The Anzacs' splendid military endeavours in Turkey had proved them worthy members of the British race. Gallipoli comprised a dramatic episode in the history of 'Imperial Relations', rather than a watershed moment in the making of the Australian nation. So removed from public sentiment was Ernest Scott's imperial interpretation of the Great War, that it was quickly forgotten.

Like Ernest Scott, the official historian Charles Bean was a devoted imperialist. Yet, under his editorship, the *Official History of Australia in the War of 1914–1918*, published in twelve volumes between 1921 and 1942, presented a very different interpretation of Australian involvement in the conflict from that offered by Scott. Bean had been developing a thesis of Australian distinctiveness during his travels as a journalist through rural New South Wales in the first decade of the twentieth century. Imbued with the racial philosophy of social Darwinism, Bean came to believe that the British race was evolving in a distinctive way in its Australian setting. The demands of the rural environment were producing a man who was suspicious of authority, resourceful, independent and loyal to his mates beyond all others. This Australian type responded magnificently when he was faced with the ultimate test of manhood: the test of war. Bean's account of Australian experience in the Great War was aligned with that held by a majority of the public, who remained steadfast to Britain but took immense pride in their soldiers' fighting skill. It was from this union of nationalist desire and martial gratification that the Anzac legend was born.

Despite their different interpretations of the meaning of the war for Australia, both Bean and Scott struggled to explain the failure of the conscription referenda in 1916 and 1917. To Scott, Australians' failure to fulfil their imperial duty by voting 'No' left them morally deficient and undeserving of the democratic rights bestowed upon them by their British-derived system of government. Charles Bean wavered between respecting the independence of mind demonstrated by the 'No' vote and lamenting the aspersion it cast upon Australians' record of martial achievement. The collaboration between Scott and Bean on Volume XI of the *Official History* proved unable to create a story of Australian effort on the home-front to match the heroic endeavour of the men in the trenches.

While Bean's *Official History* and public ceremonies of mourning and commemoration dominated remembrance of the Great War in the first decades after the war, the Australian academy remained mostly silent. Ernest Scott's colleagues in the history departments of the six Australian universities showed no inclination to scrutinise the conflict. Military history was not considered a suitable subject for academic historians, no matter that Charles Bean's magnum opus had left little unsaid about the subject. More surprising is that the official historian's thesis regarding the realisation of an Australian national consciousness was neither countered nor affirmed by academic historians, but ignored. The identity of the 'Independent Australian Briton', famously described in Keith Hancock's *Australia* (1930), derived in no part from events in Turkey on 25 April 1915.

The silence of academic historians matched that of the former soldiers in the years following the Great War. While veterans determined the form of commemorative ceremonies, mostly through their membership of returned soldiers' organisations, there was a broadly felt desire to forget about the war and to 'get on with life'. This reticence was put aside briefly in the early 1930s by a number of former soldiers who published books about their wartime experience. The boom in Australian books about the war followed a few years behind that begun in Europe with publications such as Erich Maria Remarque's *All Quiet on the Western Front* (1929) and Robert Graves' *Goodbye to All That* (1929). While a dominant theme of the bestselling European books was disillusionment and futility, the most popular Australian war novels and memoirs, such as Joseph Maxwell's *Hell's Bells and Mademoiselles* (1932) and HR Williams' *The Gallant Company* (1933), were those in which the tragedy and brutality of the war were redeemed by the nobility of the soldiers and the cause for which they fought. A catastrophe for which men like Remarque and Graves could find no redemptive purpose was replete with meaning to Maxwell and Williams. Experience may have tempered their martial nationalist rhetoric, but still the tragedy of the war was ameliorated by the righteousness of its cause. Those Australian soldiers who wrote sensitive and disillusioned books about their war experience failed to find a readership.

The international pacifist and anti-war movements of the interwar years were legacies of the Great War, just as the chest-beating martial nationalism of the prewar period was a casualty of it.

The unprecedented devastation caused by the 'war to end wars' lent credence to Marxist analysis, which argued that the workers had been sent to die for the profit of their capitalist masters. The collapse of international investment, trade and finance between 1929 and 1931, and the rise of fascist regimes in Italy, Germany and Spain gave further impetus to Marxist ideology. When the Second World War spread from Western Europe to the East in 1941, young Australian radicals fought willingly in the belief that the defeat of fascism was the prelude to the establishment of a new social order. A group of intellectuals who were born after the Great War and served in the Second World War established an influential school of historiography in the decades after 1945. Historians such as Russel Ward, Ian Turner and Geoffrey Serle sought to challenge the orthodox interpretation of Australian history that saw Britain as a benevolent power. According to their socialist philosophy, the working class embodied an authentic and radical Australian nationalism, which was thwarted by those bourgeois Australians and Britons who sought to maintain a rigid class structure and a dependent relationship with Britain.

The Great War made an awkward fit for radical nationalism. Initially, radical historians studied the period for its relevance to issues such as worker conditions and industrial conflict. Notions such as the martial baptism were irrelevant to scholars concerned with the welfare of the working class. Yet, as the historian Ken Inglis brought to general attention in the mid-1960s, the Great War demonstrated that the characteristics of the iconographic working-class Australian male – larrikinism, anti-authoritarianism, mateship, independence, practicality – were not necessarily coupled with political radicalism or anti-British sentiment. Eventually, the radical nationalists came to see the Great War as the wrecker of the progressive zeal of Australian prewar governments. According to this analysis, the conservatives demonised the Labor Party by associating it with communism and hostility to the cause of the war, which doomed it to opposition until 1929. Furthermore, the conservatives took advantage of Labor's incapacitation by gaining a stranglehold on Anzac commemoration that the left was unable to break.

By the 1960s when Ken Inglis began raising questions about the meaning of the rituals of Anzac Day, those rituals were in noticeable decline. The diggers, most of whom had been born in the last decade of the previous century, were dying. Opposition to Australian participation in the war in Vietnam widened to include opposition to the commemoration of war, and the allegation that the Anzac legend glorified war. Britain's turn from its former Empire towards Europe in the 1960s compelled Australians to seek an alternative to their Australian-Briton nationalism. The New Nationalism of the late 1960s and early 1970s was incompatible with an Anzac legend that prized the British attachment. In the liberalised social environment of the 1960s and 1970s, the old diggers appeared chauvinistic, racist and anachronistic.

It was during this period in which commemoration of the Great War was widely considered to be in terminal decline, that it finally gained a foothold inside the academy. In the late 1960s, Lloyd Robson pioneered an academic tradition of challenging the Anzac canon, while Bill Gammage's research restated significant elements of the legend, yet gave emphasis to the tragedy and horror of warfare. From these beginnings, the Great War has increasingly been the subject of academic study. Many cultural historians who study subjects such as shell shock, mourning and trauma are concerned to show how the experience of Australians during and after the Great War did not accord with the Anzac legend. Others such as Bruce Scates continue in the tradition of Bill Gammage, illuminating the suffering and tragedy of war yet stopping short of questioning the foundations of Anzac commemoration.

Gammage's book, *The Broken Years*, published in 1974, proved to be the portent of the second coming of Anzac. Gammage's sympathetic eye for the diggers and his tragic tone caught the attention of the film-maker Peter Weir, who translated these sentiments into his extraordinarily successful film *Gallipoli* (1981). By grafting the Gallipoli story onto the legend of the sacrificial young warrior, Weir gave Australians the makings of the national myth they had been seeking since the decline of British race patriotism in the 1960s. Gradually, during the 1980s, the hostility and apathy that had characterised popular attitudes towards the Great War for two decades were replaced by sympathy and curiosity.

Also during the 1980s, another group began to add its voice to the record of Great War memory in Australia: the descendants of men who had fought. These family historians were inspired partly by the resurgence of Anzac and partly by the rising international interest in genealogy. The majority of family historians of the war publish their material with an unself-conscious confidence that these documents occupy a significant place in the national story. A growing number, however, are inclined to ask psychological questions about the war: Was my father traumatised by the war? Could that explain his silences, his mood-swings, his alcoholism?

In 1990 the Prime Minister Bob Hawke gambled successfully that public sentiment about Anzac had shifted from its hostile phase when he travelled to Gallipoli with a group of elderly veterans. The success of this seventy-fifth anniversary 'pilgrimage' sealed a new relationship between politicians and the commemoration of war in Australia. Paul Keating is the only aberration among a succession of political leaders who have sought to position themselves in the draft of Australia's most powerful collective story. Political patronage of military history has mustered the resources of the state behind the production of educational resources and contributed substantially to the Anzac glut.

The dominant interpretation of the Great War in contemporary Australia is one of subdued martial nationalism. The elements of racial superiority and imperial unity that fuelled the original version of the Anzac legend have been discarded. In their place is an emphasis on tragedy and mateship that borrows much from the memory boom and its desire to assuage trauma. Nevertheless, the fundamental conceit of the martial baptism remains in place: the insistence that the Australian nation was born at Gallipoli.

I began this book with a question: 'why are Australians of the twenty-first century so emotionally attached to a military event that took place nearly one hundred years ago?' The historians who have applied themselves to this question over the past few years have often done so in anger, pointing the finger of blame at the state and its massive subsidisation of military education through schools and war museums. This argument is not entirely convincing. First, the Anzac revival was underway in the 1980s, a decade before the state began opening its coffers. Second, it assumes that popular consciousness is the plaything of politicians, when Australians gather their impressions about the nation's military history from many sources. A better, if less easily measurable, explanation for the extraordinary currency of the Anzac legend can be found in the nature of Australian nationalism.

In 1943 the historian Manning Clark wrote an article in *Meanjin* about the anxious status of Australian nationhood, an anxiety that is common to nations that began as European colonies in the eighteenth and nineteenth centuries. Australians were 'tortured by doubt', he said. Torn between our European heritage and our antipodean setting, we were forced to 'ask the dreadful question … do we belong here?'[3] In the twenty-first century, Australians are still asking the 'dreadful question', though it is more often posed about issues such as Indigenous dispossession, immigration and environmental degradation than the question of civilisation versus savagery.

Another historian, Mark McKenna, has shown how the collapse of British race patriotism during the 1960s and the difficulty of constructing a national identity around European settlement led Australians back to (a revised version of) Anzac with renewed vigour.[4] Put simply, Australians keep returning to the Gallipoli well because it provides the best (or least offensive) answer to Manning Clark's 'dreadful question'. It is a testament to the inventiveness of the human imagination that the bungled invasion of an isolated Turkish peninsula has become our favourite story of national genesis. In its contemporary form, Anzac represents universal values such as courage, comradeship and sacrifice. It is a legend based in war that says remarkably little about killing and violence. It accommodates contemporary interest in family history and trauma psychology. It can bend leftwards to teach us about suspicion of authority, egalitarianism, larrikinism, even tolerance and diversity. Alternatively, it can bend to the right to tell us about loyalty, respect for tradition and pride in our British heritage.

While it is difficult to be offended by the benign form of the contemporary Anzac legend, we should remain vigilant against politicians and others who seek to marshal national sentiment to their own ends. We should also take the opportunity of the centenary of the Gallipoli landing to scrutinise the mentality behind the Anzac legend. In perpetuating the fairytale that Australia was born at Gallipoli, we also perpetuate the cringe that is the scourge of colonial settler societies. After all, national characteristics such as mateship, egalitarianism and larrikinism were *not* invented by the diggers during the Great War. They existed in the Australian character before 1914. The 'birth of the nation' conceit did not emerge because those qualities were demonstrated for the first time, but because there was an international audience to validate them. In the twenty-first century we no longer believe that nations are made in war. Indeed, we have seen a number of them fall apart recently as the result of military intervention. Nor should we feel that Australian traits and mores require the endorsement of more powerful nations. One hundred years on, it is time to separate myth from history: the Great War was a devastating event in which young Australians fought for the interests of a nation that was born on 1 January 1901.

# NOTES

## The Anzac Ascendancy

1. Raise a Glass Appeal, 'Excuses', <www.raiseaglass.com.au/>.
2. Steve Waugh, ABC News, 24 April 2012, <www.abc.net.au/news/2012-04-20/anzac-day-cricket-special/3962992>; Jay Clark, 'Collingwood Coach Mick Malthouse tells his players they "let down the Anzacs"', *Sunday Herald Sun*, 26 April 2009, <www.theaustralian.com.au/news/we-let-down-the-anzacs-malthouse/story-e6frg6n6-1225704076351>.
3. KS Inglis, *Sacred Places: War Memorials in the Australian Landscape*, 3rd edn, Melbourne University Press, 2008 [1998] is the definitive account of war memorials in Australia. Michael McKernan has written a history of the Australian War Memorial: *Here Is Their Spirit: A History of the Australian War Memorial, 1917–1990*, University of Queensland Press, Brisbane, 1991. Bruce Scates has published a history of Melbourne's Shrine of Remembrance, *A Place to Remember: A History of the Shrine of Remembrance*, Cambridge University Press, 2009. Scates is the principal researcher in a collaborative team that is writing a comprehensive history of Anzac Day; see <arts.monash.edu.au/anzac-remembered/>. For another perspective on Anzac Day, see Jenny Macleod, 'The Fall and Rise of Anzac Day: 1965 and 1990 Compared', *War and Society*, vol. 20, no. 1, 2002, pp. 149–68. For a history of Anzac Day in South Australia, see Janice Pavils, *Anzac Day: The Undying Debt*, Lythrum Press, Adelaide, 2007. For the history of the RSL, see GL Kristianson, *The Politics of Patriotism: The Pressure Group Activities of the Returned Servicemen's League*, ANU Press, Canberra, 1966; also Martin Crotty, 'The Anzac Citizen: Towards a History of the RSL', *Australian Journal of Politics and History*, vol. 53, no. 2, 2007, pp. 183–93.

## 1   Before 1914: Nationalism and war

1. See Mark McKenna, 'The History Anxiety', in Alison Bashford and Stuart Macintyre (eds), *The Cambridge History of Australia*, vol. 2, Cambridge University Press, 2013, pp. 561–80; Gérard Bouchard, *The Making of the Nations and Cultures of the New World: An Essay in Comparative History*, McGill-Queen's University Press, Montreal and Kingston, ON, 2008, pp. 19–20; Stefan Berger, 'Introduction: Towards a Global History of National Historiographies', in Stefan Berger (ed.), *Writing the Nation: A Global Perspective*, Palgrave Macmillan, Basingstoke, Hants, 2007, pp. 5–6.
2. *Bulletin*, 18 August 1883, cited in KS Inglis, *The Rehearsal: Australians at War in the Sudan, 1885*, Rigby, Sydney, 1985, p. 66.
3. Charles Pearson, *Reviews and Critical Essays*, Methuen, London, 1896, p. 216.
4. *Royal Readers*, no. VI, Thomas Nelson and Sons, London, 1894, p. 195.
5. George Essex Evans, 'Ode for Commonwealth Day', quoted in Deryck Schreuder and Stuart Ward (eds), *Australia's Empire*, Oxford University Press, 2008, p. 154.
6. AG Hales, 'Australia's Appeal to England', *Campaign Pictures of the War in South*

*Africa (1899–1900)*, Cassell and Company, London, 1900, p. x.

7    Henry Lawson, 'The Star of Australasia', *In the Days When the World was Wide and Other Verses*, Angus & Robertson, Sydney, 1900.

8    Melbourne *Argus*, 27 August 1898, p. 11.

9    Graham Dawson, *Soldier Heroes: British Adventure, Empire and the Imagining of Masculinities*, Routledge, London, 1994, p. 233.

10   Joseph Bristow, *Empire Boys: Adventures in a Man's World*, HarperCollins Academic, London, 1991, p. 41.

11   Philip Warner, *The Best of British Pluck: The Boy's Own Paper*, Macdonald and Jane's, London, 1976, p. 140.

12   Supplement to the *Victorian Education Gazette and Teacher's Aid*, October 1901.

13   *Argus*, 5 June 1896, p. 6.

14   WH Fitchett, *Deeds that Won the Empire: Historic Battle Scenes*, Melbourne, 1897, Preface.

15   Craig Wilcox, *Red Coat Dreaming: How Colonial Australia Embraced the British Army*, Cambridge University Press, 2009, p. 118.

16   Ailsa Thomson Zainu'ddin, *They Dreamt of a School: A Centenary History of Methodist Ladies' College, Kew: 1882–1982*, Hyland House, Melbourne, 1982, p. 92; Wilcox, *Red Coat Dreaming*, p. 119.

17   LM Field, *The Forgotten War: Australian Involvement in the South African Conflict of 1899–1902*, Melbourne University Press,1979, p.1.

18   *Sydney Morning Herald*, 2, 18 January 1901 and Sydney *Daily Telegraph*, 2 January 1901, quoted in Neville Meaney, *A History of Australian Defence and Foreign Policy, 1901–1923: The Search for Security*, 2nd edn, Sydney University Press, 2009 [1976], p. 41.

19   'Two Ideals of Empire', *Daily Telegraph*, 11 November 1899, quoted in RM Crawford, *'A Bit of a Rebel': The Life and Work of George Arnold Wood*, Sydney University Press, 1975, p. 155; Arnold Wood, 'The War in the Transvaal', *Daily Telegraph*, 10 October 1899, quoted at *ibid.*, p. 154.

20   *Victorian Parliamentary Debates*, vol. 92, pp. 1765, 1773–4, quoted in John Rickard, *HB Higgins: The Rebel as Judge*, George Allen & Unwin, Sydney, 1984, p. 109; Higgins' speech to Victorian Legislative Assembly, 10 October 1899, quoted in *Argus*, 12 February 1900, p. 5.

21   Higgins' speech to Victorian Legislative Assembly, 10 October 1899; Hales, *Campaign Pictures of the War in South Africa*, p. 55; James Green, *The Story of the Australian Bushmen (Being Notes of a Chaplain)*, William Brooks, Sydney, 1903, p. 1.

22   Craig Wilcox, 'Boer War, Second', in Peter Dennis, Jeffrey Grey, Ewan Morris and Robin Prior (eds), *The Oxford Companion to Australian Military History*, 2nd edn, Oxford University Press, Melbourne, 2008 [1995], p. 94.

23   *Bulletin*, 10 February 1900, quoted in CN Connolly, 'Class, Birthplace, Loyalty: Australian Attitudes to the Boer War', *Historical Studies*, vol. 18, no. 71, October 1978, p. 221; *Geelong Advertiser*, 20 October 1900, quoted in Rickard, *HB Higgins*, p. 119.

24   Green, *The Story of the Australian Bushmen*, p. 3.

25   Thomson Zainu'ddin, *They Dreamt of a School*, p. 107.

26   *Daily Telegraph*, 10 December 1901, p. 8, quoted in Craig Wilcox, *Australia's Boer War: The War in South Africa, 1899–1902*, Oxford University Press, Melbourne, 2002, p. 315; *Review of Reviews for Australasia*, 20 February 1902, pp. 120, 121.

27   Edmund Barton to University of Sydney Chancellor Sir Normand MacLaurin, 2 May 1902, University of Sydney Archives, quoted in Geoffrey Bolton, *Edmund*

*Barton*, Allen & Unwin, Sydney, 2000, pp. 264–5; JHM Abbott, *Tommy Cornstalk: Being Some Account of the Less Notable Features of the South African War From the Point of View of the Australian Ranks*, Longmans, Green, London, 1902, p. 140; Australia's casualties were split almost evenly between military action and disease, see Field, *The Forgotten War*, p. 185.

28 AJN Tremearne, *Some Austral-African Notes and Anecdotes*, John Bale, Sons and Danielson, London, 1913, p. 1; Abbott, *Tommy Cornstalk*, p. 66; JHM Abbott, 'The Silver Trumpet', in *Some Stories by Ten Famous Australian Writers*, New Century, Sydney, 1940, p. 34, quoted in Wilcox, *Red Coat Dreaming*, p. 34; Tasmanian officer quoted in Field, *The Forgotten War*, p. v.

29 Adelaide *Advertiser*, 3 March 1902, p. 6; *Review of Reviews*, 20 January 1903, p. 43.

30 For example: *Argus*, 12 February 1901, p. 5 and *Advertiser*, 21 October 1901, p. 4.

31 NAA B168 1901/3859, quoted in Wilcox, *Australia's Boer War*, p. 208; Wilcox, 'Boer War, Second', p. 96; Wilcox, *Australia's Boer War*, p. 315.

32 *Review of Reviews*, 20 April 1902, p. 338; *Westralian Worker*, 11 April 1902, quoted in Bobbie Oliver, 'A Wanton Deed of Blood and Rapine': Opposition to Australian Participation in the Boer War', Peter Dennis and Jeffrey Grey (eds), *The Boer War: Army, Nation and Empire*, Army History Unit, Department of Defence, Canberra, 2000, p. 198; F[rank]. R[enar i.e. Frank Fox]., 'Beatification of The Breaker (with some literary remains)', *Bulletin*, 12 April 1902, Red Page. I thank Craig Wilcox for providing this reference.

33 Adelaide *Register*, 6 June 1904, quoted in KS Inglis, *Sacred Places: War Memorials in the Australian Landscape*, 3rd edn, Melbourne University Press, 2008 [1998], p. 59

34 *Advertiser*, 2 February 1903, p. 6; Frank Crowley (ed.), *A New History of Australia*, William Heinemann, Melbourne, 1974, p. 271, cited in Richard White, *Inventing Australia: Images and Identity, 1688–1980*, George Allen and Unwin, Sydney, 1981, p. 73; Inglis, *Sacred Places*, p. 54; CEW Bean, *Anzac to Amiens: A Shorter History of the Australian Fighting Services in the First World War*, 1946, Australian War Memorial (AWM), Canberra, p. 9; Abbott, *Tommy Cornstalk*, p. 67.

35 *Review of Reviews*, 20 January 1903, p. 43; letter from Frank Wilkinson to Robert Collins, Secretary for Defence, 7 August 1901; minute from Robert Collins to Minister for Defence, 6 August 1901; handwritten comment by Acting Minister for Defence, Prime Minister Edmund Barton, on minute from Collins to Minister for Defence, 6 August 1901, NAA B168 B168/0, 1902/2399.

36 Minute from Edward Hutton to Secretary of Defence, 21 July 1902; letter from Edward Hutton to Alfred Deakin, 31 December 1903, NAA B168 B168/0, 1902/2399.

37 Letter from Lord Tennyson to Prime Minister Deakin, 7 December 1903; letter from Prime Minister Deakin, 8 December 1903, NAA B168 B168/0, 1902/2399.

38 Melbourne *Age*, 15 September 1903, pasted into Commonwealth Government's file on 'History of South African War', NAA B168 B168/0, 1902/2399.

39 Wilcox's *Australia's Boer War* is the official history of Australian involvement in the Boer War. It was published in 2002; Inglis, *Sacred Places*, p. 47; Jenny Macleod, *Reconsidering Gallipoli*, Manchester University Press, 2004, p. 56.

40 Inglis, *Sacred Places*, p. 65.

41 *Argus*, 29 September 1913.

42 *Argus*, 4 June 1940, p. 4; 'Order of Dedication Service of the New South Wales South African Soldiers' War Memorial', 2 June 1940, <www.warmemorialsnsw.asn.au/pdf/RocksMemorial.pdf>.

43 Newspapers carried rose-coloured reports of 'very creditable' numbers of troops

participating in a march through the streets of Sydney and then travelling by
ferry to Clontarf for a picnic, followed by patriotic speeches by politicians,
*Advertiser*, 3 March 1902, p. 5. In truth, the march was poorly attended, speakers
at Clontarf were heckled by soldiers angry about money they believed they were
owed, and men complained about having to pay for their modest picnic lunches,
while official guests were served pastries and wine in a grand tent, Wilcox,
*Australia's Boer War*, pp. 332–3.

44  Abbott, *Tommy Cornstalk*, pp. 3, 5, 10, 11, 12, 213.
45  Handcock confessed to Witton that he had killed Daniel Heese, though he and
    Morant were acquitted of the missionary's murder at court martial, and Witton
    failed to mention the confession in his book. The news of Handcock's confession
    was contained in a letter from Witton to the men's lawyer JF Thomas and had
    been lodged at the Mitchell Library in 1929 with the stipulation that it not be
    released until 1970. RL Wallace uncovered the shocking letter while writing *The
    Australians at the Boer War*, Australian Government Publishing Service, Canberra,
    1976, see p. viii; Wilcox, *Australia's Boer War*, p. 358.
46  Alfred Buchanan, *The Real Australia*, T Fisher Unwin, London, 1907, p. 308.
47  Hales, *Campaign Pictures of the War in South Africa*, p. 291.

## 2  1916–1936: Early histories of the Great War

1   Melbourne *Argus*, 24 July 1894, p. 5. For more information on Ernest Scott, see
    the biography by Stuart Macintyre, *A History for a Nation: Ernest Scott and the Making
    of Australian History*, Melbourne University Press, 1994.
2   Ernest Scott, 'Australian Nationalism', lecture to University of Melbourne
    Historical Society, 26 September 1917, Scott Papers, NLA MS 703 Series 7–9.
3   *Round Table Studies*, no publisher, London, unspecified date [1914], pp. 333, 375,
    quoted in Macintyre, *A History for a Nation*, pp. 32–3.
4   *Terre Napoléon: A History of French Explorations and Projects in Australia*, Methuen,
    London, 1910; *Lapérouse*, Angus & Robertson, Sydney, 1912; *The Life of Matthew
    Flinders*, Angus & Robertson, Sydney, 1914.
5   Macintyre, *A History for a Nation*, p. 75.
6   Ernest Scott, *A Short History of Australia*, Oxford University Press, London, 1916,
    p. v.
7   Ibid., p. 336.
8   Ibid. In saying that Australians seized 'every one' of the German possessions,
    Scott ignored the role of the Japanese in seizing Nauru, the Caroline Islands and
    Ladrone (Mariana) Islands. The error was picked up by a reviewer in the *Sydney
    Morning Herald*, 10 March 1917, p. 8, but still stood in the final 1947 edition of
    the book.
9   Ibid.
10  Lecture by Ernest Scott, undated [post-1918], 'The Making of Australia', Scott
    Papers, NLA MS 703 Series 7–9; Scott, *A Short History of Australia*, 2nd edn, 1918,
    p. 336.
11  For example, *Argus*, 9 February 1917, p. 5.
12  *Sydney Morning Herald*, 10 March 1917, p. 8.
13  Careless editing meant that 'Anzacs' remained in the headnotes for the last
    chapter on 'Imperial Relations', despite the fact that the subject had been moved
    to the new chapter on 'Australia in the Great War'.
14  Scott's bibliography praised what he cited incorrectly as Charles Bean's '*Official
    History of Australia in the Great War*'. He described the *History* as consisting of

twelve volumes, without the qualification that only five had been published to date.

15  Scott, *A Short History of Australia*, 5th edn, pp. 348–51; John Masefield, *Gallipoli*, new edn, Rigby, Adelaide, 1978 [1916], p. 19.

16  Scott had married for a second time in 1915. His wife Emily was the sister of the economist and progressive businessman Edward Dyason.

17  John Monash, *The Australian Victories in France in 1918*, Hutchinson, London, 1920, p. 290.

18  Scott, 'Australian Nationalism'.

19  Scott, *A Short History of Australia*, 5th edn, p. 354. 'Rancid' had been changed to 'rancorous' in the 1947 edition, revised by Herbert Burton and published following Scott's death.

20  Dudley McCarthy, *Gallipoli to the Somme: The Story of CEW Bean*, John Ferguson, Sydney, 1983, pp. 299, 309.

21  KS Inglis, *CEW Bean: Australian Historian*, University of Queensland Press, Brisbane, 1970, p. 6; AW Bazley, 'Obituary, CEW Bean', *Historical Studies*, vol. 14, no. 53, 1969, p. 147; quoted (unattributed) in McCarthy, *Gallipoli to the Somme*, p. 31.

22  Scott, 'Australian Nationalism'; Bean, *Sydney Morning Herald*, 22 June 1907, p. 6; *Sydney Morning Herald*, 6 July 1907, p. 7.

23  CEW Bean, *On the Wool Track*, new edn, Sirius Books, Sydney, 1963 [1910], p. vii; CEW Bean, *The Dreadnought of the Darling*, new edn, Angus & Robertson, Sydney, 1956 [1911], pp. 216–18, 221, 223.

24  CEW Bean, *Flagships Three*, Alston Rivers, London, 1913, p. 261.

25  Bean to Lucy and Edwin Bean, 16 December 1918, AWM 3DRL 7447/7; Bean wrote: vol. I, *The Story of Anzac: From the Outbreak of War to the End of the First Phase of the Gallipoli Campaign*, 1921, vol. II, *The Story of Anzac: From 4 May 1915 to the Evacuation of the Gallipoli Peninsula*, 1924, vol. III, *The Australian Imperial Force in France, 1916*, 1929, vol. IV, *The Australian Imperial Force in France, 1917*, 1933, vol. V, *The Australian Imperial Force in France During the Main German Offensive*, vol. VI, *The Australian Imperial Force in France During the Allied Offensive*, 1942. Bean edited: HS Gullett, vol. VII, *The Australian Imperial Force in Sinai and Palestine, 1914–1918*, 1923; FM Cutlack, vol. VIII, *The Australian Flying Corps in the Western and Eastern Theatres of War, 1914–1918*, 1923; Arthur W Jose, vol. IX, *The Royal Australian Navy, 1914–1918*, 1928; SS McKenzie, vol. X, *The Australians at Rabaul: The Capture and Administration of the German Possessions in the Southern Pacific*, 1927; Ernest Scott, vol. XI, *Australia During the War*, 1936. Gullett and Bean produced vol. XII, *A Photographic Record of the War*, 1923.

26  *Sydney Morning Herald*, 27 August 1934, p. 9; Bean quoted (unattributed) in McCarthy, *Gallipoli to the Somme*, p. 104; Bean to Capt. R Muirhead Collins, 12 May 1916, Bean Papers, AWM38 3DRL 6673, item 271, quoted in Jenny Macleod, *Reconsidering Gallipoli*, Manchester University Press, 2004, p. 68; Bean, *Anzac to Amiens*, new edn, AWM, Canberra, 1983 [1946], p. viii.

27  Address by CEW Bean on 29 October 1930 to New South Wales Institute of Journalists, quoted in *Reveille: Official Journal of the Returned Sailors' and Soldiers' Imperial League of Australia (New South Wales Branch)*, 29 November 1930, p. 15; Bean, *The Australian Imperial Force in France During the Allied Offensive*, p. 1095.

28  LL Robson, 'The Origin and Character of the First AIF, 1914–1918: Some Statistical Evidence', *Historical Studies*, vol. 15, no. 61, 1973, p. 745. John Barrett suggested that Bean's position was unfairly represented by Robson and that Bean prioritised democracy over rural origins as the explanation for the soldiers' skill:

'No Straw Man: CEW Bean and Some Critics', *Australian Historical Studies*, vol. 23, no. 90, 1988, pp. 102–14; DA Kent, '*The Anzac Book* and the Anzac Legend: CEW Bean as Editor and Image-Maker', *Historical Studies*, vol. 21, no. 84, 1985, pp. 376–90; Alistair Thomson, *Stragglers or Shirkers: An Anzac Imperial Controversy*, University of London, 1991.

29   Thomson, *Stragglers or Shirkers*, p. 1.

30   Bean's Diary, undated, quoted in McCarthy, *Gallipoli to the Somme*, p. 276.

31   Bean Papers, undated, quoted in McCarthy, *Gallipoli to the Somme*, pp. 244, 248, 290; Masefield, *Gallipoli*, p. 19; quote unattributed, McCarthy, *Gallipoli to the Somme*, p. 290.

32   Bean, *The Story of Anzac*, p xviii.

33   See, for example, LL Robson, *The First AIF: A Study of its Recruitment, 1914–1918*, Melbourne University Press, 1970, p. 203. For more information on the reasons that eligible men did not enlist, see Bart Ziino, 'Enlistment and non-Enlistment in Wartime Australia: Response to the 1916 Call to Arms', *Australian Historical Studies*, vol. 41, no. 2, 2010, pp. 217–32.

34   Michael McKernan, 'Introduction' to Ernest Scott, *Australia During the War*, new edn, University of Queensland Press, 1989 [1936]; CEW Bean to JM Fowler, MHR, 14 November 1921, Bean Papers, AWM 3 DRL 7953, item 15; cited in McKernan, 'Introduction', *Australia During the War*, p. xxix; Bean to H Kneebone, 20 December 1921, AWM 3DRL 7953/15 Part 1, McKernan, 'Introduction', *Australia During the War*, p. xxx; letter from Bean to Heney, 11 June 1925, AWM 3DRL 7953/15 Part 1.

35   Bean to Secretary, Department of Defence, 25 July 1925, AWM 3DRL 7953/15 Part 1; White to Bean, 21 July 1927, AWM 3DRL 7953/15 Part 2; Bean to Newman (Secretary, Department of Defence), 25 July 1925 and Newman to Bean, 4 August 1925; AWM 3DRL 7953/15 Part 1; Bean to Archibald Strong, 6 October 1925, AWM 3DRL 7953/15 Part 2; Archibald Strong to Bean, 23 April 1926, AWM 3DRL 7953/15 Part 2.

36   Scott to Bean, 24 February 1928, AWM 3DRL 7953/16.

37   Bean to Scott, 9 November 1928, AWM 3DRL 7953/16.

38   Bean to Garran, 10 April 1934, AWM 3DRL 7953/16 Part 2; Bean to Scott, 13 April 1934, AWM 3DRL 7953/16 Part 2; Scott to Bean, 15 May 1933, AWM 3DRL 7953/16.

39   Bean to Scott, 31 January 1934, AWM 3DRL 7953/16 Part 2; Scott to Bean, 2 May 1933, AWM 3DRL 7953/16; Bean to Scott, 13 April 1934, AWM 3DRL 7953/16 Part 2.

40   Manning Clark, *The Quest for Grace*, Penguin, Melbourne, 1990, p. 4; Scott to Bean, 8 May 1934, AWM 3DRL 7953/16 Part 3; Scott to Lady Novar, 2 June 1934, noted in Macintyre, *A History for a Nation*, p. 170. See *Australia During the War*, p. 347, for Scott's use of the information; Scott to Bean, undated [1934], AWM 3DRL 6673 Item 202; Scott to Major John Treloar, Director of AWM, undated [1934], AWM 3DRL 6673 Item 771.

41   Scott, *Australia During the War*, 1936, pp. 19–20.

42   Bean to Scott, 16 July 1936, AWM 3DRL 7953/17 Part 2. Bean wrote that he was thinking of making a general editor's note that the papers of Lord Novar (Sir Ronald Munro-Ferguson) could not be checked.

43   Scott, *Australia During the War*, 1936, pp. 862, 864.

44   *Argus*, 2 January 1937, p. 14; *The Times Literary Supplement* (London), 29 September 1937.

45  Scott, 'Australian Nationalism'.
46  Charles Bean to Lucy and Edwin Bean, 12 January 1919, Bean Papers, AWM 3 DRL 7447/7.
47  Scott, 'Australian Nationalism'.
48  Scott to Bean, 12 November 1936, AWM 3DRL 7953/17 Part 2.
49  McCarthy, Gallipoli to the Somme, p. 390.
50  CEW Bean, War Aims of a Plain Australian, Angus & Robertson, Sydney, 1943, p. 159.

## 3    1920s–1930s: The Great War in Australian literature

1  Sydney Morning Herald, 13 August 1937, p. 6; Sydney Morning Herald, 16 August 1937, p. 4.
2  Hobart Mercury, 17 March 1925, p. 4; Mercury, 30 April 1929, p. 14.
3  Protection of Word 'Anzac' Regulations, <www.dva.gov.au/commems_oawg/commemorations/protection_of_Anzac/Pages/index.aspx>.
4  JT Laird, Other Banners: An Anthology of Australian Literature of the First World War, AWM and Australian Government Publishing Service, Canberra, 1971, p. 2; JD Burns, For England!, in Laird (ed.), Other Banners, p. 10; Harley Matthews, Saints and Soldiers, WF Floesell, Sydney, 1918; R Hugh Knyvett, Over There with the Australians, Hodder and Staughton, London, 1918. By 1932 there were 21 completed unit histories of infantry battalions and 10 incomplete histories; Reveille, 1 June 1932, p. 15.
5  Sydney Morning Herald, 4 February 1931, p. 12; Alistair Thomson, 'The Return of a Soldier', Meanjin, vol. 47, no. 4, 1988, p. 711; Melbourne Argus, 11 October 1930. The author of Australia had his own reasons for wishing to forget the war; he had been prevented from enlisting by his parents who had already sent two sons overseas, one of whom had been killed on the Somme. Hancock was haunted by nightmares about his dead brother 'in which he came back to us mutilated and mad', and admitted to a lasting sense of failure about not having fought: 'I used sometimes to find myself lying about my age – giving out that I was thirty instead of thirty-two, for fear that people would work the sum backwards to 1918 and ask me: "I suppose you were in France?"', WK Hancock, Country and Calling, Faber and Faber, London, 1954, p. 65.
6  The 'late unmentionable war' was a phrase coined by Sir Philip Gibbs, an official British war correspondent. Gibbs later renounced his embellished war reporting; Stuart Macintyre, A Concise History of Australia, 3rd edn, Cambridge University Press, 2009 [1999], p. 169.
7  Jeffrey Grey, A Military History of Australia, 3rd edn, Cambridge University Press, 2008 [1990], pp. 128–9, 136, 294.
8  Argus, 15 December 1924, p. 21.
9  Rosa Maria Bracco, Merchants of Hope: British Middlebrow Writers and the First World War, 1919–1939, Berg, Providence, 1993, pp. 147–8, 155.
10  New York Times, 22 September 1929, p. 7, quoted in Harley U Taylor Jnr, Erich Maria Remarque: A Literary and Film Biography, Peter Lang, New York, 1989, pp. 62, 63; All About Books, vol. 1, no. 10, 20 September 1929, p. 313.
11  Sydney Morning Herald, 12 April 1930, p. 14.
12  Sydney Morning Herald, 5 February 1930, p. 14; All About Books, vol. 2, no. 2, 24 February, 1930, p. 38. For a history of All About Books, see David Carter, '"Some Means of Learning of the Best New Books": All About Books and the Modern Reader', Australian Literary Studies, vol. 22, no. 3, 2006, pp. 329–41.

13   *All About Books*, vol. 2, no. 4, 19 April 1930, p. 100.

14   *Queenslander*, 31 October 1929, p. 64; *All About Books*, vol. 2, no. 4, 19 April 1930,
      p. 100.

15   *Sydney Morning Herald*, 16 January 1930, p. 8; Brisbane *Courier*, 16 January 1930,
      p. 10; Adelaide *Advertiser*, 16 January 1930, p. 19; Peter Coleman, *Obscenity,
      Blasphemy and Sedition: Censorship in Australia*, Jacaranda Press, Brisbane, 1962,
      p. 38.

16   Coleman, *Obscenity, Blasphemy and Sedition*, p. 38. The Commonwealth's stance had
      hardened by 1931, when Ernest Hemingway's war novel, *A Farewell to Arms*, was
      deemed obscene and added to the growing list of banned books.

17   *Sydney Morning Herald*, 24 July 1930, p. 10; *All About Books*, vol. 1, no. 8, 18 July
      1929, p. 313; Humphrey McQueen, '"Emu into Ostrich": Australian Literary
      Responses to the Great War', *Meanjin*, vol. 35, no. 1, April 1976, p. 84.

18   *Courier*, 29 July 1930, p. 19.

19   *Argus*, 19 February 1930, p. 12; *Argus*, 28 March 1930, p. 23; *Argus*, 21 April
      1930, p. 4; *Mercury*, 21 April 1930, p. 10.

20   *Argus*, 19 February 1930, p. 12; *Canberra Times*, 22 March 1930, p. 4.

21   *Argus*, 8 May 1930, p. 11; *Canberra Times*, 22 March 1930, p. 4.

22   *Sydney Morning Herald*, 14 May 1930, p. 14.

23   *Sydney Morning Herald*, 14 February 1930, p. 12.

24   Ibid.; 14 February 1930, p. 12; *Sydney Morning Herald*, 17 February 1930, p. 5.

25   *Courier*, 4 February 1930, p. 13; *Sydney Morning Herald*, 4 February 1930, p. 11;
      *Sydney Morning Herald*, 22 March 1930, p. 13.

26   Martyn Lyons and Lucy Taksa, *Australian Readers Remember: An Oral History of
      Reading, 1890–1930*, Oxford University Press, Melbourne, 1992, pp. xvii, 67.

27   Miles Franklin to Nettie Palmer, quoted in Geoffrey Dutton (ed.), *The Literature
      of Australia*, Penguin, Melbourne, 1964, p. 184. For more information about the
      middlebrow literary culture and literary transnationalism during this period,
      see David Carter, 'Modernity and the Gendering of Middlebrow Book Culture
      in Australia', in Kate Macdonald (ed.), *The Masculine Middlebrow, 1880–1950*,
      Palgrave Macmillan, Basingstoke, Hants, 2011, pp. 135–49.

28   Nettie Palmer, *Fourteen Years: Extracts from a Private Journal, 1925–1939*, Meanjin
      Press, Melbourne, 1948, p. 25, quoted in John Barnes, 'The Man of Letters',
      *Meanjin*, vol. 18, no. 2, July 1959, p. 196; *Argus*, 9 March 1935, p. 11.

29   *All About Books*, vol. 3, no. 10, 13 October 1931, p. 194.

30   *Queenslander*, 5 May 1932, p. 44; *Courier*, 23 April 1932, p. 18; *Reveille*, 1 May
      1932, vol. 5, no. 8, p. 8; *All About Books*, vol. 4, no. 5, 14 May 1932, p. 71.

31   *Reveille*, 1 April 1936, quoted in Robin Gerster, *Big-Noting: The Heroic Theme in
      Australian War Writing*, Melbourne University Press, 1987, p. 33; *Reveille*, 30 June
      1931, vol. 4, no. 10, p. 26; *Courier*, 22 October 1932, p. 20.

32   Joseph Maxwell, *Hell's Bells and Mademoiselles*, Angus & Robertson, Sydney, 1932,
      pp. 16, 80–1, 87.

33   Ibid., pp. 1–2; King Henry V's speech to English soldiers on St Crispen's Day
      before the Battle of Agincourt; William Shakespeare, *Henry V*, Act 4, Scene 3;
      *Canberra Times*, 17 November 1932, p .4.

34   *All About Books*, vol. 6, no. 2, 14 February 1934, p. 27; *Argus*, 26 May 1928, p. 31.

35   HR Williams, *The Gallant Company: An Australian Soldier's Story of 1915–18*, Angus &
      Robertson, Sydney, 1933, pp. 90, 93, 105–106.

36   HR Williams, *Comrades of the Great Adventure*, Angus & Robertson, Sydney, 1935,
      pp. 305–306.

37 Extract from *The Times Literary Supplement*, reprinted in Williams, *Comrades of the Great Adventure; Sydney Morning Herald*, 23 March 1935, p. 11.

38 Nettie Palmer to FD Davison, 31 October 1933, NLA MS 1945, quoted in McQueen, '"Emu into Ostrich"', p. 84.

39 Leonard Mann, *Flesh in Armour*, Phaedrus, Melbourne, 1932.

40 Vivian Smith (ed.), *Letters of Vance and Nettie Palmer: 1915–1963*, NLA, Canberra, 1977, p. 192; *Argus*, 9 March 1935, p. 11; *Bulletin*, Review of *Flesh in Armour*, 2 November 1932, p. 5; *Camperdown Chronicle*, 16 December 1933, p. 3.

41 *All About Books*, vol. 4, no. 4, 13 April 1933, p. 50.

42 Ibid., p. 51.

43 Palmer, *Fourteen Years*, p. 126; Reader's report, 15 October 1933, MLMSS 3269/246 vol. 453, item 9, cited in Christina Spittel, 'A Portable Monument?: Leonard Mann's *Flesh in Armour* and Australia's Memory of the First World War', *Book History*, vol. 14, 2011, p. 199; *Mercury*, 27 January 1933, p. 3.

44 George Maxted, AWM, Melbourne, to John Treloar, AWM, Canberra, 4 October 1937, AWM 93 21/1/69, 'Proposal to Sell War Novels', cited in Spittel, 'A Portable Monument?', p. 199.

45 JP McKinney, *Crucible*, Angus & Robertson, Sydney, 1935, pp. 123, 132, 241–2; *Reveille*, vol. 8, no. 12, 1 August 1935, p. 29.

46 *All About Books*, vol. 6, no. 6, 12 June 1934, p. 115; Edgar Morrow, *Iron in the Fire*, Angus & Robertson, Sydney, 1934, pp. 267, 268.

47 Williams, *The Gallant Company*, p. v; Morrow, *Iron in the Fire*, p. vii.

48 Harry Heseltine, 'Australian Fiction since 1920', in Dutton (ed.), *The Literature of Australia*, p. 183.

49 AG Butler, *Official History of the Australian Army Medical Services in the War of 1914–1918*, vol. III, *Special Problems and Services*, AWM, Canberra, 1943, p. 142, quoted in Marina Larsson, *Shattered Anzacs: Living with the Scars of War*, UNSW Press, Sydney, 2009, p. 151. For terms describing traumatised soldiers, see Larsson, *Shattered Anzacs*, p. 152. For a discussion of the stigma of psychological illness, see ibid., pp. 157–61; *Western Argus*, 19 December 1933, p. 27.

50 Ric Throssell, 'Introduction', Katharine Susannah Prichard, *Intimate Strangers*, new edn, Angus & Robertson, Sydney, 1990, [1937], p. vi; Prichard, *Intimate Strangers*, p. 10; *West Australian*, 14 March 1934, p. 3.

51 Harry Heseltine, *Vance Palmer*, University of Queensland Press, Brisbane, 1970, p. 43; HM Green quoted in David Holloway (ed.), *'Dark Somme Flowing': Australian Verse of the Great War, 1914–1918*, Robert Andersen, Melbourne, 1975, p. 110.

52 Palmer expressed his preference in an interview in the *Queensland Times*, 11 September 1958, quoted in Heseltine, *Vance Palmer*, p. 94; Vance Palmer, *Daybreak*, Stanley Paul, London, 1932, pp. 10, 14, 287.

53 Gerster, *Big-Noting*, pp. ix, 132.

54 See for instance, Christina Spittel, 'Remembering the War: Australian Novelists of the Inter-War Years', *Australian Literary Studies*, vol. 23, no. 2, 2007, pp. 121–39 and 'A Portable Monument?'; Clare Rhoden, 'What's Missing in this Picture? The *"Middle Parts of Fortune"* in Australian War Literature', *Philament: Borders, Regions, Worlds*, no. 16, August 2010, pp. 21–33; Claire Woods, 'There and Back: Two Soldiers Shape their Experience of World War I', in Nigel Starck (ed.), *Legacies of War*, Australian Scholarly Publishing, Melbourne, 2013, pp. 141–62. The argument of Gerster (and others before and after him, such as David Walker and John F Williams) that Australians were resistant to modernism has also been challenged by scholars who have shown that modernist ideas appeared in various

cultural forms both during and before the 1930s, for example, Robert Dixon and Veronica Kelly (eds), *Impact of the Modern: Vernacular Modernities in Australia, 1870s–1960s*, Sydney University Press, 2008; Jill Julius Matthews, *Dance Hall and Picture Palace: Sydney's Romance with Modernity*, Currency Press, Sydney, 2005.

55    Alistair Thomson, *Anzac Memories: Living with the Legend*, 2nd edn, Monash University Publishing, Melbourne, 2013 [1994], p. 13.

56    For a discussion of this, see Peter Stanley, *Bad Characters: Sex, Crime, Mutiny, Murder and the Australian Imperial Force*, Pier 9, Sydney, 2010, pp. 96–100. Stanley shows how differences between Australian and British troops regarding physique, discipline and attitudes to soldiering cannot be dismissed as Australian big-noting.

57    Charles Bean to John Treloar, 31 January 1920, Bean Papers, AWM38 3DRL6673/667a, quoted in Spittel, 'Remembering the War', p. 121.

## 4    1940s–1960s: Marxism and memory of the Great War

1    Ian Turner, 'Introduction', in Brian Fitzpatrick, *A Short History of the Australian Labour Movement*, 2nd edn, Macmillan, Melbourne, 1968 [1940], p. 4.

2    Sheila Fitzpatrick, *My Father's Daughter: Memories of an Australian Childhood*, Melbourne University Publishing 2010, p. 13.

3    HV Evatt, 'Preface', in Frances Clancy, *They Built a Nation*, New Century Press, Sydney, 1939, p. vi, quoted in Stuart Macintyre, 'Australia and the Empire', in Robin W Winks and Alaine M Low (eds), *Oxford History of the British Empire: Historiography*, vol. 5, Oxford University Press, 1999, p. 172.

4    Brian Fitzpatrick, *The British Empire in Australia: An Economic History, 1834–1939*, new edn, Macmillan, Melbourne, 1969 [1941], p. 348.

5    Brian Fitzpatrick, *The Australian People: 1788–1945*, new edn, Melbourne University Press, 1951 [1946], p. 237.

6    Geoffrey Blainey, 'Foreword', in Fitzpatrick, *The British Empire in Australia*, p. vii; Ian Turner, 'Australian Nationalism and Australian History', in Stephen Murray-Smith and Leonie Sandercock (eds), *Room for Manoeuvre: Writings on History, Politics, Ideas and Play*, Drummond, Melbourne, 1982, p. 10.

7    For the increase in self-confidence, see, for example, Geoffrey Serle, *From Deserts the Prophets Come: The Creative Spirit in Australia, 1788–1972*, William Heinemann, Melbourne, 1973, p. 177; Russel Ward, *A Radical Life: The Autobiography of Russel Ward*, Macmillan, Melbourne, 1988, p. 147; for the unifying effect of war service, see Janet McCalman, *Journeyings: The Biography of a Middle-Class Generation, 1920–1990*, Melbourne University Press, 1993, p. 178.

8    Ward, *A Radical Life*, pp. 54, 207.

9    Russel Ward, *The Australian Legend*, new edn, Oxford University Press, Melbourne, 1974 [1958], p. 226

10    Ibid., pp. 230, 231, 233.

11    Russel Ward, *A Nation for a Continent: The History of Australia 1901–1975*, rev. edn, Heinemann Education Australia, Melbourne, 1983 [1977], pp. 126–7.

12    Ibid., pp. 104, 127.

13    Stuart Macintyre, *A Concise History of Australia*, 3rd edn, Cambridge University Press, 2009 [1999], p. 131.

14    Turner, 'My Long March', in Murray-Smith and Sandercock (eds), *Room for Manoeuvre*, p. 106. Turner's father Frank cut Ian out of his will.

15    Ibid., pp. 115, 116, 117.

16    Amirah Inglis, *The Hammer & Sickle and the Washing Up: Memories of an Australian Woman Communist*, Hyland House, Melbourne, 1995, p. 16.

17  Turner, 'Australian Nationalism and Australian History', p. 10; Turner, 'Temper Democratic, Bias Australian', in Murray-Smith and Sandercock (eds), *Room for Manoeuvre*, p. 164.
18  Turner, 'My Long March', pp. 122, 131, 132, 143.
19  Ian Turner, *Industrial Labour and Politics: The Dynamics of the Labour Movement in Eastern Australia, 1900–1921*, 2nd edn, Hale & Iremonger, Sydney, 1979 [1965], p. xvii. For a history of the study of labour history in Australia, see Stuart Macintyre, 'Labour History and Radical Nationalism', in Anna Clark and Paul Ashton (eds), *Australian History Now*, NewSouth Publishing, Sydney, 2013, pp. 40–55; Ian Turner, 'Socialist History and the Socialist Historian', in Murray-Smith and Sandercock (eds), *Room for Manoeuvre*, p. 180.
20  Ian Turner (ed.), *The Australian Dream: A Collection of Anticipations about Australia from Captain Cook to the Present Day*, Sun Books, Melbourne, 1968, p. xix. The book is dedicated to Manning Clark 'who taught me and many others that knowledge comes from doubt, and love from understanding'.
21  Turner, 'Australian Nationalism and Australian History', p. 6; Turner, *The Australian Dream*, p. xviii.
22  Ian Turner, '1914–1919', in FK Crowley (ed.), *A New History of Australia*, William Heinemann, Melbourne, 1974, p. 323.
23  See Robert Bollard, *In the Shadow of Gallipoli: The Hidden History of World War I*, NewSouth, Sydney, 2013 and Joan Beaumont, *Broken Nation: Australians in the Great War*, Allen & Unwin, Sydney, 2013 for more information about radical attitudes to the Great War and industrial unrest.
24  Turner, '1914–1919', p. 352.
25  CJ Dennis, *Digger Smith*, Angus & Robertson, Sydney, 1918, p. 105, quoted in Turner, '1914–1919', p. 156.
26  Turner, 'Temper Democratic, Bias Australian', p. 157; Ian Turner, 'The Life of the Legend' in *Room for Manoeuvre*, p. 27
27  KS Inglis, 'The Anzac Tradition', *Meanjin Quarterly*, vol. 24, no. 1, 1965, pp. 34–5, 44.
28  Interview with Ken Inglis, 6 December 2010; Craig Wilcox (ed.), *Observing Australia: 1959–1999, KS Inglis*, Melbourne University Press, 1999, Introduction, p. 5.
29  Serle, *From Deserts the Prophets Come*, p. xii; Geoffrey Serle, 'Austerica Unlimited?', *Meanjin Quarterly*, vol. 26, no. 3, 1967, p. 21, quoted in John Thompson, *The Patrician and the Bloke: Geoffrey Serle and the Making of Australian History*, Pandanus, Canberra, 2006, p. 64.
30  Geoffrey Serle, *Robin Boyd: A Life*, Melbourne University Press, 1995, p. 77; McCalman, *Journeyings*, p. 223.
31  McCalman, *Journeyings*, p. 223; Manning Clark, *The Quest for Grace*, Penguin, Melbourne, 1990, pp. 149, 165; Geoffrey Serle, 'Autobiographical Notes', 1994, privately held, quoted in Thompson, *The Patrician and the Bloke*, p. 17.
32  Geoffrey Serle, 'The Digger Tradition and Australian Nationalism', *Meanjin*, June 1965, pp. 149, 152, 156, 158.
33  Geoffrey Serle, *John Monash: A Biography*, new edn, Melbourne University Publishing, 2002 [1982], p. 524.
34  KS Inglis, *Sacred Places: War Memorials in the Australian Landscape*, new edn, Melbourne University Publishing, 2010 [1998], see Foreword by Jay Winter.
35  Ken Inglis opened his *Meanjin* essay by lamenting conservative historian John Ward's failure to acknowledge Bean's *Official History* in a 1964 survey of Australian historiography, 'The Anzac Tradition', p. 25.

36  See chapter 7.
37  Turner, 'Temper Democratic, Bias Australian', p. 157.
38  Eric Hobsbawm, *The Age of Extremes: The Short Twentieth Century, 1914–1991*, Michael Joseph, London, 1994.
39  Turner, *The Australian Dream*, p. xvii.

## 5  1965–1985: The fall and rise of memory of the Great War

1  Melbourne *Argus*, 28 March 1953, p. 3.
2  *Argus*, 14 April 1953, p. 3.
3  Launceston *Examiner*, 6 May 1950, p. 24; *Argus*, 23 April 1954, p. 7; *Argus*, 26 April 1954, p. 6.
4  Rockhampton *Morning Bulletin*, 2 January 1951, p. 4; AP Rowe, Anzac Day Address, 25 April 1957, cited in Melbourne *Age*, 25 April 2003.
5  Alan Seymour, *The One Day of the Year*, in *Three Australian Plays*, Penguin, Melbourne, 1994, pp. 79, 80, 86.
6  KS Inglis, *This is the ABC: The Australian Broadcasting Commission, 1932–1983*, Melbourne University Publishing, 1983, pp. 220, 221; GL Kristianson, 'The RSL and *Four Corners*', *Australian Quarterly*, vol. 36, no. 1, 1964, p. 22.
7  Letter to the editor, *Australian Women's Weekly*, 21 May 1969, p. 125.
8  Women Working Together Towards Suffrage and Onwards, <home.vicnet.net.au/~women/14.%20Working%20Collectively.html>.
9  Anne Blair, *Ruxton: A Biography*, Allen & Unwin, Sydney, 2004, pp. 130–1; Bruce Scates, *A Place to Remember: A History of the Shrine of Remembrance*, Cambridge University Press, 2009, p. 244.
10  James Curran and Stuart Ward make the argument about the relationship between the withdrawal of Britain and the rise of the New Nationalism in *The Unknown Nation: Australia After Empire*, Melbourne University Publishing, 2010; 'National identity' is a term derived from Erik Erikson's theory of human social development, which carries with it the implication that nations, like humans, pass through infancy, childhood and adolescence before attaining independent adulthood.
11  Harold Holt quoted in James Curran, 'The "Thin Dividing Line": Prime Ministers and the Problem of Australian Nationalism, 1972–1996', *Australian Journal of Politics and History*, vol. 48, no. 4, 2002, p. 474; Donald Horne, 'Republican Australia', quoted in Curran and Ward, *The Unknown Nation*, p. 112.
12  John Gorton cited in *Bulletin*, 5 October 1968, quoted in Curran and Ward, *The Unknown Nation*, p. 6: Donald Horne applied the term 'New Nationalism' to Gorton's rhetorical style.
13  Stuart Ward, '"Culture up to our Arseholes": Projecting Post-Imperial Australia', *Australian Journal of Politics and History*, vol. 51, no. 1, 2005, p. 65.
14  Mark McKenna, *An Eye for Eternity: The Life of Manning Clark*, Miegunyah Press, Melbourne University Publishing, 2011, p. 397; Curran and Ward, *The Unknown Nation*, p. 115; *Argus*, 9 March 1935, p. 11; Sidney Nolan, 'Q & A', *The Studio*, London, October 1960, p. 30, quoted in Damian Smith, 'Nolan Through Kelly', Heide, MOMA, 2006, <www.wordsforart.com.au/Images/PDF/NOLAN%20THROUGH%20KELLY.pdf>; Patrick White, 'The Prodigal Son', *Macquarie Pen Anthology of Australian Literature*, Allen & Unwin, Sydney, 2009, pp. 557–60, quoted in McKenna, *An Eye for Eternity*, p. 370.
15  Whitlam cited in *Australian*, 6 December 1972; Whitlam, 'Relations with the United Kingdom', cablegram, Canberra, 18 December 1972, NAA A1838 67/1/3

Part 7, both quoted in Curran and Ward, *The Unknown Nation*, p. 135; Gough Whitlam, *Australian*, 20 November 1972, p. 1, quoted in Anne Pender, 'The Mythical Australian: Barry Humphries, Gough Whitlam and "New Nationalism"', *Australian Journal of Politics and History*, vol. 51, no. 1, 2005, p. 69.

16  Gough Whitlam, 'National Anthem', Australia Day Broadcast, 26 January 1973, cited in Curran and Ward, *The Unknown Nation*, p. 165.

17  Pender, 'The Mythical Australian', p. 70; Curran and Ward, *The Unknown Nation*, pp. 168, 176; *Age*, 21 January 1976; cited in ibid. The national anthem was changed to 'Advance Australia Fair' for all occasions by the Hawke Labor government in 1984.

18  Brisbane *Courier-Mail*, 26 April 1973, quoted in Curran and Ward, *The Unknown Nation*, p. 198; *Sydney Morning Herald*, 26 April 1976, quoted in ibid., p. 198.

19  Adrian Howe, 'Anzac Mythology and the Feminist Challenge', in Joy Damousi and Marilyn Lake (eds), *Gender and War: Australians at War in the Twentieth Century*, Cambridge University Press, 1995, pp. 302–10.

20  McKenna, *An Eye for Eternity*, p. 211; Bill Gammage, 'The Broken Years', *Journal of the Australian War Memorial*, vol. 24, April 1994, p. 34; Bill Gammage, speech at Australian Defence Force Academy (ADFA), Canberra, 19 April 2002.

21  Gammage, 'The Broken Years', p. 34.

22  Ibid.; Bill Gammage, speech to Estaminet Club, 27 May 2010.

23  Interview with Bill Gammage, 24 March 2011.

24  LL Robson, *The First AIF: A Study of its Recruitment, 1914–1918*, new edn, Melbourne University Press, 1982 [1970], p. 1. See also LL Robson, 'The Origin and Character of the First AIF, 1914–1918: Some Statistical Evidence', *Historical Studies*, vol. 15, no. 61, 1973, pp. 737–49.

25  Gammage, 'The Broken Years', p. 34; Bill Gammage, 'Australians and the Great War', *Journal of Australian Studies*, vol. 6, 1980, pp. 26–35; interview with Gammage; 'Manning Clark, *The Quest for Grace*, Penguin, Melbourne, 1990; p. 212.

26  Interview with Gammage.

27  Bill Gammage, '*The Broken Years*: Australian soldiers in the Great War, 1914–18', in Ann Curthoys and Ann McGrath (eds), *Writing Histories: Imagination and Narration*, Monash University, Melbourne, 2000, p. 14; interview with Gammage; speech at ADFA.

28  For example, Jeffrey Grey wrote in *A Military History of Australia*, 3rd edn, Cambridge University Press, 2008 [1999], p. 307; 'Bill Gammage, *The Broken Years* … had the effect of placing the Great War on the popular and scholarly agenda for a new generation of readers, although his actual argument does not add anything to the positions advanced by Bean fifty years previously'.

29  Bill Gammage, *The Broken Years: Australian Soldiers in the Great War*, new edn, Melbourne University Publishing, 2010 [1974], pp. 241, 248.

30  Gammage, *The Broken Years*, p. 153.

31  Ibid., pp. 248, 249, 252–5.

32  Bill Gammage, speech to Queenscliff Carnival of Words, 10 November 2002; speech at ADFA.

33  Gammage, speech to Estaminet Club.

34  Gammage, speech at ADFA.

35  Gammage, *The Broken Years*, pp. 96, 212, 215.

36  In fact, Charles Bean would have liked to have been more frank about the less heroic and salubrious aspects of the AIF, but felt unable to deliver anything

other than glowing praise to the Australian public. In his war diary he expressed
frustration about 'the tender Australian public, which only tolerates flattery, and
that in its cheapest form', Charles Bean, war diary, 26 September 1915, 'Records
of CEW Bean', AWM38 3 DRL 606 Diaries, <www.awm.gov.au/collection/
records/awm38/3drl606/>.

37    Gammage, *The Broken Years*, pp. 50, 101, 257–8.
38    CEW Bean, *Anzac to Amiens: A Shorter History of the Australian Fighting Services in the
      First World War*, 5th edn, AWM, Canberra, 1968 [1946], p. viii; CEW Bean,
      *The Story of Anzac: From 4 May 1915 to the Evacuation of the Gallipoli Peninsula*, vol.
      II, *The Official History of Australia in the War of 1914–1918*, new edn, Queensland
      University Press, Brisbane, 1981 [1924], p. 910; Gammage, speech to Estaminet
      Club. Charles Bean's views about nationalism, war and Britain changed
      profoundly over his lifetime. He eventually rejected the martial nationalism
      upon which his initial understanding of Australian participation in the Great War
      was built, see chapter 2.
39    WE Murphy, *NZ Listener*, July 1974; Gerald Lyons, 1974; frontispiece, Gammage,
      *The Broken Years*, 2010.
40    Roslyn Russell (ed.), *Ever, Manning: Selected Letters of Manning Clark, 1938–1991*,
      Allen & Unwin, Sydney, 2008, p. 360.
41    Gammage, *'The Broken Years'*, p. 14.
42    Ibid., pp. 147, 182, 193, 205.
43    See Christina Twomey, 'Trauma and the Reinvigoration of Anzac: An Argument',
      *History Australia*, vol. 10, no. 3, 2013, pp. 85–108.
44    Nettie Palmer, *Argus*, 9 March 1935, p. 11.
45    Jenny Macleod, *Reconsidering Gallipoli*, Manchester University Press, 2004, p. 221.
46    Patsy Adam-Smith, *The Anzacs*, new edn, Sphere Books, Melbourne, 1981 [1978],
      pp. vii, ix, 8.
47    Ibid., p. 8.
48    Robert C Miller, Washington *United Press International*, 5 April 1981.
49    Brisbane *Sunday Mail*, 17 April 2005, p. 119.
50    David Williamson, *'The Removalist*: A Conjunction of Limitations', *Meanjin
      Quarterly*, vol. 33, no. 4, 1974, pp. 413–14.
51    Bill Gammage, David Williamson and Peter Weir, *The Story of Gallipoli*, Penguin,
      Melbourne, 1981, p. 6.
52    Michael Bodey, 'Gallipoli', in Scott Hocking and Bill Collins, *100 Greatest Films of
      Australian Cinema*, Scribal, Melbourne, 2006, p. 104.
53    The most extreme example of the demilitarising trend is found in Simon
      Wincer's *The Lighthorsemen* (1987), when one of the soldiers realises that he
      has no desire to kill Turks and becomes a stretcher-bearer; see Stuart Ward,
      'A War Memorial in Celluloid: The Gallipoli Legend in Australian Cinema,
      1940s–1980s', in Jenny Macleod (ed.), *Gallipoli: Making History*, Frank Cass,
      London, 2004, pp. 66, 69, 71; Macleod, *Reconsidering Gallipoli*, p. 225; Gammage,
      Williamson and Weir , *The Story of Gallipoli*, p. 90; Joy Damousi has written
      about the 'post-imperial' generation of film-makers, among whom she includes
      Peter Weir and Bruce Beresford, who made *Breaker Morant*. These directors
      'cinematically restaged' Australian involvement in war, such that the 'Empire
      and the British [were] positioned as the villain'; 'War and Commemoration', in
      Deryck M Schreuder and Stuart Ward (eds), *Australia's Empire*, Oxford University
      Press, 2008, pp. 308–309; Mark McKenna, 'How Did it Become Australia's
      National Day?', in Marilyn Lake, Henry Reynolds, Mark McKenna, Joy Damousi

and Carina Donaldson, *What's Wrong with Anzac? The Militarisation of Australian History*, NewSouth, Sydney, 2010, pp. 110–34; Daniel Reynaud, *Celluloid Anzacs: The Great War through Australian Cinema*, Australian Scholarly Publishing, Melbourne, 2007, pp. 192–4.

54 *The Times*, 18 December 1981, quoted in Ward, 'A War Memorial in Celluloid', p. 71.

55 Peter Weir, *Cineaste*, p. 42, quoted in Jonathan Rayner, *The Films of Peter Weir*, Cassell, London, 1998, p. 101.

56 New York *Newsweek*, 7 September 1981; Rick Groen, '*Gallipoli*: Australian Film a Dishonest Look at War', Toronto *Globe and Mail*, 4 September 1981; Derek Malcolm, 'Over the Top', *Manchester Guardian Weekly*, 20 December 1981, p. 20; Sylvia Lawson, 'Gallipoli: You are Being Told What to Remember', Sydney *Film News*, November–December 1981, p. 11, quoted in Macleod, *Reconsidering Gallipoli*, p. 225.

# 6    1980s–present: The Great War as family history

1 <www.facebook.com/news.com.au/posts/407301092630603>;
  <www.anzaccentenary.vic.gov.au/wwi-centenary-poppy-tile-project/>.

2 For discussion about why this phenomenon did not begin until the 1960s, see Jay Winter in Duncan Bell (ed.), *Memory, Trauma and World Politics: Reflections on the Relationship Between Past and Present*, Palgrave Macmillan, Basingstoke, Hants, 2006, p. 60 and Peter Novick, *The Holocaust in American Life*, Houghton Mifflin, Boston, 1999, cited in RJB Bosworth, 'The Second World Wars and Their Clouded Memories', *History Australia*, vol. 8, no. 3, 2011, p. 87.

3 Jay Winter, 'The Memory Boom in Contemporary Historical Studies', *Raritan*, vol. 21, no. 15, 2001, p. 52.

4 Italian scholars Alessandro Portelli and Luisa Passerini were pioneers of oral history. See, for example, Luisa Passerini, 'Work Ideology and Consensus under Italian Fascism', *History Workshop Journal*, vol 8, no 1, 1979, pp. 82–108.

5 Membership of genealogical societies grew ten-fold during the 1970s and 1980s: Richard Waterhouse, 'Locating the New Social History: Transnational Historiography and Australian Local History', *Journal of the Royal Australian Historical Society*, vol. 95, no. 1, 2009, p. 8; Graeme Davison, 'The Broken Lineage', in Donna Merwick (ed.), *Dangerous Liaisons: Essays in Honour of Greg Dening*, History Department, University of Melbourne, 1994, p. 334; 36 new historical societies were established in South Australia in the 1970s and a further 54 in the 1980s, Graeme Davison, *The Use and Abuse of Australian History*, Allen & Unwin, Sydney, 2000, p. 197. In 2012, the state of Victoria was host to 103 historical, genealogical and family history societies, 'Family History and Historical Societies in Australia', <www.coraweb.com.au/society.htm>.

6 NAA, 'Mapping our Anzacs', <mappingouranzacs.naa.gov.au>.

7 Jay Winter, *Sites of Memory, Sites of Mourning: The Great War in European Cultural History*, Cambridge University Press, 1995, p. 115.

8 Novick, *The Holocaust in American Life*, quoted in Bosworth, 'The Second World Wars and Their Clouded Memories', p. 89.

9 Allan M Nixon (ed.), *Somewhere in France: Letters to Home, The War Years of Sgt. Roy Whitelaw, 1st AIF*, Five Mile Press, Melbourne, 1989, Preface.

10 Eunice Laidler, *Walter's War: Letters of Walter James Mcpherson, 59th Battalion AIF During World War I, 1914–1918*, Rosewold Publications, St Arnaud, Vic, 1998, p. 124.

11   Ronald Sinclair, *Dear Ad...Love Ron: The Complete Collection of the Handwritten Letters and Diary Entries of Ronald Augustine Sinclair, Australian Imperial Forces, Fifth Division Artillery, 14th Field Army Brigade, 114th Howitzer Battery on Active Service in Egypt, France and Belgium, 1915–1919*, The Sisters of Mercy, Singleton, NSW, 1996, p. 64.

12   Laidler, *Walter's War*, pp. 52, 124.

13   JG Rogers (ed.), *For King and Country: The War Diaries of J.M. Laidlaw*, self-published, Moe, Vic, 1985, Foreword, p. 118.

14   George Kirk, *Tales from Tangerine and World War I Diary of Pte A.G. Kirk MM*, self-published, Maryborough, Qld, 2002, p. 68.

15   David Nott, *Somewhere in France: The Collected Letters of Lewis Windermere Nott*, HarperPerennial, Sydney, 1996, pp. 31, 44.

16   Noni Faragher, *Prelude Fugue and Variations: Letters to a Loved One from Chaplain TC Rintoul in World War One*, Spectrum, Melbourne, 1989, p. 141.

17   Eric Evans, *So Far From Home: The Remarkable War Diaries of Eric Evans, an Australian Soldier during World War I*, Kangaroo Press, Sydney, 2002, Foreword; Gilbert Mant (ed.), *Soldier Boy: The Letters of Gunner WJ Duffell, 1915–18*, Kangaroo Press, Sydney, 1992, p. 7; Elizabeth Whiteside, *A Valley in France: World War I Letters to His Parents and Sister While on Active Service from Egypt, France and Great Britain, 1915–1918*, self-published, Melbourne, 1999, p. ix.

18   Sinclair, *Dear Ad...Love Ron*, pp. vii, xi.

19   Mant (ed.), *Soldier Boy*, p. 8.

20   Joy Damousi, 'Why Do We Get So Emotional About Anzac?', in Marilyn Lake, Henry Reynolds, Joy Damousi, Mark McKenna and Carina Donaldson, *What's Wrong with Anzac? The Militarisation of Australian History*, NewSouth, Sydney, 2010, p. 103. As part of the Victorian conservative government's Anzac centenary commemorations, Victorians are encouraged to trace soldier-forebears who sailed on the HMAT *Orvieto*, the lead ship in the first convoy to leave Victoria in the Great War, see 'Victorian Families Renew Connections to their Anzac Ancestors', 21 October 2013, <www.premier.vic.gov.au/media-centre/media-releases/8154-victorian-families-renew-connections-to-their-anzac-ancestors. html>.

21   Claire Skelton, *In My Own Shadow: Including the War Diary of WB Wilson and Memoirs of LE Wilson*, self-published, Ascot, Qld, 1999, p. 5, cited in Bart Ziino, '"A Lasting Gift to His Descendants": Family Memory and the Great War in Australia', *History and Memory: Studies in Representation of the Past*, vol. 22, no. 2, p. 131; Narelle I Wynn, *Behind the Lines: War Time Stories from 1914–1918 with the 5th Light Horse Brigade as told by Peter William Kerr, 1896–1984*, self-published, Brisbane, 1997, p. 10.

22   Lynette Oates, *With the Big Guns: An Australian Artilleryman in the Great War*, Shannon Books, Melbourne, 2006, p. v.

23   Winsome McDowell Paul, *Blessed with a Cheerful Nature: A Reading of the Letters of Lieutenant George Stanley McDowell MC, 13th Battalion AIF, 1914–1917*, self-published, Adelaide, 2005, pp. 8–9.

24   Rogers (ed.), *For King and Country*, Foreword.

25   Laidler, *Walter's War*, p. 75.

26   John Davidson, *The Dinkum Oil of Light Horse and Camel Corps*, self-published, Robina, Qld, 1996, Introduction.

27   Patsy Adam-Smith, *The Anzacs*, new edn, Sphere Books, Melbourne, 1981 [1978], pp. viii, 9.

28   Sinclair, *Dear Ad...Love Ron*, p. xi.

29   Mary Reddrop, *Jim's Story: With the 37th Battalion-AIF*, Spectrum, Melbourne, 1982,

pp. 1–2.
30 McDowell Paul, *Blessed with a Cheerful Nature*, pp. 334, 340–1.
31 Ibid., pp. 79, 152, 180.
32 Ibid., pp. 180, 315–16.
33 Interview with Winsome McDowell Paul, 11 June 2012.
34 Oates, *With the Big Guns*, pp. v, 173.
35 Whiteside, *A Valley in France*, p. 180 and Preface.
36 George Bevan, *Jum's War: Finding My Father, William 'Jum' Bevan, 5th FAB AIF*, Pier 9, Sydney, 2007, p. 7.
37 Ibid., pp. 5, 414.
38 Interview with David Noonan, 17 February 2012; David Noonan, *My Dearest Violet: Letters of Love and War, 1916 to 1919*, self-published, Melbourne, 2005, p. iii.
39 Interview with Julie Cattlin, 13 March 2012. The diaries are published as Julie Cattlin (ed.), *The World War I Diaries of Sergeant Jim Osborn*, self-published, Melbourne, 2010.
40 Ibid.
41 Ibid.
42 Sinclair, *Dear Ad...Love Ron*, p. xi.
43 On the emergence of the digger as a victim, see Christina Twomey, 'Trauma and the Reinvigoration of Anzac: An Argument', *History Australia*, vol. 10, no. 3, 2013, pp. 85–108. On the rise of 'trauma culture', see Didier Fassin and Richard Rechtman, *The Empire of Trauma: An Inquiry into the Condition of Victimhood*, trans. Rachel Gomme, Princeton University Press, 2009 and Allan Young, *The Harmony of Illusions: Inventing Post-Traumatic Stress Disorder*, Princeton University Press, 1995.

## 7 Since 1990: Politicians and commemoration of the Great War

1 PJ Keating, *After Words: The Post–Prime Ministerial Speeches of Paul Keating*, Allen & Unwin, Sydney, 2011, p. 70.
2 Kevin Rudd interview on Macquarie Radio Network, quoted in *Sydney Morning Herald*, 31 October 2008; *Australian*, 1 November 2008.
3 John Lack (ed.), *Remembering Anzac: Selected Writings of KS Inglis*, History Department, University of Melbourne, 1998, p. 3.
4 Marilyn Lake, 'How do Schoolchildren Learn about Anzac?', in Marilyn Lake, Henry Reynolds, Mark McKenna, Joy Damousi and Carina Donaldson, *What's Wrong with Anzac? The Militarisation of Australian History*, NewSouth, Sydney, 2010, pp. 147–54.
5 For a discussion of the genesis of Anzac Day and the concerns raised by members of the community, see Tanja Luckins, *The Gates of Memory: Australian People's Experiences and Memories of Loss and the Great War*, Curtin University Books, Perth, 2004, pp. 81–106.
6 Clem Lloyd and Jacqui Rees, *The Last Shilling: A History of Repatriation in Australia*, Melbourne University Press, 1994, p. 188.
7 This process of battlefield 'pilgrimage', as it quickly came to be known, is recorded in Bruce Scates, *Return to Gallipoli: Walking the Battlefields of the Great War*, Cambridge University Press, 2006. See also David W Lloyd, *Battlefield Tourism: Pilgrimage and the Commemoration of the Great War in Britain, Australia and Canada, 1919–1939*, Berg, Oxford, 1998; 'Graves, "Visit of Mr Bruce"', NAA A 458/1, R 337/7, <recordsearch.naa.gov.au/scripts/Imagine.asp>.
8 There is a vast literature on grief and mourning after the Great War: see, for

example, Bart Ziino, *A Distant Grief: Australians, War Graves and the Great War*, UWA Press, Perth, 2007, Scates, *Return to Gallipoli*; Luckins, *The Gates of Memory*; 'Graves, "Visit of Mr Bruce"'.

9 'Graves, "Visit of Mr Bruce"'.

10 *Canberra Times*, 22 June 1935, p. 1; Perth *Daily News*, 24 June 1937, p. 4.

11 Melbourne *Argus*, 26 March 1938, p. 3.

12 *Cairns Post*, 19 March 1938, p. 6; letter from LC Robson, Headmaster, Sydney Church of England Grammar School to Peter Board, Chairman of the School, dated (Kent) 24 July 1938, RSL Papers, ANL MS 6609, Series B, Box 64, file 8180, cited in Scates, *Return to Gallipoli*, p. 144.

13 AW Martin, *Menzies: A Life, vol. 1, 1894–1943*, Melbourne University Press, 1996, p. 30; AWM, John Curtin, 11 November 1941, 93 File # 2/5/25/4, quoted in James Curran, *The Power of Speech: Australian Prime Ministers Defining the National Image*, Melbourne University Press, 2006, p. 31.

14 KS Inglis, *Sacred Places: War Memorials in the Australian Landscape*, new edn, Melbourne University Press, 2010 [1998], p. 381.

15 KS Inglis, 'Return to Gallipoli' in Lack (ed.), *Remembering Anzac*, pp. 29–39; correspondence with Ken Inglis, 3 May 2012.

16 Bruce Scates, 'Soldiers' Journeys: Returning to the Battlefields of the Great War', *Journal of the Australian War Memorial*, no. 40, 2007; <www.awm.gov.au/journal/j40/>.

17 Interview with Malcolm Fraser, 16 June 2012.

18 *Ten Days of Glory: The Gallipoli Pilgrimage*, video, Australian Broadcasting Corporation, Sydney, 1991.

19 For Ken Inglis' attitude, see chapter 4; interview with Bob Hawke, 21 May 2012.

20 Curran, *The Power of Speech*, p. 242; interview with Hawke.

21 Graham Freudenberg, speech to Walkley Foundation, 27 July 2010, <www. walkleys.com/books/790/>; for a discussion of the Bicentenary and Australia Day, see Mark McKenna, 'How Did it Become Australia's National Day?', in Lake et al., *What's Wrong with Anzac?*, pp. 113–16.

22 Interview with Kim Beazley, 15 May 2012.

23 Interview with Beazley.

24 Ibid.; Freudenberg, speech to Walkley Foundation.

25 Graham Freudenberg, *A Figure of Speech: A Political Memoir*, John Wiley, Brisbane, 2005, p. 4; interview with Hawke. Freudenberg wrote the Dawn Service speech and Stephen Mills wrote the Lone Pine speech, delivered later on the morning of 25 April 1990.

26 Bob Hawke, speech at Dawn Service, Gallipoli, April 1990; Bob Hawke, speech at Lone Pine, Gallipoli, April 1990.

27 *Sydney Morning Herald*, Editorial, 26 April 1990, quoted in McKenna, 'How Did it Become Australia's National Day?', p. 119.

28 'Paul Keating: The Interviews' with Kerry O'Brien, ABC Television, November 2013, Part 4.

29 Don Watson, *Recollections of a Bleeding Heart: A Portrait of Paul Keating PM*, Knopf Books, Sydney, 2002, pp. 181, 182.

30 Mark Ryan (ed.), *Advancing Australia: The Speeches of Paul Keating, Prime Minister*, Big Picture, Sydney, 1995, pp. 279–80.

31 Watson, *Recollections of a Bleeding Heart*, p. 181; Paul Kelly, *The March of Patriots: The Struggle for Modern Australia*, new edn, Melbourne University Publishing, 2011 [2009], pp. 153, 155.

32 Author interview with Paul Keating, 26 June 2013; Watson, *Recollections of a*

*Bleeding Heart*, p. 181.

33 Ruxton quoted in Watson, *Recollections of a Bleeding Heart*, p. 184; interview with Keating.

34 Watson, *Recollections of a Bleeding Heart*, p. 182; Keating, *After Words*, p. 27.

35 'Paul Keating: The Interviews', Part 4.

36 Author interview with Keating.

37 Ibid.

38 Ibid.

39 Ibid.

40 Author interview with Keating; PJ Keating, maiden speech to Commonwealth Parliament, 17 March 1970.

41 Author interview with Keating; Ryan (ed.), *Advancing Australia*, p. 287; Watson, *Recollections of a Bleeding Heart*, p. 443; interview with Michael McKernan, 14 January 2014.

42 Paul Keating, speech at AWM, 11 November 2013; Mervyn Bendle, 'Keating's Remembrance Day Speech Echoed Leninist Nihilism', *Australian*, 18 November 2013, <www.theaustralian.com.au/national-affairs/opinion/keatings-remembrance-day-speech-echoed-leninist-nihilism/story-e6frgd0x-1226762070866#>; also John Roskam, 'Sacrifice Should not be Politicised', *Australian Financial Review*, 15 November 2013, p. 46.

43 Letter from Geoffrey Blainey to Peter Gration, 5 April 1998, Minutes of Council of the AWM Meeting, 21–22 May 1998, Freedom of Information request, 13 February 2014.

44 Minutes of Council of the AWM Meeting, 11–12 May 1999, Freedom of Information request, 13 February 2014.

45 Interview with Geoffrey Blainey, 23 April 2014.

46 Ibid.

47 Interview with McKernan; Inglis, *Sacred Places*, pp. 496–7; Miranda Devine, 'A Row over God's Place: War Memorial Retreats on Secret Plan to Replace Christian Epitaph with Keating Speech', Sydney *Daily Telegraph*, 29 October 2013, <www.dailytelegraph.com.au/news/nsw/a-row-over-gods-place-war-memorial-retreats-on-secret-plan-to-replace-christian-epitaph-with-keating-speech/story-fni0cx12-1226748591790>; for Brendan Nelson's explanation of the 2013 changes to the tomb of the Unknown Soldier, see 'Twentieth Anniversary of the Reinterment of the Unknown Australian Soldier', <www.youtube.com/watch?v=3tlOWU66D7Y>.

48 See Liz Reed, *Bigger than Gallipoli: War, History and Memory in Australia*, UWA Press, Perth, 2004.

49 Author interview with Keating.

50 Inglis, *Sacred Places*, pp. 471, 509, cited in Kate Darian-Smith, *On the Home Front: Melbourne in Wartime: 1939–1945*, 2nd edn, Melbourne University Publishing, 2009 [1990], p. x.

51 'Howard Vows to Protect Kokoda from Mining', *Sydney Morning Herald*, 29 September 2006, <www.smh.com.au/news/world/howard-vows-to-protect-kokoda-from-mining/2006/09/29/1159337335458.html>; Kevin Rudd, speech at inauguration of Battle for Australia Day, 3 September 2008; *Sydney Morning Herald*, 1 November 2008; author interview with Keating.

52 Author interview with Keating.

53 Interview with John Howard, 22 May 2012.

54 Ibid.

55    Curran, *The Power of Speech*, p. 326; John Howard, speech at Anzac Day Dawn
      Service, Gallipoli, 25 April 2005.
56    Interview with Howard.
57    Ibid.
58    John Howard, *Future Directions*, 1985, cited in Mark McKenna, 'Different
      Perspectives on Black Armband History', Research Paper 5, 1997–98,
      Parliamentary Library, <www.aph.gov.au/About_Parliament/Parliamentary_
      Departments/Parliamentary_Library/pubs/rp/RP9798/98RP05>, p. 4; Anne
      Curthoys, 'History in the Howard Era', talk to professional historians,
      History House, Sydney, 19 July 2006, <www.phansw.org.au/publications/
      HistoryintheHowardEra2.pdf>, p. 1; Manning Clark, 'The Beginning of
      Wisdom', *Time Australia*, 25 January 1988, cited in McKenna, 'Different
      Perspectives on Black Armband History', p. 3; Geoffrey Blainey, *Eye on Australia:
      Speeches and Essays of Geoffrey Blainey*, Schwartz Books, Melbourne, 1991, p. 272;
      GA Blainey, 'Balance Sheet on Our History', *Quadrant*, July 1993, pp. 10–15,
      cited in McKenna, 'Different Perspectives on Black Armband History', p. 3.
59    John Howard, speech to Liberal Students Foundation, University of Sydney,
      8 July 1996, transcript DPMCL, cited in Curran, *The Power of Speech*, p. 345;
      John Howard, Sir Thomas Playford Memorial Lecture, 5 July 1996, transcript
      DPMCL, cited in Curran, *The Power of Speech*, p. 344.
60    Interview with Howard.
61    Interview with Howard; author interview with Keating.
62    John Howard, interview on *Four Corners*, ABC Television, 19 November 1996;
      interview with Howard.
63    Interview with Howard; John Howard, speech to Queensland Liberal Party,
      22 September 1996, cited in Kelly, *The March of Patriots*, p. 368.
64    See, for example, Keith Windschuttle, *The Fabrication of Australian History,
      Volume I, Van Diemen's Land, 1803–1847*, Macleay Press, Sydney, 2002; John
      Howard, speech to *Quadrant* Magazine 50th Anniversary Dinner, Sydney,
      3 October 2006, extracted in *Australian*, 4 October 2006, <www.theaustralian.
      com.au/opinion/john-howard-standard-bearer-in-liberal-culture/story-
      e6frg6zo-1111112306534>.
65    John Howard, speech at National Press Club, Canberra, 26 January 2006;
      Howard, *Quadrant* speech.
66    Interview with Howard.
67    Interview with Howard; Bernard Keane, 'Running a Flagpole up Glenn Milne.
      Salute', Crikey, 28 September 2012, <www.crikey.com.au/2009/08/31/running-a-
      flagpole-up-glenn-milne-salute/?wpmp_switcher=mobile>.
68    'Aspiring Citizens Should Know about Gallipoli', Melbourne *Age*, 13 December
      2006, cited in Nick Dyrenfurth, 'John Howard's Hegemony of Values: The
      Politics of 'Mateship' in the Howard Decade', *Australian Journal of Political Science*,
      vol. 42, no. 2, 2007, pp. 220, 221; Kelly, *The March of Patriots*, p. 340. See also
      Judith Brett's 'Claiming the Australian Legend' in *Australian Liberals and the Moral
      Middle Class: From Alfred Deakin to John Howard*, Cambridge University Press, 2003,
      pp. 202–206.
69    Interview with Howard.
70    Ibid.
71    'Egalitarianism of manners' is a term coined by John Hirst, see *Sense and Nonsense in
      Australian History*, Black Inc., Melbourne, 2009, pp. 149–73.
72    *Canberra Times*, 24 April 2012; *Canberra Times*, 17 April 2012; for example, Tony

Abbott, speech at Shrine of Remembrance, Melbourne, 17 April 2014.

73 *How Australia May Commemorate the Anzac Centenary*, The National Commission on the Commemoration of the Anzac Centenary, Department of Veterans' Affairs, Canberra, March 2011, p. xi; 'Abbott Flags Arlington-style National War Cemetery for ACT', *Sydney Morning Herald*, 18 October 2013, <www.smh.com.au/national/abbott-flags-arlingtonstyle--national-war-cemetery-for-act-20131018-2vrvm.html>.

74 James Brown, *Anzac's Long Shadow: The Cost of our National Obsession*, Black Inc, Melbourne, 2014, p. 71.

## Epilogue

1 Edward P Thompson, *The Making of the English Working Class*, Victor Gollancz, London, 1963, Preface.

2 CEW Bean, *Anzac to Amiens: A Shorter History of the Australian Fighting Services in the First World War*, 5th edn, AWM, Canberra, 1968 [1946], p. vi; George Pearce, quoted in 'The Relevance of Anzac', Australian Parliament House Research Publications, <www.aph.gov.au/About_Parliament/Parliamentary_Departments/Parliamentary_Library/pubs/anzac_day/relevance>; Marilyn Lake, *A Divided Society: Tasmania During World War I*, Melbourne University Press, 1975, p. 191.

3 Manning Clark, 'A Letter to Tom Collins', *Meanjin Papers*, vol. 2, no. 3, 1943, p. 40.

4 Mark McKenna, 'Anzac Day: How Did it Become Australia's National Day?', in Marilyn Lake, Henry Reynolds, Mark McKenna, Joy Damousi and Carina Donaldson, *What's Wrong with Anzac? The Militarisation of Australian History*, NewSouth, Sydney, 2010, pp. 110–34. This argument needs some qualification, given what has happened to Australia Day in the past decade. While historians have been preoccupied with the Anzac renaissance, Australia Day has emerged as a celebratory occasion to sit alongside Christmas and Easter. There now exists an Australia Day tradition of gathering for a barbecue with family and friends, bearing merchandise such as thongs, board shorts, t-shirts and tattoos decorated with the Australian flag.

# SELECT BIBLIOGRAPHY

## Archives

### Australian War Memorial

Bean Papers and papers on the writing of Volume XI of the *Official History of Australia in the War of 1914–1918*, AWM38.

Correspondence with Carnegie Endowment, 3DRL 6673, Item 16.

Correspondence of C.E.W. Bean, 3DRL 6673, Item 202.

Correspondence Relating to the Acquisition of Lord Novar's Papers Dated 1934–1935, 3DRL 6673, Item 771.

Letters, 1918–1920; Letters from C.E.W. Bean to His Parents Covering the Australian Historical Mission, the Australian War Museum etc., 3DRL 7447/7.

Private Correspondence of C.E.W. Bean, 3DRL 7447/9–10.

Official History 1914–18 War Records of Charles E.W. Bean Correspondence 1919–28 Concerns the Writing of Volume XI of the Official History by T.W. Heney Part 1, 3DRL 7953/15, Part 1.

Official History of 1914–18 War Records of Charles E.W. Bean Correspondence 1919–28 Concerns the Writing of Volume XI of the Official History by T.W. Heney Part 2, 3DRL 7953/15, Part 2.

Official History 1914–18 War Records of Charles E.W. Bean Correspondence 1928–34 Documents the Writing of Volume XI of the Official History Part 1, 3DRL 7953/16.

Official History 1914–18 War Records of Charles E.W. Bean Correspondence 1928–34 Documents the Writing of Volume XI of the Official History Part 2, 3DRL 7953/16, Part 2.

Official History 1914–18 War Records of Charles E.W. Bean Correspondence 1928–34 Documents the Writing of Volume XI of the Official History Part 3, 3DRL 7953/16, Part 3.

Official History 1914–1918 War Records of Charles E.W. Bean Correspondence 1933–39 Relates to the Writing and Publication of Volume XI of the Official History Part 1, 3DRL 7953/17, Part 1.

Official History 1914–1918 War Records of Charles E.W. Bean Correspondence 1933–39 Relates to the Writing and Publication of Volume XI of the Official History Part 2, 3DRL 7953/17, Part 2.

### National Archives of Australia

Papers on the writing of a history of the Boer War: NAA B168.

Commonwealth Military Forces, History of South African War, 1902/2399.

Papers on battlefield pilgrimage and Prime Minister S.M. Bruce's visit to Gallipoli: NAA A 458/1.

Graves. Visit of Mr Bruce, 1924, R 337/7, <recordsearch.naa.gov.au/scripts/Imagine. asp>. Accessed 2 June 2012.

### National Library of Australia
Papers of Sir Ernest and Lady Scott: MS 703.
MS 703/7–9: Papers of Sir Ernest and Lady Scott.
MS 703/4/1–85: Correspondence Relating to Historical Writings.
MS 703/5/36–110: Articles by Ernest Scott.
MS 703/10/1–83: Papers of Sir Ernest Scott.

### University of Melbourne Archives
Boobooks Records.
Melbourne University Historical Society Papers, 79: 177 & 81/4.
Ernest Scott's Notecards.

### University of Melbourne special collections
Australasian Federation League of Victoria, 'Manifesto of the Australasian Federation League of Victoria', Ballieu Library, Australiana Collection, 1898, AX 321.021 A 938.
Registrar's Correspondence, 1913.

## Private papers
Papers of Adjunct Professor Bill Gammage, ANU, Canberra.

## Official publications
*Commonwealth Parliamentary Debates*
*Victorian Parliamentary Debates*

## Interviews and personal communications
The Hon. Kim Beazley, 15 May 2012
Professor Geoffrey Blainey, 23 April 2014
Ms Julie Cattlin, 13 March 2012
The Rt Hon. Malcolm Fraser, 15 June 2012
Professor Bill Gammage, 24 March 2011
The Hon. Bob Hawke, 21 May 2012
The Hon. John Howard, 22 May 2012
Professor Ken Inglis, 2010–2012
The Hon. Paul Keating, 26 June 2013
Ms Winsome McDowell Paul, 2011–2012
Dr Michael McKernan, 14 January 2014
Dr David Noonan, 17 February 2012

## Broadcast media

*Gallipoli*, film, director Peter Weir, producer Pat Lovell, Associated R&R Films, 1981.
'Keating: The Interviews', interviewer Kerry O'Brien, ABC and Binna Burra Media co-production, ABC Television, November–December 2013.
*Ten Days of Glory: The Gallipoli Pilgrimage*, video, Australian Broadcasting Corporation, Sydney, 1991.

## Online sources

'Anzac Remembered', <arts.monash.edu.au/anzac-remembered/>. Accessed 25 October 2012.
AWM, 'The Anzac Day Tradition', <www.awm.gov.au/commemoration/anzac/anzac_tradition.asp>. Accessed 12 August 2012.
Bean, CEW, War Diary, 26 September 1915, 'Records of C.E.W. Bean', AWM38, 3 DRL 606 Diaries, <www.awm.gov.au/collection/records/awm38/3drl606/>. Accessed 2 September 2012.
Bendle, Mervyn F, 'Anzac in Ashes', *Quadrant Online*, no. 4, 2010, <www.quadrant.org.au/magazine/issue/2010/4/anzac-in-ashes>. Accessed 14 May 2012.
—— 'Gallipoli: Second Front in the History Wars', *Quadrant Online*, no. 6, 2009, <www.quadrant.org.au/magazine/issue/2009/6/gallipoli-second-front-in-the-history-wars>. Accessed 14 May 2012.
—— 'Keating's Remembrance Day Speech Echoed Leninist Nihilism', 18 November 2013, <www.theaustralian.com.au/national-affairs/opinion/keatings-remembrance-day-speech-echoed-leninist-nihilism/story-e6frgd0x-1226762070866#>. Accessed 7 January 2014.
Curthoys, Anne, 'History in the Howard Era', talk to professional historians, History House, Sydney, 19 July 2006, <www.phansw.org.au/wp-content/uploads/2012/11/CurthoysHistoryintheHowardEra.pdf>. Accessed 8 May 2014.
Department of Veterans' Affairs, 'Understanding Anzac Day – Past, Present, Future', <www.dva.gov.au/commems_oawg/commemorations/education/Documents/Gallipoli_Anzacs_Unit7.pdf>. Accessed 16 May 2012.
Devine, Miranda, 'A Row over God's Place: War Memorial Retreats on Secret Plan to Replace Christian Epitaph with Keating Speech', Sydney *Daily Telegraph*, 29 October 2013, <www.dailytelegraph.com.au/news/nsw/a-row-over-gods-place-war-memorial-retreats-on-secret-plan-to-replace-christian-epitaph-with-keating-speech/story-fni0cx12-1226748591790>. Accessed 7 January 2014.
Europeana 1914–1918: Your Family History of World War One, <www.europeana1914–1918.eu/en>. Accessed 18 September 2012.
'France to Leave Britain Behind with First World War Centenary Plans', <www.telegraph.co.uk/news/worldnews/europe/france/8858265/France-to-leave-Britain-behind-with-First-World-War-centenary-plans.html>. Accessed 29 October 2012.
Freudenberg, Graham, 'Lurching to the Right', speech to the Walkley Foundation, 17 July 2010, <www.walkleys.com/books/790/>. Accessed 18 May 2012.
Family History and Historical Societies in Australia, <www.coraweb.com.au/society.htm>. Accessed 20 November 2011.
Gillard, The Hon. Julia, Speech at Anzac Day Dawn Service, Gallipoli, 25 April 2012, <www.smh.com.au/opinion/a-place-shining-with-honour-pm-honours-diggers-turks-and-the-mates-they-left-behind-20120425-1xkok.html>. Accessed

20 May 2012.

Hawke, The Hon. Bob, Speech at Anzac Day Dawn Service, Gallipoli, 25 April 1990, <www.library.unisa.edu.au/bhpml/speeches/Prime/2-1-17-8.pdf>. Accessed 15 May 2012.

—— Speech at Anzac Day Lone Pine Service, Gallipoli, 25 April 1990, <www.archivaldatabase.library.unisa.edu.au/fedora/get/uuid:I1743/CONTENT0>. Accessed 15 May 2012.

Hirst, John, 'Australia: The Official History', *Monthly*, February 2008, <www.themonthly.com.au/official-history-australia-john-hirst-781>. Accessed 5 May 2012.

Howard, The Hon. John, Speech at Anzac Day Dawn Service, Gallipoli, 25 April 2005, <parlinfo.aph.gov.au/parlInfo/download/media/pressrel/CBUF6/upload_binary/cbuf65.pdf;fileType=application%2Fpdf#search=%22media/pressrel/cbuf6)%22>. Accessed 18 May 2012.

—— Speech at *Quadrant* Magazine 50th Anniversary Dinner, Sydney, 3 October 2006, <www.theaustralian.com.au/opinion/john-howard-standard-bearer-in-liberal-culture/story-e6frg6zo-1111112306534>. Accessed 24 May 2012.

—— Speech to National Press Club, Canberra, Australia Day, 26 January 2006, <australianpolitics.com/2006/01/25/john-howard-australia-day-address.html>. Accessed 24 May 2012.

Keane, Bernard, 'Running a Flagpole up Glenn Milne. Salute', Crikey, 28 September 2012, <www.crikey.com.au/2009/08/31/running-a-flagpole-up-glenn-milne-salute/?wpmp_switcher=mobile>. Accessed 25 May 2012.

Liberal Party, 'Centenary of ANZAC Funding Announcement', 26 April 2012, <www.liberal.org.au/latest-news/2012/04/26/centenary-anzac-funding-announcement>. Accessed 3 June 2012.

Lieutenant George Witton, Ancestor Details, <www.bwm.org.au/site/George_WittonDD.asp>. Accessed 9 December 2010.

McKenna, Mark, 'Different Perspectives on Black Armband History', *Research Paper 5*, 1997–98, Parliamentary Library, <www.aph.gov.au/About_Parliament/Parliamentary_Departments/Parliamentary_Library/pubs/rp/RP9798/98RP05>. Accessed 16 May 2012.

—— 'Writing the Past: History, Literature & the Public Sphere in Australia', public lecture, 1 December 2005, Queensland College of Art, Brisbane, <www.humanitieswritingproject.net.au/Mark_McKenna.pdf>. Accessed 27 September 2012.

NAA, 'Mapping our Anzacs', <mappingouranzacs.naa.gov.au/>. Accessed 15 September 2012.

National Commission on the Commemoration of the Anzac Centenary, 'How Australia May Commemorate the Anzac Centenary', Department of Veterans' Affairs, Canberra, 2011, <www.anzaccentenary.gov.au/subs/2010/reports/anzac_centenary_report.pdf>. Accessed 18 September 2012.

Nelson, Brendan, 'Twentieth Anniversary of the Reinterment of the Unknown Australian Soldier', <www.youtube.com/watch?v=3tlOWU66D7Y>. Accessed 5 January 2014.

'Order of Dedication Service of the New South Wales South African Soldiers' War Memorial', 2 June 1940, <www.warmemorialsnsw.asn.au/pdf/rocksmemorial.pdf>. Accessed 29 November 2009.

'The Relevance of Anzac', Australian Parliament House Research Publications, <www.aph.gov.au/About_Parliament/Parliamentary_Departments/

Parliamentary_Library/pubs/anzac_day/relevance>. Accessed 27 September 2012.

Scates, Bruce, 'Soldiers' Journeys: Returning to the Battlefields of the Great War', *Journal of the Australian War Memorial*, <www.awm.gov.au/journal/j40/scates.asp>. Accessed 25 May 2012.

Smith, Damian, 'Nolan Through Kelly', Heide, MOMA, 2006, <www.wordsforart. com.au/Images/PDF/NOLAN%20THROUGH%20KELLY.pdf>. Accessed 6 June 2011.

Women Working Together Towards Suffrage and Onwards, <home.vicnet.net. au/~women/14.%20Working%20Collectively.html>. Accessed 26 May 2011.


## Books and book chapters

Abbott, JHM, *Plain and Veldt: Being Studies, Stories and Sketches of My Own People, in Peace and at War*, Methuen and Co., London, 1903.

—— *Tommy Cornstalk: Being Some Account of the Less Notable Features of the South African War from the Point of View of the Australian Ranks*, Longmans, Green and Company, London, 1902.

Adam-Smith, Patsy, *The Anzacs*, new edn, Sphere Books, Melbourne, 1981 [1978].

Ashmead Bartlett, E and CEW Bean, *Australians in Action: The Story of Gallipoli*, Department of Public Instruction, NSW, Sydney, 1915.

Bashford, Alison and Stuart Macintyre (eds), *The Cambridge History of Australia*, vol. 2, Cambridge University Press, 2013.

Bean, CEW, *Anzac to Amiens: A Shorter History of the Australian Fighting Services in the First World War*, new edns, AWM, Canberra, 1968, 1983 [1946].

—— *The Dreadnought of the Darling*, new edn, Angus & Robertson, Sydney, 1956 [1911].

—— *Flagships Three*, Hodder and Stoughton, London, 1916.

—— *Gallipoli Mission*, new edn, ABC Enterprises, Sydney, 1990 [1948].

—— *Here, My Son: An Account of the Independent and Other Corporate Boys' Schools of Australia*, Angus & Robertson, Sydney, 1950.

—— *In Your Hands, Australians*, 2nd edn, Cassell, London, 1919 [1918].

—— *Letters from France*, Cassell, London, 1917.

—— *The Official History of Australia in the War of 1914–1918*, Angus & Robertson, Sydney, 1921–1942.

vol. I, *The Story of Anzac: From the Outbreak of War to the End of the First Phase of the Gallipoli Campaign*, Angus & Robertson, Sydney, 1921.

vol. II, *The Story of Anzac: From 4 May 1915 to the Evacuation of the Gallipoli Peninsula*, Angus & Robertson, Sydney, 1924.

vol. III, *The Australian Imperial Force in France, 1916*, Angus & Robertson, Sydney, 1929.

vol. IV, *The Australian Imperial Force in France, 1917*, Angus & Robertson, Sydney, 1933.

vol. V, *The Australian Imperial Force in France During the Main German Offensive*, Angus & Robertson, Sydney, 1937.

vol. VI, *The Australian Imperial Force in France During the Allied Offensive*, Angus & Robertson, Sydney, 1942.

—— and HS Gullett, vol. XII, *Photographic Record of the War: Reproduction of Pictures taken by the Australian Official Photographers (Captains G.H. Wilkins, M.C. and J.F.*

*Hurley, Lieutenants H.F. Baldwin and J.P. Campbell) and Others*, Angus & Robertson, Sydney, 1923.

—— *On the Wool Track*, new edn, Alston Rivers, London, 1913 [1910].

—— *Two Men I Knew: William Bridges and Brudenell White, Founders of the AIF*, Angus & Robertson, Sydney, 1957.

—— *War Aims of a Plain Australian*, Angus & Robertson, Sydney, 1943.

—— (ed.), *The Anzac Book: Written and Illustrated in Gallipoli by the Men of Anzac*, Cassell, London, 1916.

Beaumont, Joan, *Broken Nation: Australians in the Great War*, Allen & Unwin, Sydney, 2013.

—— (ed.), *Australia's War 1914–18*, Allen & Unwin, Sydney, 1995.

Bevan, George, *Jum's War: Finding My Father, William 'Jum' Bevan, 5th FAB AIF*, Pier 9, Sydney, 2007.

Bliss, Michael, *Dreams within a Dream: The Films of Peter Weir*, Southern Illinois University Press, Carbondale, Ill., 2000.

Borchardt, DH and W Kirsop (eds), *The Book in Australia: Essays Towards a Cultural and Social History*, Australian Reference Publications, Melbourne, 1988.

Bouchard, Gérard, *The Making of the Nations and Cultures of the New World*, McGill-Queen's University Press, Montreal and Kingston, ON, 2008.

Bracco, Rosa Maria, *Merchants of Hope: British Middlebrow Writers and the First World War, 1919–1939*, Berg, Providence, Mass., 1993.

Brett, Judith, *Australian Liberals and the Moral Middle Class: From Alfred Deakin to John Howard*, Cambridge University Press, 2003.

Bristow, Joseph, *Empire Boys: Adventures in a Man's World*, HarperCollins Academic, London, 1991.

Buchanan, Alfred, *The Real Australia*, T. Fisher Unwin, London, 1907.

Bufton, John, *Tasmanians in the Transvaal War*, S.G. Loone, Hobart, 1905.

Carlyon, Les, *Gallipoli*, Pan Macmillan, Sydney, 2001.

—— *The Great War*, Pan Macmillan, Sydney, 2006.

Carter, David, 'Modernity and the Gendering of Middlebrow Book Culture in Australia', in Kate Macdonald (ed.), *The Masculine Middlebrow, 1880–1950*, Palgrave Macmillan, Basingstoke, Hampshire, 2011, pp. 135–49.

Cattlin, Julie (ed.), *The World War I Diaries of Sergeant Jim Osborn*, self-published, Melbourne, 2010.

Clark, Anna, *History's Children*, UNSW Press, Sydney, 2008.

Clark, CMH, *Manning Clark on Gallipoli*, Melbourne University Publishing, 2005.

—— *Occasional Writings and Speeches*, Fontana/Collins, Melbourne, 1980.

—— *The Quest for Grace*, Penguin, Melbourne, 1990.

—— *A Short History of Australia*, new edn, Mentor, New York, 1969 [1963].

Coleman, Peter, *Obscenity, Blasphemy and Sedition: Censorship in Australia*, Jacaranda Press, Brisbane, 1962.

—— (ed.), *Australian Civilization*, Cheshire, Melbourne, 1962.

Crawford, RM, *Australia*, Hutchinson University Library, London, 1952.

—— *'A Bit of a Rebel': The Life and Work of George Arnold Wood*, Sydney University Press, 1975.

Crowley, FK (ed.), *A New History of Australia*, William Heinemann, Melbourne, 1974.

Curran, James, *The Power of Speech: Australian Prime Ministers Defining the National Image*, Melbourne University Press, 2006.

—— and Stuart Ward, *The Unknown Nation: Australia after Empire*, Melbourne University Press, 2010.

Curthoys, Anne and Ann McGrath (eds), *Writing Histories: Imagination and Narration*, Monash University, Melbourne, 2000.

Damousi, Joy, *Freud in the Antipodes: A Cultural History of Psychoanalysis in Australia*, UNSW Press, Sydney, 2005.

—— *The Labour of Loss: Mourning, Memory and Wartime Bereavement in Australia*, Cambridge University Press, 1999.

—— *Living with the Aftermath: Trauma, Nostalgia and Grief in Post-War Australia*, Cambridge University Press, 2001.

—— and Marilyn Lake (eds), *Gender and War: Australians at War in the Twentieth Century*, Cambridge University Press, 1995.

Darian-Smith, Kate and Paula Hamilton (eds), *Memory and History in Twentieth-Century Australia*, Oxford University Press, Melbourne, 1994.

Davidson, Jim, *A Three-Cornered Life: The Historian W.K. Hancock*, UNSW Press, Sydney, 2010.

Davidson, John, *The Dinkum Oil of Light Horse and Camel Corps*, self-published, Robina, Qld, 1996.

Davison, Graeme, *The Use and Abuse of Australian History*, Allen & Unwin, Sydney, 2000.

Dawes, JNI and LL Robson, *Citizen to Soldier: Australia Before the Great War, Recollections of Members of the First AIF*, Melbourne University Press, 1977.

Dawson, Graham, *Soldier Heroes: British Adventure, Empire and the Imagining of Masculinities*, Routledge, London, 1994.

Dennis, Peter and Jeffrey Grey (eds), *The Boer War: Army, Nation and Empire*, Army History Unit, Department of Defence, Canberra, 2000.

——, ——, Ewan Morris and Robin Prior (eds), *The Oxford Companion to Australian Military History*, 2nd edn, Oxford University Press, Melbourne, 2008 [1995].

Dixson, Miriam, *The Real Matilda: Women and Identity in Australia, 1788 to 1975*, Penguin, Melbourne, 1976.

Duffell, WJ (ed.), *Soldier Boy: The Letters of Gunner W.J. Duffell, 1915–1918*, Kangaroo Press, Sydney, 1992.

Eby, Cecil Degrotte, *The Road to Armageddon: The Martial Spirit in English Popular Literature, 1870–1914*, Duke University Press, Durham, NC, 1987.

Errington, Wayne and Peter van Onselen, *John Winston Howard: The Definitive Biography*, Melbourne University Press, 2008.

Evans, Eric, *So Far from Home: The Remarkable War Diaries of Eric Evans, An Australian Soldier During World War*, Kangaroo Press, Sydney, 2002.

Faragher, Noni, *Prelude Fugue and Variations: Letters to a Loved One from Chaplain T.C. Rintoul in World War One*, Spectrum, Melbourne, 1989.

Fewster, Kevin (ed.), *Frontline Gallipoli: C.E.W. Bean, Diaries from the Trenches*, 2nd edn, Allen & Unwin, Sydney, 1990 [1983].

Field, LM, *The Forgotten War: Australian Involvement in the South African Conflict of 1899–1902*, Melbourne University Press, 1979.

Fitchett, WH, *Deeds That Won the Empire*, Ward, Lock and Company, Melbourne, 1897.

Fitzpatrick, Brian, *The Australian Commonwealth: A Picture of the Community, 1901–1955*, F.W. Cheshire, Melbourne, 1956.

—— *The Australian People: 1788–1945*, new edn, Melbourne University Press, 1951 [1946].

—— *The British Empire in Australia: An Economic History, 1834–1939*, new edn, Macmillan, Melbourne, 1969 [1941].

—— *British Imperialism and Australia, 1783–1833: An Economic History of Australasia*, George Allen & Unwin, London, 1939.
—— *A Short History of the Australian Labour Movement*, new edn, Macmillan, Melbourne, 1968 [1940].
Fitzpatrick, Kathleen, *Solid Bluestone Foundations and Other Memories of a Melbourne Girlhood, 1908–1928*, Macmillan, Melbourne, 1983.
Fitzpatrick, Sheila, *My Father's Daughter*, Melbourne University Publishing, 2010.
Freudenberg, Graham, *A Figure of Speech: A Political Memoir*, John Wiley & Sons, Brisbane, 2005.
Fussell, Paul, *Doing Battle: The Making of a Sceptic*, Little, Brown, Boston, 1996.
—— *The Great War and Modern Memory*, new edn, Oxford University Press, 2000 [1975].
Gammage, Bill, *The Broken Years: Australian Soldiers in the Great War*, new edns, Penguin, Melbourne, 1975; Melbourne University Publishing, 2010 [1974].
——, David Williamson and Peter Weir, *The Story of Gallipoli*, Penguin, Melbourne, 1981.
Garton, Stephen, *The Cost of War: Australians Return*, Oxford University Press, Melbourne, 1996.
Gerster, Robin, *Big-Noting: The Heroic Theme in Australian War Writing*, Melbourne University Press, 1987.
Gollan, Robin, *Radical and Working Class Politics: A Study of Eastern Australia, 1850–1910*, Melbourne University Press, 1960.
Graves, Robert, *Goodbye to All That*, new edn, Cassell, London, 1957 [1929].
Green, James, *The Story of the Australian Bushmen: (Being Notes of a Chaplain)*, William Brooks and Company, Sydney, 1903.
Grey, Jeffrey, *A Military History of Australia*, 3rd edn, Cambridge University Press, 2008 [1990].
Grimshaw, Patricia, Marilyn Lake, Ann McGrath and Marian Quartly, *Creating a Nation, 1788–1990*, McPhee Gribble, Melbourne, 1994.
Hales, AG, *Campaign Pictures of the War in South Africa: (1899–1900)*, Cassell and Company, London, 1900.
Hancock, WK, *Australia*, Ernest Benn, London, 1930.
—— *Country and Calling*, Faber and Faber, London, 1954.
Hawke, Bob, *The Hawke Memoirs*, William Heinemann, Melbourne, 1994.
Hirst, John, *Looking for Australia: Historical Essays*, Black Inc., Melbourne, 2010.
—— *Sense and Nonsense in Australian History*, Black Inc., Melbourne, 2009.
Holloway, David, *'Dark Somme Flowing': Australian Verse of the Great War, 1914–1918*, Robert Andersen, Melbourne, 1987.
Howard, John, *Lazarus Rising: A Personal and Political Autobiography*, HarperCollins, Sydney, 2010.
Idriess, Ion, *The Desert Column*, Angus & Robertson, Sydney, 1934.
Inglis, Amirah, *The Hammer & Sickle and the Washing Up: Memories of an Australian Woman Communist*, Hyland House, Melbourne, 1995.
Inglis, KS, *C.E.W. Bean: Australian Historian*, University of Queensland Press, Brisbane, 1969.
—— *The Rehearsal: Australians at War in the Sudan 1885*, Rigby, Sydney, 1985.
—— *Sacred Places: War Memorials in the Australian Landscape*, new edn, Melbourne University Publishing, 2008 [1998].
—— *This Is the ABC: The Australian Broadcasting Commission, 1932–1983*, Melbourne University Press, 1983.

Jose, Arthur W, *The Royal Australian Navy, 1914–1918*, vol. IX, *Official History of Australia in the War of 1914–1918*, Angus & Robertson, Sydney, 1928.

Keating, PJ, *After Words: The Post-Prime Ministerial Speeches of P.J. Keating*, Allen & Unwin, Sydney, 2011.

—— *Paul Keating Prime Minister: Major Speeches of the First Year*, Australian Labor Party, Canberra, 1993.

Kelly, Paul, *The March of Patriots: The Struggle for Modern Australia*, new edn, Melbourne University Press, 2011 [2009].

Kirk, George, *Tales from Tangerine and World War I Diary of Pte A.G. Kirk M.M.*, self-published, Maryborough, Qld, 2002.

Knyvett, R Hugh, *'Over There' with the Australians*, Hodder and Stoughton, London, 1918.

Kristianson, GL, *The Politics of Patriotism: The Pressure Group Activities of the Returned Servicemen's League*, ANU Press, Canberra, 1966.

Lack, John (ed.), *Anzac Remembered: Selected Writings of K.S. Inglis*, History Department, University of Melbourne, 1998.

Laidler, Eunice, *Walter's War: Letters of Walter James Mcpherson, 59th Battalion AIF During World War I, 1914–1918*, Rosewold Publications, St Arnaud, Vic, 1998.

Laird, JT, *The Australian Experience of War: Illustrated Stories and Verse Selected by John Laird*, Mead and Beckett, Sydney, 1988.

—— (ed.), *Other Banners: An Anthology of Australian Literature of the First World War*, AWM and Australian Government Publishing Service, Canberra, 1971.

Lake, Marilyn, *A Divided Society: Tasmania During World War I*, Melbourne University Press, 1975.

—— *The Limits of Hope: Soldier Settlement in Victoria, 1915–38*, Oxford University Press, Melbourne, 1987.

—— and Henry Reynolds, *Drawing the Global Colour Line: White Men's Countries and the Question of Racial Equality*, Melbourne University Publishing, 2008.

——, Henry Reynolds, Mark McKenna, Joy Damousi and Carina Donaldson, *What's Wrong with Anzac? The Militarisation of Australian History*, NewSouth, Sydney, 2010.

Larsson, Marina, *Shattered Anzacs: Living with the Scars of War*, UNSW Press, Sydney, 2009.

Lawson, Henry, *In the Days When the World Was Wide and Other Verses*, Angus & Robertson, Sydney, 1900.

Lemon, Pamela J (ed.), *A Man Called Searcy: Including His Diary of the Great War, 1914–1918*, self-published, Main Beach, Qld, 1999.

Lewis, RC, *On the Veldt: A Plain Narrative of Service Afield in South Africa*, J Walch and Sons, Hobart, 1902.

Lloyd, Clem and Jacqui Rees, *The Last Shilling: A History of Repatriation in Australia*, Melbourne University Press, 1994.

Lloyd, David W, *Battlefield Tourism: Pilgrimage and the Commemoration of the Great War in Britain, Australia and Canada, 1919–1939*, Berg, Oxford, 1998.

Luckins, Tanja, *The Gates of Memory: Australian People's Experience and Memories of Loss and the Great War*, Curtin University, Perth, 2004.

Lyons, Martyn and John Arnold (eds), *A History of the Book in Australia, 1891–1945: A National Culture in a Colonised Market*, University of Queensland Press, Brisbane, 2001.

Macintyre, Stuart, *A Concise History of Australia*, 3rd edn, Cambridge University Press, 2009 [1999].

—— *A History for a Nation: Ernest Scott and the Making of Australian History*, Melbourne

University Press, 1994.

—— *The Oxford History of Australia. Volume 4: The Succeeding Age, 1901–1942*, Oxford University Press, Melbourne, 1986.

—— *The Reds: The Communist Party of Australia, From Origins to Illegality*, Allen & Unwin, Sydney, 1998.

—— and Anna Clark, *The History Wars*, Melbourne University Press, 2003; new edn, 2004.

—— and RJW Selleck, *A Short History of the University of Melbourne*, Melbourne University Press, 2003.

—— and John Faulkner (eds), *True Believers: The Story of the Federal Parliamentary Labor Party*, Allen & Unwin, Sydney, 2001.

——, Juam Maiguashca and Attila Pok (eds), *The Oxford History of Historical Writing, Volume 4, 1800–1945*, Oxford University Press, 2011.

—— and Julian Thomas (eds), *The Discovery of Australian History, 1890–1939*, Melbourne University Press, 1995.

—— and Sheila Fitzpatrick (eds), *Against the Grain: Brian Fitzpatrick and Manning Clark in Australian History and Politics*, Melbourne University Publishing, 2007.

Macleod, Jenny, *'Battle of the Nations': Remembering Gallipoli*, Menzies Centre for Australian Studies, London, 2005.

—— *Reconsidering Gallipoli*, Manchester University Press, 2004.

—— (ed.), *Gallipoli, Making History*, Frank Cass, London, 2004.

—— and Pierre Purseigle (eds), *Uncovered Fields: Perspectives in First World War Studies*, Brill, Leiden, NL, 2004.

Mann, Leonard, *Flesh in Armour*, Phaedrus, Melbourne, 1932.

Manning, Frederic, *Her Privates We*, new edn, Serpent's Tail, London, 1999 [1929].

—— *The Middle Parts of Fortune*, new edn, Granada Publishing, London, 1977 [1930].

Mant, Gilbert (ed.), *Soldier Boy: The Letters of Gunner W.J. Duffell, 1915–18*, Kangaroo Press, Sydney, 1992.

Martin, AW, *Menzies: A Life*, vol. 1, Melbourne University Press, 1996.

Masefield, John, *Gallipoli*, new edn, Rigby, Adelaide, 1978 [1916].

Maxwell, Joseph, *Hell's Bells and Mademoiselles*, Angus & Robertson, Sydney, 1932.

McCalman, Janet, *Journeyings: The Biography of a Middle-Class Generation, 1920–1990*, Melbourne University Press, 1993.

McCarthy, Dudley, *Gallipoli to the Somme: The Story of C.E.W. Bean*, John Ferguson, Sydney, 1983.

McDowell Paul, Winsome, *Blessed with a Cheerful Nature: A Reading of the Letters of Lieutenant George Stanley McDowell MC, 13th Battalion AIF, 1914–1917*, self-published, Adelaide, 2005.

McKenna, Mark, *An Eye for Eternity: The Life of Manning Clark*, Miegunyah Press, Melbourne, 2011.

McKernan, Michael, *Here Is Their Spirit: A History of the Australian War Memorial, 1917–1990*, University of Queensland Press, Brisbane, 1991.

—— *This War Never Ends: The Pain of Separation and Return*, University of Queensland Press, Brisbane, 2001.

—— and M Browne (eds), *Australia: Two Centuries of War and Peace*, AWM, Canberra, 1988.

McKinney, JP, *Crucible*, Angus & Robertson, Sydney, 1935.

McMullin, Ross, *Farewell, Dear People: Biographies of Australia's Lost Generation*, Scribe, Melbourne, 2012.

McQueen, Humphrey, *A New Britannia: An Argument Concerning the Social Origins of*

*Australian Radicalism and Nationalism*, new edn, Penguin, Melbourne, 1986
[1970].

Meaney, Neville, *A History of Australian Defence and Foreign Policy, 1901–1923: The Search for Security*, 2nd edn, Sydney University Press, 2009 [1976].

Monash, John, *The Australian Victories in France in 1918*, Hutchinson, London, 1920.

Morrison, Geoff (ed.), *Letters Home: The Letters Home from Alfred F. Morrison*, Graffiti Publications, Castlemaine, Vic, 2005.

Morrow, Edgar, *Iron in the Fire*, Angus & Robertson, Sydney, 1934.

Mosse, George L, *Fallen Soldiers: Reshaping the Memory of the World Wars*, Oxford University Press, New York, 1990.

Murray, PL, *Official Records of the Australian Military Contingents to the War in South Africa*, Department of Defence, Melbourne, 1911.

Murray-Smith, Stephen and Leonie Sandercock (eds), *Room for Manoeuvre: Writings on History, Politics, Ideas and Play*, Drummond, Melbourne, 1982.

Nixon, Allan M, *'Somewhere in France': Letters to Home, The War Years of Sgt. Roy Whitelaw 1st AIF*, Five Mile Press, Melbourne, 1989.

Noonan, David C and Isaac Miller, *My Dearest Violet: Letters of Love and War, 1916 to 1919*, self-published, Melbourne, 2005.

Nott, David, *Somewhere in France: The Collected Letters of Lewis Windermere Nott*, HarperPerennial, Sydney, 1996.

Oates, Lynette, *With the Big Guns: An Australian Artilleryman in the Great War*, Shannon Books, Melbourne, 2006.

Palmer, Nettie, *Fourteen Years: Extracts from a Private Journal*, Meanjin Press, Melbourne, 1948.

Palmer, Vance, *Daybreak*, Stanley and Paul, London, 1932.

—— *The Legend of the Nineties*, new edn, Melbourne University Press, 1963 [1954].

Pearson, Charles H, *Reviews and Critical Essays*, Methuen, London, 1896.

Pierce, Peter (ed.), *The Cambridge History of Australian Literature*, Cambridge University Press, 2009.

Preston, Richard (ed.), *Contemporary Australia: Studies in History, Politics and Economics*, Duke University Press, Durham, NC, 1969.

Prichard, Katharine Susannah, *Intimate Strangers*, new edn, Angus & Robertson, Sydney, 1990 [1937].

Prior, Robin, *Gallipoli: The End of the Myth*, UNSW Press, Sydney, 2009.

Reddrop, Mary, *Jim's Story: With the 37th Battalion–AIF*, Spectrum, Melbourne, 1982.

Reed, Liz, *Bigger Than Gallipoli: War, History and Memory in Australia*, University of Western Australia Press, Perth, 2004.

Remarque, Erich Maria, *All Quiet on the Western Front*, new edn, Vintage, London, 1996 [1929].

Renar, Frank, *Bushman and Buccaneer: Harry Morant, His 'Ventures and Verses*, H.T. Dunn, Sydney, 1902.

Reynaud, Daniel, *Celluloid Anzacs: The Great War through Australian Cinema*, Australian Scholarly Publishing, Melbourne, 2007.

Rickard, John, *H.B. Higgins: The Rebel as Judge*, George Allen & Unwin, Sydney, 1984.

Robson, LL, *Australia and the Great War, 1914–1918*, Macmillan, Melbourne, 1970.

—— *The First AIF: A Study of its Recruitment, 1914–1918*, Melbourne University Press, new edn, 1982 [1970].

Rogers, JG (ed.), *For King and Country: The War Diaries of J.M. Laidlaw*, self-published, Moe, Vic, 1985.

Roper, Michael, *The Secret Battle: Emotional Survival in the Great War*, Manchester

University Press, 2009.

*Royal Readers*, no. VI, Thomas Nelson and Sons, London, 1894.

Ryan, Mark (ed.), *Advancing Australia: The Speeches of Paul Keating, Prime Minister*, Big Picture, Sydney, 1995.

Scates, Bruce, *A Place to Remember: A History of the Shrine of Remembrance*, Cambridge University Press, 2009.

—— *Return to Gallipoli: Walking the Battlefields of the Great War*, Cambridge University Press, 2006.

Schreuder, Deryck M and Stuart Ward (eds), *Australia's Empire*, Oxford University Press, 2008.

Scott, Ernest, *Australia During the War*, vol. XI, *The Official History of Australia in the War of 1914–1918*, Angus & Robertson, Sydney, 1936; new edn, University of Queensland Press, in association with AWM, Brisbane, 1989.

—— *Laperouse*, Angus & Robertson, Sydney, 1912.

—— *The Life of Matthew Flinders*, Angus & Robertson, Sydney, 1914.

—— *A Short History of Australia*, Oxford University Press, London, 1916; new edns, 1918, 1925, 1928, 1947.

—— *Terre Napoléon: A History of French Explorations and Projects in Australia*, Methuen, London, 1910.

—— *University of Melbourne War Lectures: The Nature of the Issue*, George Robertson, Melbourne, 1915.

—— (ed.), *Australia: Cambridge History of the British Empire*, Volume VII, Part I, new edn, Cambridge University Press, 1988 [1936].

Seal, Graham, *Inventing Anzac: The Digger and National Mythology*, University of Queensland Press, Brisbane, 2004.

Serle, Geoffrey, *From Deserts the Prophets Come: The Creative Spirit in Australia, 1788–1972*, William Heinemann, Melbourne, 1973.

—— *John Monash: A Biography*, new edn, Melbourne University Press, 2002 [1982].

Seymour, Alan, *The One Day of the Year*, new edns, Angus & Robertson, Sydney; Penguin, Melbourne; 1993, 1994 [1961].

Sherriff, RC, *Journey's End: A Play in Three Acts*, Victor Gollancz, London, 1929.

Sinclair, Ronald, *Dear Ad...Love Ron: The Complete Collection of the Handwritten Letters and Diary Entries of Ronald Augustine Sinclair, Australian Imperial Forces, Fifth Division Artillery, 14th Field Army Brigade, 114th Howitzer Battery on Active Service in Egypt, France and Belgium, 1915–1919*, The Sisters of Mercy, Singleton, NSW, 1996.

Skelton, Claire Meredith, *In My Own Shadow: Including the War Diary of W.B. Wilson and Memoirs of L.E. Wilson*, self-published, Ascot, Qld, 1999.

Smith, Vivian (ed.), *Letters of Vance and Nettie Palmer: 1915–1963*, NLA, Canberra, 1977.

Stanley, Peter, *Bad Characters: Sex, Crime, Mutiny, Murder and the Australian Imperial Force*, Pier 9, Sydney, 2010.

St John Adcock, A, *Australasia Triumphant! With the Australians and New Zealanders in the Great War on Land and Sea*, Simpkin, Marshall, Hamilton, Kent, London, 1916.

Thompson, John, *The Patrician and the Bloke: Geoffrey Serle and the Making of Australian History*, Pandanus, Canberra, 2006.

Thomson, Alistair, *Anzac Memories: Living with the Legend*, new edn, Monash University Publishing, Melbourne, 2013 [Oxford University Press, Melbourne, 1994].

—— *Stragglers or Shirkers: An Anzac Imperial Controversy*, University of London, 1991.

Todman, Dan, *The Great War: Myth and Memory*, Hambledon and London, London, 2005.

Trainor, Luke, *British Imperialism and Australian Nationalism: Manipulation, Conflict and Compromise in the Late Nineteenth Century*, Cambridge University Press, 1994.

Tremearne, AJN, *Some Austral-African Notes and Anecdotes*, John Bale, Sons and Danielsson, London, 1913.

Triolo, Rosalie, *Our Schools and the War*, Australian Scholarly Publishing, Melbourne, 2012.

Turner, Ian, *The Australian Dream: A Collection of Anticipations about Australia from Captain Cook to the Present Day*, Sun Books, Melbourne, 1968.

—— *Industrial Labour and Politics: The Dynamics of the Labour Movement in Eastern Australia, 1900–1921*, new edn, Hale & Iremonger, Sydney, 1979 [1965].

Tyquin, Michael, *Madness and the Military: Australia's Experience of the Great War*, Australian Military History Publications, Sydney, 2006.

Wallace, RL, *The Australians at the Boer War*, Australian Government Publishing Service, Canberra, 1976.

Ward, Russel, *Australia*, new edn, Walkabout, Sydney, 1969 [1965].

—— *The Australian Legend*, new edn, Oxford University Press, Melbourne, 1966 [1958].

—— *A Nation for a Continent: The History of Australia, 1901–1975*, rev. edn, Heinemann Education Australia, Melbourne, 1983 [1977].

—— *A Radical Life: The Autobiography of Russel Ward*, Macmillan, Melbourne, 1988.

Ward, Stuart, *Australia and the British Embrace*, Melbourne University Press, 2001.

Warner, Philip, *The Best of British Pluck: The Boy's Own Paper*, Macdonald and Jane's, London, 1976.

Watson, Don, *Brian Fitzpatrick: A Radical Life*, Hale & Iremonger, Sydney, 1979.

—— *Recollections of a Bleeding Heart: A Portrait of Paul Keating PM*, Knopf Books, Sydney, 2002; new edn, Vintage, Sydney, 2011.

White, Richard, *Inventing Australia: Images and Identity, 1688–1980*, George Allen & Unwin, Sydney, 1981.

Whiteside, Elizabeth, *A Valley in France: World War I Letters to His Parents and Sister while on Active Service from Egypt, France and Great Britain, 1915–1918*, self-published, Beaconsfield, Vic, 1999.

Wilcox, Craig, *Australia's Boer War: The War in South Africa, 1899–1902*, Oxford University Press, Melbourne, 2002.

—— *Red Coat Dreaming: How Colonial Australia Embraced the British Army*, Cambridge University Press, 2009.

—— (ed.), *Observing Australia, 1959 to 1999, K.S. Inglis*, Melbourne University Press, 1999.

Williams, HR, *Comrades of the Great Adventure*, Angus & Robertson, Sydney, 1935.

—— *The Gallant Company: An Australian Soldier's Story of 1915–18*, Angus & Robertson, Sydney, 1933.

Williams, John F, *Anzacs, the Media and the Great War*, UNSW Press, Sydney, 1999.

—— *The Quarantined Culture: Australian Reactions to Modernism, 1913–1939*, Cambridge University Press, 1995.

Winter, Denis, *Making the Legend: The War Writings of C.E.W. Bean*, University of Queensland Press, Brisbane, 1992.

Winter, Jay, *Sites of Memory, Sites of Mourning: The Great War in European Cultural History*, Cambridge University Press, 1995.

—— and Antoine Prost, *The Great War in History: Debates and Controversies, 1914 to the Present*, Cambridge University Press, 2005.

—— and Emmanuel Sivan (eds), *War and Remembrance in the Twentieth Century*, Cambridge University Press, 1999.

Witton, George R, *Scapegoats of the Empire: The Story of the Bushveldt Carbineers*, D.W. Paterson, Melbourne, 1907.

Woods, Claire, 'There and Back: Two Soldiers Shape their Experience of World War I', in Nigel Starck (ed.), *Legacies of War*, Australian Scholarly Publishing, Melbourne, 2013, pp. 141–62.

Wynn, Narelle I (ed.), *Behind the Lines: War Time Stories from 1914–1918 with the 5th Light Horse Brigade as Told by Peter William Kerr, 1896–1984*, self-published, Brisbane, 1997.

Zainu'ddin, Ailsa G Thomson, *They Dreamt of a School: A Centenary History of Methodist Ladies' College, Kew, 1882–1982*, Hyland House, Melbourne, 1982.

Ziino, Bart, *A Distant Grief: Australians, War Graves and the Great War*, University of Western Australia Press, Perth, 2007.

# Articles

Adam-Smith, Patsy, 'All Those Empty Pages', *La Trobe Library Journal*, vol. 4, no. 14, 1974, pp. 25–52.

Barnes, John, 'The Man of Letters', *Meanjin*, vol. 18, no. 2, July 1959, pp. 193–205.

Barrett, John, 'No Straw Man, C.E.W. Bean and Some Critics', *Australian Historical Studies*, vol. 23, no. 90, 1988, pp. 102–14.

Bazley, AW, 'Obituary: C.E.W. Bean', *Historical Studies*, vol. 14, no. 53, 1969, pp. 147–54.

Beaumont, Joan, 'The State of Australian History of War', *Australian Historical Studies*, vol. 34, no. 121, 2003, pp. 165–8.

Bongiorno, Frank, '"Real Solemn History" and Its Discontents: Australian Political History and the Challenge of Social History', *Australian Journal of Politics and History*, vol. 56, no. 1, 2010, pp. 6–20.

—— and Grant Mansfield, 'Whose War Was It Anyway? Some Australian Historians and the Great War', *History Compass*, vol. 6, no. 1, 2008, pp. 62–90.

Bonnell, Andrew and Martin Crotty, 'Australia's History under Howard: 1996–2007', *The Annals of the American Academy of Political and Social Science*, no. 617, 2008, pp. 149–65.

Bosworth, RJB, 'The Second World Wars and their Clouded Memories', *History Australia*, vol. 8, no. 3, 2011, pp. 75–94.

Carter, David, '"Some Means of Learning of the Best New Books": All About Books and the Modern Reader', *Australian Literary Studies*, vol. 22 no. 3, 2006, pp. 329–41.

Clark, Anna, 'Politicians Using History', *Australian Journal of Politics and History*, vol. 56, no. 1, 2010, pp. 120–31.

Clark, CMH, 'A Letter to Tom Collins: Mateship', *Meanjin Papers*, vol. 2, no. 3, 1943, pp. 40–1.

Cooper, Anthony, 'The Australian Historiography of the First World War: Who is Deluded?', *Australian Journal of Politics and History*, vol. 40, no. 1, 1994, pp. 16–35.

Crotty, Martin, 'The Anzac Citizen: Towards a History of the RSL', *Australian Journal of Politics and History*, vol. 53, no. 2, 2007, pp. 183–93.

—— 'Review Essay, War Stories in Australia: Scholarship, Memory and Public Intellectualism', *Australian Historical Studies*, vol. 42, 2011, pp. 148–54.

—— and Craig Melrose, 'Anzac Day, Brisbane, Australia: Triumphalism, Mourning and Politics in Interwar Commemoration', *Round Table*, vol. 96, no. 393, 2007, pp. 679–92.

Curran, James, 'The "Thin Dividing Line": Prime Ministers and the Problem of Australian Nationalism, 1972–1996', *Australian Journal of Politics and History*, vol. 48, no. 4, 2002, pp. 469–86.

Damousi, Joy, 'Australian Medical Intellectuals and the Great War', *Australian Journal of Politics and History*, vol. 53, no. 3, 2007, pp. 436–50.

Davison, Graeme, 'The Use and Abuse of Australian History', *Australian Historical Studies*, vol. 23, no. 91, 1988, pp. 55–76.

Dyrenfurth, Nick, 'John Howard's Hegemony of Values: The Politics of "Mateship" in the Howard Decade', *Australian Journal of Political Science*, vol. 42, no. 2, 2007, pp. 211–30.

Fewster, Kevin, 'Ellis Ashmead Bartlett and the Making of the Anzac Legend', *Journal of Australian Studies*, no. 10, 1982, pp. 17–30.

Firth, Stewart, Review of *The Broken Years*, *Labour History*, no. 27, 1974, pp. 81–2.

Gammage, Bill, 'Australians and the Great War', *Journal of Australian Studies*, vol. 6, 1980, pp. 26–35.

—— 'The Broken Years', *Journal of the Australian War Memorial*, no. 24, 1994, pp. 34–5.

Garton, Stephen, 'Freud Versus the Rat: Understanding Shell Shock in World War I', *Australian Cultural History*, vol. 16, 1997/98, pp. 45–59.

Higgins, Esmonde and Henry Minogue, 'Australia and the Round Table', *Melbourne University Magazine*, vol. 11, no. 1, May 1917, pp. 14–16.

'Historical Society', *Melbourne University Magazine*, vol. 11, no. 3, 1917, pp. 127–8.

Inglis, KS, 'The Anzac Tradition', *Meanjin Quarterly*, vol. 24, no. 1, 1965, pp. 25–44.

—— 'Entombing Unknown Soldiers: From London and Paris to Baghdad', *History and Memory*, vol. 5, no. 2, 1993, pp. 7–31.

Johnson, Paul E, 'Looking Back at Social History', *Reviews in American History*, vol. 39, 2011, pp. 379–88.

Kent, DA, 'The Anzac Book and the Anzac Legend: C.E.W. Bean as Editor and Image-Maker', *Historical Studies*, vol. 21, no. 84, 1985, pp. 376–90.

Kristianson, GL, 'The RSL and Four Corners', *Australian Quarterly*, vol. 36, no. 1, 1964, pp. 20–30.

Laird, JT, 'Australian Poetry of the First World War: A Survey', *Australian Literary Studies*, vol. 4, no. 3, 1970, pp. 241–50.

—— 'A Checklist of Australian Literature of World War I', *Australian Literary Studies*, vol. 4, no. 2, 1969, pp. 148–63.

Larsson, Marina, 'A Disenfranchised Grief: Post-War Death and Memorialisation in Australia after the First World War', *Australian Historical Studies*, vol. 40, no. 1, 2009, pp. 79–95.

Luckins, Tanja, 'Collecting Women's Memories: The Australian War Memorial, the Next of Kin and Great War Soldiers' Diaries and Letters as Objects of Memory in the 1920s and 1930s', *Women's History Review*, vol. 19, no. 1, 2010, pp. 21–37.

Macintyre, Stuart, 'Reviewing the History Wars', *Labour History*, vol. 85, 2003, pp. 213–15.

Macleod, Jenny, 'The Fall and Rise of Anzac Day: 1965 and 1990 Compared', *War and Society*, vol. 20, no. 1, 2002, pp. 149–68.

Main, JM, 'Recruiting the First AIF: Book Review', *Meanjin Quarterly*, vol. 30, 1971, pp. 476–7.

Mann, Leonard, 'A Double Life', *Southerly*, vol. 29, no. 3, 1969, pp. 163–74.

Martin, AW, Review of *John Monash: A Biography*, *Historical Studies*, vol. 20, no. 80, 1983, pp. 464–7.

McKernan, Michael, Review of *What's Wrong with Anzac?*, *Labour History*, no. 99, 2010, pp. 231–3.

McLachlan, Noel, 'Nationalism and the Divisive Digger', *Meanjin Quarterly*, vol. 27, no. 3, 1968, pp. 306–307.

McQueen, Humphrey, '"Emu into Ostrich": Australian Literary Responses to the Great War', *Meanjin*, vol. 35, no. 1, 1976, pp. 78–93.

Meaney, Neville, 'Britishness and Australian Identity: The Problem of Nationalism in Australian History and Historiography', *Australian Historical Studies*, vol. 32, no. 116, 2001, pp. 76–90.

Pender, Anne, 'The Mythical Australian: Barry Humphries, Gough Whitlam and "New Nationalism"', *Australian Journal of Politics and History*, vol. 51, no. 1, 2005, pp. 67–78.

Picken, DK, 'The Round Table Movement', *Melbourne University Magazine*, vol. 10, no. 3, 1916, pp. 76–7.

'Review of *Gallipoli* by John Masefield', *Melbourne University Magazine*, vol. 11, no. 1, 1917, p. 38.

Rhoden, Clare, 'What's Missing in this Picture? The "*Middle Parts of Fortune*" in Australian War Literature', *Philament: Borders, Regions, Worlds*, no. 16, August 2010, pp. 21–33.

Robson, LL, 'The Origin and Character of the First AIF, 1914–1918: Some Statistical Evidence', *Historical Studies*, vol. 15, no. 61, 1973, pp. 737–49.

Scates, Bruce, 'The First Casualty of War', *Australian Historical Studies*, vol. 38, no. 130, 2007, pp. 312–21.

—— 'The Price of War: Labour Historians Confront Military History', *Labour History*, vol. 84, 2003, pp. 133–43.

Scott, Ernest (ed.), 'The Referenda', *Round Table*, vol. 1, no. 4, 4 August, 1911, pp. 500–508.

Serle, Geoffrey, 'Austerica Unlimited', *Meanjin*, vol. 26, no. 3, 1967, pp. 237–50.

—— 'The Digger Tradition and Australian Nationalism', *Meanjin Quarterly*, vol. 24, no. 2, 1965, pp. 148–58.

—— 'The State of the Profession in Australia', *Historical Studies*, vol. 15, no. 61, 1973, pp. 686–702.

Spittel, Christina, '"The Deepest Sorrow in their Hearts": Grief and Mourning in Australian Novels about the First World War', When the Soldiers Return: November 2007 Conference Proceedings, University of Queensland, Brisbane, 2009, pp. 26–33.

—— 'A Portable Monument?: Leonard Mann's *Flesh in Armour* and Australia's Memory of the First World War', *Book History*, vol. 14, 2011, pp. 187–220.

—— 'Remembering the War: Australian Novelists in the Interwar Years', *Australian Literary Studies*, vol. 23, no. 2, 2007, pp. 121–39.

Supplement, Victorian *Education Gazette and Teacher's Aid*, October 1901.

Thomson, Alistair, 'Anzac Memories: Putting Popular Memory Theory into Practice in Australia', *Oral History*, vol. 18, no. 1, 1990, pp. 25–31.

—— 'Memory as a Battlefield: Personal and Political Investments in the National Military Past', *Oral History Review*, vol. 22, no. 2, 1996, pp. 55–73.

—— 'The Return of a Soldier', *Meanjin*, vol. 47, no. 4, 1988, pp. 709–16.

—— Review of *Anzac Remembered: Selected Writings of K.S. Inglis*, *Australian Historical*

*Studies*, vol. 29, no. 113, 1999, pp. 350–1.

—— '"Steadfast until Death"? C.E.W. Bean and the Representation of Australian Military Manhood', *Australian Historical Studies*, vol. 23, no. 93, 1989, pp. 462–78.

Twomey, Christina, 'Trauma and the Reinvigoration of Anzac: An Argument', *History Australia*, vol. 10, no. 3, 2013, pp. 85–108.

Ward, Stuart, '"Culture up to Our Arseholes": Projecting Post-Imperial Australia', *Australian Journal of Politics and History*, vol. 51, no. 1, 2005, pp. 53–66.

—— and Mark McKenna, '"It Was Really Moving, Mate": The Gallipoli Pilgrimage and Sentimental Nationalism in Australia', *Australian Historical Studies*, vol. 38, no. 129, 2007, pp. 141–51.

Winter, Jay, 'The Memory Boom in Contemporary Historical Studies', *Raritan*, vol. 21, no. 15, 2001, pp. 52–66.

Ziino, Bart, 'Enlistment and non-Enlistment in Wartime Australia: Response to the 1916 Call to Arms', *Australian Historical Studies*, vol. 41, no. 2, 2010, pp. 217–32.

—— '"A Lasting Gift to His Descendants": Family Memory and the Great War in Australia', *History and Memory, Studies in Representation of the Past*, vol. 22, no. 2, 2010, pp. 125–46.

# INDEX